Handbook of Computational Linguistics and Natural Language Processing

Handbook of Computational Linguistics and Natural Language Processing

Edited by Martin Whitehead

CLANRYE
INTERNATIONAL
www.clanryeinternational.com

Clanrye International,
750 Third Avenue, 9th Floor,
New York, NY 10017, USA

ISBN: 978-1-63240-975-1

Cataloging-in-Publication Data

Handbook of computational linguistics and natural language processing /
edited by Martin Whitehead.
    p. cm.
Includes bibliographical references and index.
ISBN 978-1-63240-975-1
1. Computational linguistics. 2. Natural language processing
(Computer science). 3. Multilingual computing. 4. Applied linguistics.
5. Cross-language information retrieval. I. Whitehead, Martin.
P98 .H36 2020
006.35--dc23

For information on all Clanrye International publications
visit our website at www.clanryeinternational.com

Contents

Preface

Computational linguistics deals with the study of the morphology of language as well as its syntax and dynamic use in order to enable machines process human language. There are numerous applications of this field, such as text-to-speech software, speech recognition and grammar checking. The ability of a computer program to understand human language is known as natural language processing. The two main techniques used with natural language processing are semantic and syntax analysis. Some of the syntax techniques are parsing, word segmentation and sentence breaking. The techniques which are associated with semantics are word sense disambiguation, named entity recognition and natural language generation. This book provides significant information of this discipline to help develop a good understanding of computational linguistics and natural language processing. It will serve as a valuable source of reference for graduate and post graduate students.

This book has been the outcome of endless efforts put in by authors and researchers on various issues and topics within the field. The book is a comprehensive collection of significant researches that are addressed in a variety of chapters. It will surely enhance the knowledge of the field among readers across the globe.

It gives us an immense pleasure to thank our researchers and authors for their efforts to submit their piece of writing before the deadlines. Finally in the end, I would like to thank my family and colleagues who have been a great source of inspiration and support.

Editor

Bimorphisms and synchronous grammars

Stuart M. Shieber
School of Engineering and Applied Sciences
Harvard University, Cambridge MA, USA

Keywords: synchronous grammars, tree transducers, tree-adjoining grammars, tree-substitution grammars

ABSTRACT

We tend to think of the study of language as proceeding by characterizing the strings and structures of a language, and we think of natural-language processing as using those structures to build systems of utility in manipulating the language. But many language-related problems are more fruitfully viewed as requiring the specification of a relation between two languages, rather than the specification of a single language.

In this paper, we provide a synthesis and extension of work that unifies two approaches to such language relations: the automata-theoretic approach based on tree transducers that transform trees to their counterparts in the relation, and the grammatical approach based on synchronous grammars that derive pairs of trees in the relation. In particular, we characterize synchronous tree-substitution grammars and synchronous tree-adjoining grammars in terms of bimorphisms, which have previously been used to characterize tree transducers. In the process, we provide new approaches to formalizing the various concepts: a metanotation for describing varieties of tree automata and transducers in equational terms; a rigorous formalization of tree-adjoining and tree-substitution grammars and their synchronous counterparts, using trees over ranked alphabets; and generalizations of tree-adjoining grammar allowing multiple adjunction.

1   INTRODUCTION

We tend to think of the study of language as proceeding by characterizing the strings and structures of a language, and we think of natural-language processing as using those structures to build systems of utility in manipulating the language. But many language-related problems are more fruitfully viewed as requiring the specification of a *relation* between two languages, rather than the specification of a single language. The paradigmatic case is machine translation, where the translation relation between the source and target natural languages is itself the goal to be characterized. Similarly, the study of semantics involves a relation between a natural language and a language of semantic representation (phonological form and logical form in one parlance). Computational interpretation of text, as in question-answering or natural-language command and control systems, requires computing that relation in the direction from natural language to semantic representation, and tactical generation in the opposite direction. Sentence paraphrase and compression can be thought of as computing a relation between strings of a single natural language. Similar examples abound.

The modelling of these relations has been a repeated area of study throughout the history of computational linguistics, proceeding in phases that have alternated between emphasizing automata-theoretic tools and grammatical tools. On the automata-theoretic side, the early pioneering work of Rounds (1970) on *tree transducers* was intended to formalize aspects of transformational grammars, and led to a long development of the formal-language theory of tree transducers. Grammatical approaches are based on the idea of synchronizing the grammars of the related languages. We use the general term *synchronous grammars* for the idea (Shieber and Schabes 1990), though early work in formalizing programming-language compilation uses the more domain-specific term *syntax-directed transduction* or *translation* (Lewis and Stearns 1968; Aho and Ullman 1969), and a variety of specific systems – inversion transduction grammars (Wu 1996, 1997), head transducers (Alshawi *et al.* 2000), multitext grammars (Melamed 2003, 2004) – forgo the use of the term. The early work on the synchronous grammar approach for natural-language application involved synchronizing tree-adjoining grammars (TAG). A recent resurgence of interest in automata-theoretic approaches in the machine translation community (Graehl and Knight 2004; Galley *et al.* 2004) has led to more powerful types of transducers (Maletti *et al.* 2009) and a far better understanding of the computational properties of and relationships among different transducer types (Maletti *et al.* 2009). Synchronous grammars have also seen a rise in application in areas such as machine translation (Nesson *et al.* 2006; DeNeefe and Knight 2009), linguistic semantics (Nesson and Shieber 2006; Han and Hedberg 2008), and sentence compression (Yamangil and Shieber 2010).

As these various models were developed, the exact relationship among them had been unclear, with a large number of seemingly unrelated formalisms being independently proposed or characterized. In particular, the grammatical approach to tree relations found in synchronous grammar formalisms and the automata-theoretic approach of tree transducers have been viewed as contrasting approaches.

A reconciliation of these two approaches was initiated in two pieces of earlier work (Shieber 2004, 2006), which the present paper unifies, simplifies, and extends. That work proposed to use the formal-language-theoretic device of bimorphisms (Arnold and Dauchet 1982), previously little known outside the formal-language-theory community, as a means for unifying the two approaches and clarifying the interrelations. It investigated the formal properties of synchronous tree-substitution grammars (STSG) and synchronous tree-adjoining grammars (STAG) from this perspective, showing that both formalisms, along with traditional tree transducers, can be thought of as varieties of bimorphisms. This earlier work has already been the basis for further extensions, such as the synchronous context-free tree grammars of Nederhof and Vogler (2012).

The present paper includes all of the results of the prior two papers, with notations made consistent, presentations clarified and expanded, and proofs simplified, and therefore supersedes those papers. It provides a definitive presentation of the formal foundations for TSG, TAG, and their synchronous versions, improving on the earlier presentations. To our knowledge, it provides the most consistent definition of TAG and STAG available, and the only one to use trees over ranked rather than unranked alphabets. It also, in passing, provides a characterization of transducers in terms of equational systems using a uniform metagrammar notation, a new characterization of the relation between tree-adjoining grammar derivation and derived trees, and a new simpler and more direct proof of the equivalence of tree-adjoining languages and the output languages of monadic macro tree transducers, formal contributions that may have independent utility. Finally, it extends the prior results to cover more linguistically appropriate variants of synchronous tree-adjoining grammars, in particular incorporating multiple adjunction.

After some preliminaries (Section 2), we present a set of known results relating context-free languages, tree homomorphisms, tree automata, and tree transducers to extend them for the tree-adjoining languages (Section 3), presenting these in terms of restricted kinds of functional programs over trees, using a simple grammatical notation for describing the programs. We review the definition of tree-substitution and tree-adjoining grammars (Section 4) and synchronous versions thereof (Section 5). We prove the equivalence between STSG and a variety of bimorphism (Section 6).

The grammatical presentation of transducers as functional programs allows us to easily express generalizations of the notions: monadic macro tree homomorphisms, automata, and transducers, which bear (at least some of) the same interrelationships that their traditional simpler counterparts do (Section 7). Finally, we use this characterization to place the synchronous TAG formalism in the bimorphism framework (Section 7.3), further unifying tree transducers and other synchronous grammar formalisms. We show that these methods generalize to TAG allowing multiple adjunction as well (Section 8).[1]

The present work, being based on and synthesizing work from some ten years ago, is by no means the last word in the general area. Indeed, since publication of the earlier articles, the connections among synchronous grammars, transducers, and bimorphisms have been considerably further clarified. The relation between bimorphisms and tree transducers has benefitted from a notion of extended top-down tree transducers, which have been shown to be strongly equivalent to the $B(LC, LC)$ bimorphism class we discuss below (Maletti 2008). Koller

---

[1] Much of the content in Sections 2–7 of this paper is based on material in previous papers (Shieber 2004, 2006), and is used by permission.

and Kuhlmann (2011) provide an elegant generalization of monolingual and synchronous systems in terms of interpreted regular tree grammars (IRTG), in spirit quite close to the idea here of reconstructing synchronous grammars as bimorphism-like formal systems. Their IRTG can be used for CFG, TSG, TAG, and synchronous versions of various sorts. Of especial interest are the formalizations of Büchse *et al.* (2012, 2014), which modify the definitions of TAG to incorporate state information at substitution and adjunction sites. This modification eliminates much of the inelegance of the formalization here that accounts for our having to couch the various equivalences we show in terms of weak rather than strong generative capacity. The presentation below should be helpful in understanding the background to these works as well.

2 PRELIMINARIES

We start by defining the terminology and notations that we will use for strings, trees, and the like.

2.1 *Basics*

We will notate sequences with angle brackets, e.g., $\langle a, b, c \rangle$, or where no confusion results, simply as abc, with the empty string written ϵ.

We follow much of the formal-language-theory literature (and in particular, the tree transducer literature) in defining trees over *ranked* alphabets, in which the symbols decorating the nodes are associated with fixed arities. (By contrast, formal work in computational linguistics typically uses unranked trees.) Trees will thus have nodes labeled with elements of a RANKED ALPHABET, a set of symbols $\mathcal{F}$, each with a non-negative integer RANK or ARITY assigned to it, determining the number of children for nodes so labeled. To emphasize the arity of a symbol, we will write it as a parenthesized superscript, for instance $f^{(n)}$ for a symbol f of arity n. Analogously, we write $\mathcal{F}^{(n)}$ for the set of symbols in $\mathcal{F}$ with arity n. Symbols with arity zero ($\mathcal{F}^{(0)}$) are called NULLARY symbols or CONSTANTS. The set of nonconstants is written $\mathcal{F}^{(\geq 1)}$.

To express incomplete trees, trees with "holes" waiting to be filled, we will allow leaves to be labeled with variables, in addition to nullary symbols. The set of TREES OVER A RANKED ALPHABET $\mathcal{F}$

AND VARIABLES $\mathcal{X}$, notated $\mathcal{T}(\mathcal{F}, \mathcal{X})$, is the smallest set such that

Nullary symbols at leaves $f \in \mathcal{T}(\mathcal{F}, \mathcal{X})$ for all $f \in \mathcal{F}^{(0)}$;

Variables at leaves $x \in \mathcal{T}(\mathcal{F}, \mathcal{X})$ for all $x \in \mathcal{X}$;

Internal nodes $f(t_1, \ldots, t_n) \in \mathcal{T}(\mathcal{F}, \mathcal{X})$ for all $f \in \mathcal{F}^{(n)}$, $n \geq 1$, and $t_1, \ldots, t_n \in \mathcal{T}(\mathcal{F}, \mathcal{X})$.

Where convenient, we will blur the distinction between the leaf and internal node notation for a nullary symbol f, allowing $f()$ as synonymous for the leaf node f.

We abbreviate $\mathcal{T}(\mathcal{F}, \emptyset)$, where the set of variables is empty, as $\mathcal{T}(\mathcal{F})$, the set of GROUND TREES over $\mathcal{F}$. We will also make use of the set of n numerically ordered variables $\mathcal{X}_n = \{x_1, \ldots, x_n\}$, and write x, y, z as synonyms for x_1, x_2, x_3, respectively.

Trees can also be viewed as mappings from TREE ADDRESSES, sequences of integers, to the labels of nodes at those addresses. The address ϵ is the address of the root, 1 the address of the first child, 12 the address of the second child of the first child, and so forth. We write $q \prec p$ to indicate that tree address q is a proper prefix of p, and $p - q$ for the sequence obtained from p by removing prefix q from the front. For instance, $1213 - 12 = 13$.

We will use the notation t/p to pick out the subtree of the node at address p in the tree t, that is, (using $\cdot$ for the insertion of an element on a sequence)

$$t/\epsilon = t$$
$$f(t_1, \ldots, t_n)/(i \cdot p) = t_i/p \qquad \text{for } 1 \leq i \leq n \qquad .$$

The notation $t@p$ picks out the label of the node at address p in the tree t, that is, the root label of t/p.

Replacing the subtree of t at address p by a tree t', written $t[p \mapsto t']$ is defined as

$$t[\epsilon \mapsto t'] = t'$$
$$f(t_1, \ldots, t_n)[(i \cdot p) \mapsto t'] = f(t_1, \ldots, t_i[p \mapsto t'], \ldots, t_n)$$
$$\text{for } 1 \leq i \leq n \qquad .$$

The HEIGHT of a tree t, notated $height(t)$, is defined as follows:

$$height(x) = 0 \qquad\qquad\qquad \text{for } x \in \mathcal{X}$$

$$height(f(t_1,\ldots,t_n)) = 1 + \max_{i=1}^{n} height(t_i) \qquad \text{for } f \in \mathcal{F}^{(n)}$$

We can use trees with variables as CONTEXTS in which to place other trees. A tree in $\mathcal{T}(\mathcal{F}, \mathcal{X}_n)$ will be called a context, typically denoted with the symbol C. The notation $C[t_1,\ldots,t_n]$ for $t_1,\ldots,t_n \in \mathcal{T}(\mathcal{F})$ denotes the tree in $\mathcal{T}(\mathcal{F})$ obtained by substituting for each x_i the corresponding t_i.

More formally, for a context $C \in \mathcal{T}(\mathcal{F}, \mathcal{X}_n)$ and a sequence of n trees $t_1,\ldots,t_n \in \mathcal{T}(\mathcal{F})$, the SUBSTITUTION OF $t_1,\ldots,t_n$ INTO C, notated $C[t_1,\ldots,t_n]$, is defined inductively as follows:

$$(f(u_1,\ldots,u_m))[t_1,\ldots,t_n] = f(u_1[t_1,\ldots,t_n],\ldots,u_m[t_1,\ldots,t_n])$$

$$x_i[t_1,\ldots,t_n] = t_i$$

2.2   *A grammatical metanotation*

We will use a grammatical notation akin to BNF to specify, among other constructs, equations defining functional programs of various sorts. As an introduction to this notation, here is a grammar defining trees over a ranked alphabet and variables (essentially identically to the definition given above):

$$f^{(n)} \in \mathcal{F}^{(n)}$$

$$x \in \mathcal{X} ::= x_1 \mid x_2 \mid \cdots$$

$$t \in \mathcal{T}(\mathcal{F}, \mathcal{X}) ::= f^{(m)}(t_1,\ldots,t_m)$$

$$\mid \quad x$$

The notation allows definition of classes of expressions (e.g., $\mathcal{F}^{(n)}$) and specifies metavariables over them ($f^{(n)}$). These classes can be primitive ($\mathcal{F}^{(n)}$) or defined ($\mathcal{X}$), even inductively in terms of other classes or themselves ($\mathcal{T}(\mathcal{F}, \mathcal{X})$). We use the metavariables and subscripted variants on the right-hand side to represent an arbitrary element of the corresponding class. Thus, the elements $t_1,\ldots,t_m$ stand for arbitrary trees in $\mathcal{T}(\mathcal{F}, \mathcal{X})$, and x an arbitrary variable in $\mathcal{X}$. Because numerically subscripted versions of x appear explicitly and individually enumerated as instances of $\mathcal{X}$ (on the right hand side of the rule defining variables), numerically subscripted variables (e.g., x_1) on the right-hand side of all rules are taken to refer to the specific elements of $\mathcal{X}$ (for instance, in the definition (1) of tree transducers), whereas otherwise subscripted elements within the metanotation (e.g., x_i, t_1, t_m) are taken as metavariables.

3   TREE TRANSDUCERS, HOMOMORPHISMS, AND AUTOMATA

We review the formal definitions of tree transducers and related constructions for defining tree languages and relations, making use of the grammatical metanotation to define them as functional program classes.

3.1   *Tree transducers*

The variation in tree transducer formalisms is extraordinarily wide and the literature vast. For present purposes, we restrict attention to simple nondeterministic tree transducers operating top-down, which transform trees by replacing each node with a subtree as specified by the label of the node and the state of the transduction at that node.

Informally, a TREE TRANSDUCER (specifically a NONDETERMINISTIC TOP-DOWN TREE TRANSDUCER ($\downarrow TT$)) specifies a nondeterministic computation from $\mathcal{T}(\mathcal{F})$ to $\mathcal{T}(\mathcal{G})$ defined such that the symbol at the root of the input tree and a current state determines an output context in which the recursive images of the subtrees are placed. Formally, we can define a transducer as a kind of functional program, that is, a set of equations characterized by the following grammar for equations *Eqn*. (The set of states is conventionally notated Q, with members notated q. One of the states is distinguished as the INITIAL STATE of the transducer.)

$$
\begin{aligned}
q &\in Q \\
f^{(n)} &\in \mathcal{F}^{(n)} \\
g^{(n)} &\in \mathcal{G}^{(n)} \\
x \in \mathcal{X} &::= x_1 \mid x_2 \mid \cdots \\
Eqn &::= q(f^{(n)}(x_1,\ldots,x_n)) \doteq \tau^{(n)} \\
\tau^{(n)} \in \mathcal{R}^{(n)} &::= g^{(m)}({\tau^{(n)}}_1,\ldots,{\tau^{(n)}}_m) \\
&\mid q_j(x_i) \quad \text{where } 1 \le i \le n
\end{aligned}
$$

(1)

Intuitively speaking, the expressions in $\mathcal{R}^{(n)}$ are right-hand-side terms using variables limited to the first n.

Given this formal description of the set of equations Eqn, a tree transducer is defined as a tuple $\langle Q, \mathcal{F}, \mathcal{G}, \Delta, q_0 \rangle$ where[2]

- Q is a finite set of STATES;
- $\mathcal{F}$ is a ranked alphabet of INPUT SYMBOLS;
- $\mathcal{G}$ is a ranked alphabet of OUTPUT SYMBOLS;
- $\Delta \subseteq Eqn$ is a finite set of EQUATIONS;
- $q_0 \in Q$ is a distinguished INITIAL STATE.

Conventional nomenclature refers to the equations as TRANSITIONS, by analogy with transitions in string automata. We use both terms interchangeably. To make clear the distinction between these equations and other equalities used throughout the paper, we use the special equality symbol $\doteq$ for these equations.

The equations define a derivation relation as follows. Given a tree transducer $\langle Q, \mathcal{F}, \mathcal{G}, \Delta, q_0 \rangle$ and two trees $t \in \mathcal{T}(\mathcal{F} \cup \mathcal{G} \cup Q)$ and $t' \in \mathcal{T}(\mathcal{F} \cup \mathcal{G} \cup Q)$, tree t DERIVES t' IN ONE STEP, notated $t \doteq t'$ if and only if there is an equation $u \doteq u' \in \Delta$ with $u \in \mathcal{T}(\mathcal{F} \cup Q, \mathcal{X}_n)$ and $u' \in \mathcal{T}(\mathcal{G} \cup Q, \mathcal{X}_n)$, and a tree $C \in \mathcal{T}(\mathcal{F} \cup \mathcal{G} \cup Q, \mathcal{X}_1)$ in which the variable x_1 occurs exactly once and trees $u_1, \ldots, u_n \in \mathcal{T}(\mathcal{F} \cup \mathcal{G})$, such that

$$t = C[u[u_1, \ldots, u_n]]$$

and

$$t' = C[u'[u_1, \ldots, u_n]] \quad .$$

We abuse notation by using the same symbol for the transition equations and the one-step derivation relation they define, and will further extend the abuse to cover the derivation relation's reflexive transitive closure.

The TREE RELATION defined by a $\downarrow TT$ $\langle Q, \mathcal{F}, \mathcal{G}, \Delta, q_0 \rangle$ is the set of all tree pairs $\langle s, t \rangle \in \mathcal{T}(\mathcal{F}) \times \mathcal{T}(\mathcal{G})$ such that $q_0(s) \doteq t$. By virtue of nondeterminism in the equations, multiple equations for a given state q and symbol f, tree transducers define true relations rather than merely functions.

---

[2] We assume without loss of generality that $\mathcal{F}$, $\mathcal{G}$, and Q are disjoint so that their union can itself be taken to be a well-formed ranked alphabet. The elements of the set Q are taken to be ranked symbols of arity 1.

By way of example, the equation grammar above allows the definition of the following set of equations defining a tree transducer:[3]

$$q(f(x)) \doteq g(q'(x), q(x))$$
$$q(a) \doteq a$$

$$q'(f(x)) \doteq f(q'(x))$$
$$q'(a) \doteq a$$

This transducer allows for the following derivation:

$$q(f(f(a))) \doteq g(q'(f(a)), q(f(a)))$$
$$\doteq g(f(q'(a)), g(q'(a), q(a)))$$
$$\doteq g(f(a), g(a, a))$$

3.2   *Subvarieties of transducers*

Important subvarieties of the basic transducers can be defined by restricting the trees τ that form the right-hand sides of equations, the elements of $\mathcal{R}^{(n)}$ used.

Recall that each equation is of the form

$$q(f^{(n)}(x_1, \ldots, x_n)) \doteq \tau^{(n)} \qquad .$$

A transducer is

- LINEAR if for each such equation defining the transducer, τ is linear, that is, no variable is used more than once;
- COMPLETE if τ contains every variable in $\mathcal{X}_n$ at least once;
- ϵ-FREE if $\tau \notin \mathcal{X}_n$;
- SYMBOL-TO-SYMBOL if $height(\tau) = 1$; and
- a DELABELING if τ is complete, linear, and symbol-to-symbol.

---

[3] We will, in general, leave off the explicit specification of the set of states, input and output ranked alphabet, and initial state when providing example transducers, in the expectation that the sets of states and symbols can be inferred from the equations, and the initial state determined under a convention that it is the state defined in the textually first equation.

Note also that we avail ourselves of consistent renaming of the variables x_1, x_2, and so forth, where convenient for readability.

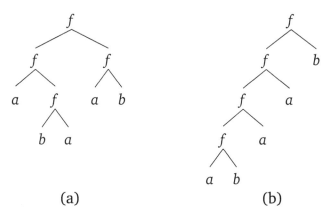

(a) (b)

Figure 1: Local rotation computed by a nonlinear tree transducer. Trees
(a) and (b) are in the tree relation of the transducer defined
in Section 3.3.

3.3 *Nonlinearity deprecated*

The following rules specify a transducer that recursively "rotates" subtrees of the form $f(t_1, f(t_2, t_3))$ to the tree $f(f(t_1, t_2), t_3)$, failing if the
required pattern is not found.

$$q(f(x,y)) \doteq f(f(q(x), q_1(y)), q_2(y))$$
$$q_1(f(x,y)) \doteq q(x)$$
$$q_2(f(x,y)) \doteq q(y)$$
$$q(a) \doteq a$$
$$q(b) \doteq b$$

The tree $f(f(a, f(b, a)), f(a, b))$ is transduced to $f(f(f(f(a, b), a), a), b)$
(as depicted graphically in Figure 1) according to the following derivation:

$$
\begin{aligned}
&q(f(f(a, f(b, a)), f(a, b))) \\
&\quad \doteq\ f(f(q(f(a, f(b, a))), q_1(f(a, b))), q_2(f(a, b))) \\
&\quad \doteq\ f(f(f(f(q(a), q_1(f(b, a))), q_2(f(b, a))), q(a)), q(b)) \\
&\quad \doteq\ f(f(f(f(a, q(b)), q(a)), a), b) \\
&\quad \doteq\ f(f(f(f(a, b), a), a), b)
\end{aligned}
$$

A variant transducer can allow f subtrees to remain unchanged (rather
than failing) when the second argument is not itself an f tree. We add
a (nondeterministic) equation to allow nonrotation,

$$q(f(x,y)) \doteq f(q(x), q'(y)),$$

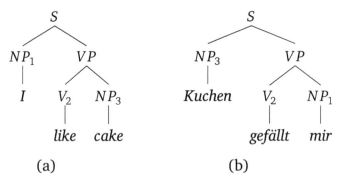

Figure 2: Example of local rotation in language translation divergence. Corresponding nodes are marked with matched subscripts.

which puts the proper constraint on its second subtree y through the new state q' defined by

$$q'(a) \doteq a$$
$$q'(b) \doteq b \quad .$$

This allows, for instance, the "already rotated" tree in Figure 1(b) to transduce to itself.

Note that intrinsic use is made in these examples of the ability to duplicate variables on the right-hand sides of rewrite rules. Transducers without such duplication are *linear*. Linear tree transducers are incapable of performing local rotations of this sort.

Local rotations are typical of natural-language applications. For instance, many of the kinds of translation divergences between languages, such as that exemplified in Figure 2, manifest such rotations. Similarly, semantic bracketing paradoxes can be viewed as necessitating rotations. Thus, linear tree transducers are insufficient for natural-language modeling purposes.

Nonlinearity per se, the ability to make copies during transduction, is not the kind of operation that is characteristic of natural-language phenomena. Furthermore, nonlinear transducers are computationally problematic. The following nonlinear transducer generates a tree that doubles in both width and depth.

$$q(f(x)) \doteq g(f(f(q(x))), f(f(q(x))))$$
$$q(g(x, y)) \doteq g(q(x), q(y))$$
$$q(a) \doteq a$$

For instance, the tree $f(a)$ transduces to

$$g(f(f(a)), f(f(a)))$$

which in turn transduces to

$$
\begin{aligned}
&g(g(f(f(g(f(f(a)),f(f(a)))))), \\
&\quad f(f(g(f(f(a)),f(f(a)))))), \\
&\quad g(f(f(g(f(f(a)),f(f(a)))))), \\
&\quad f(f(g(f(f(a)),f(f(a))))))) \quad .
\end{aligned}
$$

Notice that the number of a's in the i-th iteration is 2^{2^i-1}. The size of this transducer's output is exponential in the size of its input. (The existence of such a transducer constitutes a simple proof of the lack of composition closure of tree transducers, as the exponential of an exponential grows faster than exponential.)

In summary, nonlinearity seems inappropriate on computational and linguistic grounds, yet is required for tree transducers to express the kinds of simple local rotations that are typical of natural-language transductions. By contrast, STSG, as described in Section 6, is intrinsically a linear formalism but can express rotations straightforwardly.

3.4 *Tree automata and homomorphisms*

Two subcases of tree transducers are especially important. First, tree transducers that implement a partial identity function over their domain are TREE AUTOMATA. These are delabeling tree transducers that preserve the label and the order of arguments. Because they compute only the identity function, tree automata are of interest for the domains over which they are defined, not the mappings they compute. This domain forms a tree language, the tree language recognized by the automaton. The tree languages so recognized are the REGULAR TREE LANGUAGES (or RECOGNIZABLE TREE LANGUAGES). Though the regular tree languages are a superset of the tree languages defined by context-free grammars (the local tree languages), the string languages defined by their yield are coextensive with the context-free languages. We take tree automata to be quadruples by dropping one of the redundant alphabets from the corresponding tree transducer quintuple.

Second, TREE HOMOMORPHISMS are deterministic tree transducers with only a single state, hence essentially stateless. The replacement of a node by a subtree thus proceeds deterministically and independently of its context. Consequently, a homomorphism $h : \mathcal{T}(\mathcal{F}) \rightarrow$

$\mathcal{T}(\mathcal{G})$ is specified by its kernel, a function $\hat{h} : \mathcal{F} \to \mathcal{T}(\mathcal{G}, \mathcal{X}_\infty)$ such that $\hat{h}(f)$ is a context in $\mathcal{T}(\mathcal{G}, \mathcal{X}_{arity(f)})$ for each symbol $f \in \mathcal{F}$. The kernel $\hat{h}$ is extended to the homomorphism h by the following recurrence:

$$h(f(t_1, \ldots, t_n)) = \hat{h}(f)[h(t_1), \ldots, h(t_n)]$$

that is, $\hat{h}(f)$ acts as a context in which the homomorphic images of the subtrees are substituted.

As with transducers (see Section 3.2), further restrictions can be imposed to generate the subclasses of linear, complete, ϵ-free, symbol-to-symbol, and delabeling tree homomorphisms.

The import of these two subcases of tree transducers lies in the fact that the tree relations defined by certain tree transducers have been shown to be also characterizable by composition from these simplified forms, via an alternate and quite distinct formalization, to which we now turn.

3.5   *The bimorphism characterization of tree transducers*

Tree transducers can be characterized directly in terms of equations defining a simple kind of functional program, as above. Bimorphisms constitute an elegant alternative characterization of tree transducers in terms of a constellation of elements of the various subtypes of transducers – homomorphisms and automata – we have introduced.

A BIMORPHISM is a triple $\langle L, h_{in}, h_{out} \rangle$ consisting of a regular tree language L (or, equivalently, a tree automaton) and two tree homomorphisms h_{in} and h_{out} (connoting the input and output respectively). The tree relation $\mathcal{L}$ defined by a bimorphism is the set of tree pairs that are generable from elements of the tree language by the homomorphisms, that is,

$$\mathcal{L}(\langle L, h_{in}, h_{out} \rangle) = \{ \langle h_{in}(t), h_{out}(t) \rangle \mid t \in L \} \qquad .$$

Depending on the type of tree homomorphisms used in the bimorphism, different classes of tree relations are defined. We can limit attention to bimorphisms in which the input or output homomorphisms are restricted to a certain type: linear (L), complete (C), ϵ-free (F), symbol-to-symbol (S), delabeling (D), or unrestricted (M). We will write $B(I, O)$ where I and O characterize a subclass of homomorphisms for the set of bimorphisms for which the input homomorphism is in the subclass indicated by I and the output homomorphism is in the subclass indicated by O. For example, $B(D,M)$ is the set of bimorphisms for which the input homomorphism is a delabeling but the output homomorphism can be arbitrary.

The tree relations definable by bottom-up tree transducers (closely related to the top-down transducers we use here) turn out to be exactly this class $B(D,M)$. (See the survey by Comon *et al.* (2008, Section 6.5) and works cited therein.) The bimorphism notion thus allows us to characterize certain tree transductions purely in terms of tree automata and tree homomorphisms.

As an example, we consider the rotation transducer of Section 3.3, expressed as a bimorphism. The tree relation for the bimorphism expresses an abstract specification of where the rotations are to occur, picking out such cases with a special symbol R of arity 3, its arguments being the three subtrees participating in the rotation.

$$q(A) \doteq A$$
$$q(B) \doteq B$$
$$q(R(x,y,z)) \doteq R(q(x),q(y),q(z))$$

The input homomorphism maps these trees onto trees prior to rotation.

$$q(A) \doteq a$$
$$q(B) \doteq b$$
$$q(R(x,y,z)) \doteq f(q(x),f(q(y),q(z)))$$

Notice that the trees rooted in R map onto a tree configuration that should be rotated.

The output homomorphism maps each tree onto the corresponding post-rotation tree:

$$q(A) \doteq a$$
$$q(B) \doteq b$$
$$q(R(x,y,z)) \doteq f(f(q(x),q(y)),q(z))$$

Again, to allow the option of nonrotating configurations, we can add to the control trees nodes labeled F that should map onto configurations that cannot be rotated. (New equations are marked with $\Leftarrow$.)

The new q' state guarantees this constraint on the F trees.

$$q(A) \doteq A$$
$$q(B) \doteq B$$
$$q(F(x,y)) \doteq F(q(x), q'(y)) \qquad \Leftarrow$$
$$q(R(x,y,z)) \doteq R(q(x), q(y), q(z))$$
$$q'(A) \doteq A \qquad \Leftarrow$$
$$q'(B) \doteq B \qquad \Leftarrow$$

The input homomorphism maps the new F states onto f trees

$$q(A) \doteq a$$
$$q(B) \doteq b$$
$$q(F(x,y)) \doteq f(q(x), q(y)) \qquad \Leftarrow$$
$$q(R(x,y,z)) \doteq f(q(x), f(q(y), q(z)))$$

as does the output homomorphism.

$$q(A) \doteq a$$
$$q(B) \doteq b$$
$$q(F(x,y)) \doteq f(q(x), q(y)) \qquad \Leftarrow$$
$$q(R(x,y,z)) \doteq f(f(q(x), q(y)), q(z))$$

4 TREE–SUBSTITUTION AND TREE–ADJOINING GRAMMARS

Tree-adjoining grammars (TAG) and tree-substitution grammars (TSG) are grammar formalisms based on tree rewriting, rather than the string rewriting of the Chomsky hierarchy formalisms. Grammars are composed of a set of elementary trees, which are combined according to simple tree operations. In the case of TAG, these operations are substitution and adjunction, in the case of TSG, substitution alone. Synchronous variants of these formalisms extend the base formalism with the synchronization idea presented in earlier work (Shieber 1994). In particular, grammars are composed of pairs of elementary trees, and certain pairs of nodes, one from each tree in a pair, are linked to indicate that operations incorporating trees from a single elementary pair must occur at the linked nodes.

We review here the definition of tree-substitution and tree-adjoining grammars, and their synchronous variants. Since TSG can be thought of as a subset of TAG, we first present TAG, describing the restriction to TSG thereafter. Our presentation of TAG differs slightly from traditional ones in ways that simplify the synchronous variants and the later bimorphism constructions.

4.1   *Tree-adjoining grammars*

A tree-adjoining grammar is composed of a set of elementary trees, such as those depicted in Figure 4, that are combined by operations of substitution and adjunction. Traditional presentations of TAG, with which we will assume familiarity, take the symbols in elementary and derived trees to be unranked; nodes labeled with a given nonterminal symbol may have differing numbers of children. (Joshi and Schabes (1997) present a good overview.) For example, foot nodes of auxiliary trees and substitution nodes have no children, whereas the similarly labeled root nodes must have at least one. Similarly, two nodes with the same label but differing numbers of children may match for the purpose of allowing an adjunction (as the root nodes of α_1 and β_1 in Figure 4). In order to integrate TAG with tree transducers, however, we move to a ranked alphabet, which presents some problems and opportunities. (In some ways, the ranked alphabet definition of TAGs is slightly more elegant than the traditional one.)

We will thus take the nodes of TAG trees to be labeled with symbols from a ranked alphabet $\mathcal{F}$; a given symbol then has a fixed arity and a fixed number of children. However, in order to maintain information about which symbols may match for the purpose of adjunction and substitution, we take the elements of $\mathcal{F}$ to be explicitly formed as pairs of an unranked label e and an arity n. (For notational consistency, we will use e for unranked and f for ranked symbols.) We will notate these elements, abusing notation, as $e^{(n)}$, and make use of a function $|\cdot|$ to unrank symbols in $\mathcal{F}$, so that $|e^{(n)}| = e$.

To handle foot nodes, for each non-nullary symbol $e^{(i)} \in \mathcal{F}^{(\geq 1)}$, we will associate a new nullary symbol e_*, which one can take to be the pair of e and $*$; the set of such symbols will be notated $\mathcal{F}_*$. Similarly, for substitution nodes, $\mathcal{F}_\downarrow$ will be the set of nullary symbols $e_\downarrow$

for all $e^{(i)} \in \mathcal{F}^{(\geq 1)}$. These additional symbols, since they are nullary, will necessarily appear only at the frontier of trees. We will extend the function $|\cdot|$ to provide the unranked symbol associated with these symbols as well, so $|e_\downarrow| = |e_*| = e$.

A TAG grammar (which we will define more precisely shortly) is based then on a set P of elementary trees, a finite subset of $\mathcal{T}(\mathcal{F} \cup \mathcal{F}_\downarrow \cup \mathcal{F}_*)$, divided into the auxiliary and initial trees depending on whether they do or do not possess a foot node, respectively. In order to allow reference to a particular tree in the set P, we associate with each tree a unique name, conventionally notated with a subscripted α or β for initial and auxiliary trees respectively. We will abuse notation by using the name and the tree that it names interchangably, and use primed and subscripted variants of α and β as variables over initial and auxiliary trees, with γ serving for elementary trees in general.

Traditionally in TAG grammars, substitutions are obligatory at substitution nodes (those with labels from $\mathcal{F}_\downarrow$) and adjunctions are optional at nodes with labels from $\mathcal{F}$. This presents two problems. First, the optionality of adjunction makes it tricky to provide a canonical fixed-length specification of what trees operate at the various nodes in the tree; such a specification will turn out to be helpful in our definitions of derivation for TAG and synchronous TAG. (This is not a problem for substitution, as the obligatoriness of substitution means that there will be exactly as many trees substituting in as there are substitution nodes.) Second, it is standard within TAG to provide further constraints that disallow adjunction at certain nodes. So far, we have no provision for such NONADJOINING CONSTRAINTS. To address these problems, we use a TAG formalism slightly modified from traditional presentations, one that loses no expressivity in weak generative capacity but is easier for analysis purposes.

First, we make all adjunction obligatory, in the sense that if a node in a tree allows adjunction, an adjunction must occur there. To get the effect of optional adjunction, for instance at a node labeled B, we add to the grammar a NONADJUNCTION TREE NA_B, a vestigial auxiliary tree of a single node B_*, which has no adjunction sites and therefore does not itself modify any tree that it adjoins into. These nonadjunction trees thus found the recursive structure of derivations.[4]

---

[4] In traditional TAG, all adjunction is optional; adding nonadjunction trees

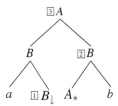

Figure 3: Sample TAG tree marked with diacritics to show the permutation of operable nodes. Note that the node at address 1 is left out of the set of operable sites; it is thus a nonadjoining node.

Second, now that it is determinate whether an operation must occur at a node, the number of children of a node in a derivation tree is determined by the elementary tree γ at that node; it is just the number of adjunction or substitution sites in γ, the OPERABLE SITES, which we will notate $\overline{\gamma}$. We take $\overline{\gamma}$ to be the set of adjunction and substitution nodes in the tree, that is, all nodes in the tree with the exception of the foot node. (Below, we will allow for nodes to be left out from the set of operable sites, and in Section 8, we generalize this to allow multiple adjunctions at a single site.)

All that is left is to provide a determinate ordering of operable sites in an elementary tree, that is, a permutation π on the operable sites $\overline{\gamma}$ (or equivalently, their addresses). This permutation can be thought of as specified as part of the elementary tree itself. For example, the tree in Figure 3, which requires operations at the nodes at addresses ϵ, 12, and 2, may be associated with the permutation $\langle 12, 2, \epsilon \rangle$. The permutation can be marked on the tree itself with numeric diacritics ⬚, as shown in the figure.

A nonadjoining constraint on a node can now be implemented merely by removing the node from the operable sites of a tree, and hence from the tree's associated permutation. In the graphical depictions, nonadjoining nodes are those non-substitution nodes that bear no numeric diacritic.

Formally, we define $\mathcal{E}(\mathcal{F})$, the ELEMENTARY TREES over a ranked alphabet $\mathcal{F}$, to be all pairs $_\square\gamma = \langle \gamma, \pi \rangle$ where $\gamma \in \mathcal{T}(\mathcal{F} \cup \mathcal{F}_\downarrow \cup \mathcal{F}_*)$ and π is a permutation of a subset of the nodes in γ. As above, we use the notation $\overline{\gamma}$ to specify the operable sites of γ, that is, the domain of π. The operable sites $\overline{\gamma}$ must contain all substitution nodes in γ.

---

for all elements of $\mathcal{F}$ is consistent with that practice. Our approach, however, opens the possibility of leaving out nonadjunction trees for one or more symbols, thereby implementing a kind of global obligatory adjunction constraint, less expressive than those variants of TAG that have node-based obligatory adjunction constraints, but more so than the purely adjunction-optional approach.

We further require that the tree γ whose root is labeled f contain at most one node labeled with $|f|_* \in \mathcal{F}_*$ and no other nodes labeled in $\mathcal{F}_*$; this node is its foot node, and its address is notated $foot(\beta)$. The foot node is not an element of $\overline{\gamma}$. Trees with a foot node are AUXILIARY TREES; those with no foot node are INITIAL TREES. The set $\mathcal{E}(\mathcal{F})$ is the set of all possible such elementary trees.

The notation $_\Box\gamma$ is used to indicate an elementary tree, the box as a mnemonic for the box diacritics labeling the permutation. We use similar notations for the particular cases where the elementary tree is initial ($_\Box\alpha$) or auxiliary ($_\Box\beta$). For convenience, for an elementary tree $_\Box\gamma$, we will use γ for its tree component when no confusion results, and will conflate the tree properties of an elementary tree $_\Box\gamma$ and its tree component γ.

A TAG grammar is then a triple $\langle \mathcal{F}, P, S \rangle$, where $\mathcal{F}$ is a ranked alphabet; P is the set of ELEMENTARY TREES, a finite subset of $\mathcal{E}(\mathcal{F})$; and $S \in \mathcal{F}_\downarrow$ is a distinguished INITIAL SYMBOL. We further partition the set P into the set I of initial trees in P and the set A of auxiliary trees in P. A simple TAG grammar is depicted in Figure 4; α_1 and α_2 are initial trees, and β_1 and β_2 are auxiliary trees.

4.2   *The substitution and adjunction operations*

We turn now to the operations used to derive more complex trees from the elementary trees. It is convenient to notationally distinguish derived trees that have the *form* of an initial or auxiliary tree, that is, (respectively) lacking or bearing a foot node. We use the bolded symbols $\boldsymbol{\alpha}$ and $\boldsymbol{\beta}$ for derived trees in $\mathcal{T}(\mathcal{F} \cup \mathcal{F}_\downarrow \cup \mathcal{F}_*)$ without and with foot nodes, respectively, again using γ when being agnostic as to the form.

The trees are combined by two operations, SUBSTITUTION and ADJUNCTION. Under substitution, a node labeled $e_\downarrow$ (at address p) in a tree γ can be replaced by an initial-form tree $\boldsymbol{\alpha}$ with the corresponding label f at the root when $|f| = e$. The resulting tree, the substitution of $\boldsymbol{\alpha}$ at p in γ, is

$$\gamma[\text{SUBST}_p \, \boldsymbol{\alpha}] \equiv \gamma[p \mapsto \boldsymbol{\alpha}] \qquad .$$

Under adjunction, an internal node of γ at p labeled $f \in \mathcal{F}$ is *split apart*, replaced by an auxiliary-form tree $\boldsymbol{\beta}$ rooted in f' when $|f| = |f'|$. The

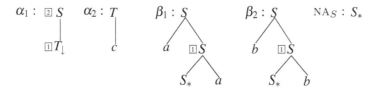

Figure 4: Sample TAG for the copy language $\{\, wcw \mid w \in \{a, b\}^* \,\}$. The initial symbol is $S_\downarrow$.

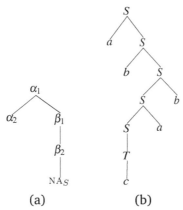

(a)   (b)

Figure 5: Derivation and derived trees for the sample grammar of Figure 4:(a) derivation tree,(b) corresponding derived tree.

resulting tree, the adjunction of β at p in γ, is

$$\gamma[\text{ADJ}_p\, \beta] \equiv \gamma[p \mapsto \beta[\text{foot}(\beta) \mapsto \gamma/p]] \qquad .$$

This definition (by requiring f to be in $\mathcal{F}$, not $\mathcal{F}_*$ or $\mathcal{F}_\downarrow$) is consistent with the standard convention, without loss of expressivity, that adjunction is disallowed at foot nodes and substitution nodes.

For uniformity, we will notate these operations with a single operator OP_p defined as follows:

$$\gamma[\text{OP}_p\, \gamma'] \equiv \begin{cases} \gamma[\text{SUBST}_p\, \gamma'] & \text{if } \gamma@p \in \mathcal{F}_\downarrow \\ \gamma[\text{ADJ}_p\, \gamma'] & \text{otherwise} \end{cases}$$

4.3   *Derivation trees and the derivation relation*

A derivation tree D records the operations over the elementary trees used to derive a given derived tree. Each node in the derivation tree specifies an elementary tree $_\square\gamma$, with the node's child subtrees D_i recording the derivations for trees that are adjoined or substituted into that tree at the corresponding operable nodes.

A DERIVATION for a grammar $G = \langle \mathcal{F}, P, S \rangle$ is a tree whose nodes are labeled with elementary trees, that is, a tree D in $\mathcal{T}(P)$. We here interpret P itself as a ranked alphabet, where for each $_\Box\gamma = \langle\gamma, \pi\rangle \in P$, we take its arity to be $arity(_\Box\gamma) \equiv |\pi|$. This requirement enforces the constraint that nodes in a derivation tree labeled with $_\Box\gamma$ will have exactly the right number of children to specify the subtrees to be used at each of the operable sites in $_\Box\gamma$. We add an additional constraint:

Labels match: For each node in D labeled with $_\Box\gamma = \langle\gamma, \pi\rangle$, and for all i where $1 \le i \le arity(_\Box\gamma)$, the root node of the i-th child of $_\Box\gamma$, labeled with $_\Box\gamma_i$, must match the corresponding operable site in $_\Box\gamma$, that is,

$$|\gamma@\pi_i| = |\gamma_i@\epsilon| \quad .$$

(The notation $\gamma@\pi_i$ can be thought of as the node in γ labeled by diacritic $_\Box$.)

A derivation is COMPLETE if it is rooted in an initial tree that is itself rooted in the initial symbol:

Initial symbol at root: The tree $_\Box\alpha_r$ at the root of the derivation tree must be an initial tree labeled at its root by the initial symbol; that is, $|\alpha_r@\epsilon| = |S|$.[5]

For example, the tree in Figure 5(a) is a well-formed complete derivation tree for the grammar in Figure 4. Note, for instance, that $|\alpha_1@\pi_2| = S = |\beta_1@\epsilon|$ as required by the label-matching constraint, and the root is an initial tree α_1 whose root is consistent with the initial symbol $S_\downarrow$.

A simple tree automaton can check these conditions, and therefore define the set of well-formed complete derivation trees. This automaton is constructed as follows. The states of the automaton are the set $\{q_N \mid N \in |\mathcal{F}|\}$, one for each unranked vocabulary symbol in the derived tree language. The start state is $q_{|S|}$. For each tree $_\Box\gamma = \langle\gamma, \pi\rangle \in P$, of arity n and rooted with the symbol N, there is a transition of the form

$$q_{|N|}(_\Box\gamma(x_1,\ldots,x_n)) \doteq _\Box\gamma(q_{|\gamma@\pi_1|}(x_1),\ldots,q_{|\gamma@\pi_n|}(x_n)) \quad . \quad (2)$$

The set of well-formed derivation trees is thus a regular tree set.

---

[5] The stripping of ranks and diacritics is necessary to allow, for instance, the initial symbol to match root nodes of differing arities.

For the grammar of Figure 4, the automaton defining well-formed derivation trees is given by

$$q_S(\alpha_1(x,y)) \doteq \alpha_1(q_T(x), q_S(y))$$
$$q_T(\alpha_2) \doteq \alpha_2$$
$$q_S(\beta_1(x)) \doteq \beta_1(q_S(x))$$
$$q_S(\beta_2(x)) \doteq \beta_2(q_S(x))$$
$$q_S(\mathrm{NA}_S) \doteq \mathrm{NA}_S$$

which recognizes the tree of Figure 5(a):

$$q_S(\alpha_1(\alpha_2, \beta_1(\beta_2(\mathrm{NA}_S)))) \doteq \alpha_1(q_T(\alpha_2), q_S(\beta_1(\beta_2(\mathrm{NA}_S))))$$
$$\doteq \alpha_1(\alpha_2, \beta_1(q_S(\beta_2(\mathrm{NA}_S))))$$
$$\doteq \alpha_1(\alpha_2, \beta_1(\beta_2(q_S(\mathrm{NA}_S))))$$
$$\doteq \alpha_1(\alpha_2, \beta_1(\beta_2(\mathrm{NA}_S)))$$

The DERIVATION RELATION $\mathcal{D}$, that is, the relation between derivation trees and the derived trees that they specify, can be simply defined via the hierarchical iterative operation of trees at operable sites. In particular, for a derivation tree with root labeled with the elementary tree $_\square\gamma = \langle \gamma, \pi \rangle$ of arity n, we define

$$\mathcal{D}(_\square\gamma(t_1, \ldots, t_n)) \equiv \gamma[\mathrm{OP}_{\pi_1} \mathcal{D}(t_1), \mathrm{OP}_{\pi_2} \mathcal{D}(t_2), \ldots, \mathrm{OP}_{\pi_n} \mathcal{D}(t_n)]$$

where, following Schabes and Shieber (1994), the right-hand side specifies the *simultaneous* application of the specified operations. We define this in terms of the *sequential* application of operations as follows:

$$\gamma[\mathrm{OP}_{p_1} \gamma_1, \mathrm{OP}_{p_2} \gamma_2, \ldots, \mathrm{OP}_{p_n} \gamma_n]$$
$$\equiv \gamma[\mathrm{OP}_{p_1} \gamma_1][\mathrm{OP}_{update(p_2, \gamma_1, p_1)} \gamma_2, \ldots, \mathrm{OP}_{update(p_n, \gamma_1, p_1)} \gamma_n] \quad (3)$$

The *update* function adjusts the paths at which later operations take place to compensate for an earlier adjunction. (Recall the notations $q \prec p$ for q a proper prefix of p and $p - q$ for the sequence obtained by removing the prefix q from p.)

$$update(p, \gamma, q) \equiv \begin{cases} p & \text{if } \gamma \text{ is an initial-form tree} \\ p & \text{if } \gamma \text{ is an auxiliary-form tree and } q \not\prec p \\ q \cdot foot(\gamma) \cdot (p - q) & \\ & \text{if } \gamma \text{ is an auxiliary-form tree and } q \prec p \end{cases}$$

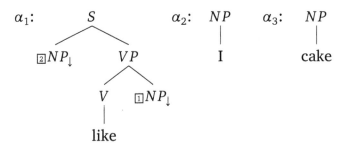

Figure 6: Grammar for a tiny English fragment.

Schabes and Shieber (1994) prove that adjunctions at distinct sites commute: if $p \neq q$ then

$$\gamma[\ldots, \text{ADJ}_p \, \gamma_1, \text{ADJ}_q \, \gamma_2, \ldots] = \gamma[\ldots, \text{ADJ}_q \, \gamma_2, \text{ADJ}_p \, \gamma_1, \ldots] \quad (4)$$

that is, that the order of adjunctions is immaterial according to this definition. The proof applies equally well to substitution and mixtures of operations. This proves that the order of the permutation over operable sites is truly arbitrary; any order will yield the same result. (In Section 8, the introduction of multiple adjunction presents the potential for noncommutativity. We address the issue in that section.)

As the base case, this definition gives, as expected,

$$\mathcal{D}(_\square \gamma) \equiv \gamma$$

for elementary trees of arity 0, that is, trees with no operable sites.

4.4   *Tree-substitution grammars*

Tree-substitution grammars are simply tree-adjoining grammars with no auxiliary trees, so that the elementary trees are only combined by substitution.

As a simple natural-language example, we consider the grammar with three elementary trees of Figure 6 and initial symbol S. The arities of the symbols should be clear from their usage and the associated permutations from the link diacritics.

As in Section 4.3, the derived tree for a derivation tree D is generated by performing all of the requisite substitutions. In this section, we provide a new definition of the derivation relation between a derivation tree and the derived tree it specifies as a simple homomorphism $h_{\mathcal{D}}$, and prove that this definition is equivalent to that of Section 4.3.

We define $h_{\mathcal{D}}$ in equational form. For each elementary tree ${}_{\square}\alpha \in P$, there is an equation of the form

$$h_{\mathcal{D}}({}_{\square}\alpha(x_1,\ldots,x_n)) \doteq \lfloor {}_{\square}\alpha \rfloor$$

where the right-hand-side transformation $\lfloor \cdot \rfloor$ is defined by

$$\lfloor A(t_1,\ldots,t_n) \rfloor = A(\lfloor t_1 \rfloor,\ldots,\lfloor t_n \rfloor)$$
$$\lfloor {}_{\boxed{k}}A_{\downarrow} \rfloor = h_{\mathcal{D}}(x_k) \tag{5}$$

Essentially, this transformation replaces each operable site π_i by the homomorphic image of the corresponding variable x_i, that is,

$$\lfloor \alpha \rfloor = \alpha[\pi_1 \mapsto h_{\mathcal{D}}(x_1)]\ldots[\pi_n \mapsto h_{\mathcal{D}}(x_n)]$$

for a tree α with n substitution sites in its permutation π.

4.5   *An example derivation*

Returning to the example, the equations corresponding to the elementary trees of Figure 6 are

$$h_{\mathcal{D}}(\alpha_1(x_1,x_2)) \doteq S(h_{\mathcal{D}}(x_2), VP(V(like), h_{\mathcal{D}}(x_1)))$$
$$h_{\mathcal{D}}(\alpha_2) \doteq NP(I)$$
$$h_{\mathcal{D}}(\alpha_3) \doteq NP(cake) \quad .$$

We define the derived tree corresponding to a derivation tree D as the application of this homomorphism to D, that is $h_{\mathcal{D}}(D)$. For the example above, the derived tree is that shown in Figure 2(a):

$$h_{\mathcal{D}}(\alpha_1(\alpha_3,\alpha_2)) \doteq S(h_{\mathcal{D}}(\alpha_2), VP(V(like), h_{\mathcal{D}}(\alpha_3)))$$
$$\doteq S(NP(I), VP(V(like), NP(cake)))$$

By composing the automaton recognizing well-formed derivation trees with the homomorphism above, we can construct a single transducer doing the work of both. We do this explicitly for TAG in Section 7.1.

Note that, by construction, each variable occurs exactly once on the right-hand side of a given equation. Thus, this homomorphism $h_{\mathcal{D}}$ is linear and complete.

4.6   *Equivalence of $\mathcal{D}$ and $h_{\mathcal{D}}$*

We can show that this definition in terms of the linear complete homomorphism $h_{\mathcal{D}}$ is equivalent to the traditional definition $\mathcal{D}$:

$$\mathcal{D}(D) = h_{\mathcal{D}}(D) \tag{6}$$

The proof is by induction on the height of D. Since $h_{\mathcal{D}}$ is the identity function everywhere except at operable sites,

$$\mathcal{D}(_{\square}\alpha) = \alpha = h_{\mathcal{D}}(_{\square}\alpha) \quad .$$

This serves as the base case for the induction.

Now suppose, that Equation (6) holds for trees of height k, and consider tree $_{\square}\alpha(D_1, \ldots, D_n)$ of height $k+1$. Then

$$
\begin{aligned}
\mathcal{D}(_{\square}\alpha(D_1, \ldots, D_n)) &= \alpha[\text{SUBST}_{\pi_1}\, \mathcal{D}(D_1), \ldots, \text{SUBST}_{\pi_n}\, \mathcal{D}(D_n)] \\
&= \alpha[\text{SUBST}_{\pi_1}\, \mathcal{D}(D_1)] \ldots [\text{SUBST}_{\pi_n}\, \mathcal{D}(D_n)] \\
&= \alpha[\pi_1 \mapsto \mathcal{D}(D_1)] \ldots [\pi_n \mapsto \mathcal{D}(D_n)] \\
&= \alpha[\pi_1 \mapsto h_{\mathcal{D}}(D_1)] \ldots [\pi_n \mapsto h_{\mathcal{D}}(D_n)] \quad\quad \Leftarrow \\
&= \alpha[\pi_1 \mapsto h_{\mathcal{D}}(x_1)] \ldots [\pi_n \mapsto h_{\mathcal{D}}(x_n)][D_1, \ldots, D_n] \\
&= \lfloor \alpha \rfloor [D_1, \ldots, D_n] \\
&= h_{\mathcal{D}}(_{\square}\alpha(D_1, \ldots, D_n)) \quad .
\end{aligned}
$$

The marked step applies the induction hypothesis.

Later, in Section 7 we will provide a similar reformulation of the derivation relation for tree-adjoining grammars. To do so, however, requires additional power beyond simple tree homomorphisms, which is the subject of that section.

5   SYNCHRONOUS GRAMMARS

We perform synchronization of tree-adjoining and tree-substitution grammars as per the approach taken in earlier work (Shieber 1994). Synchronous grammars consist of pairs of elementary trees with a linking relation between operable sites in each tree. Simultaneous operations occur at linked nodes. In the case of synchronous tree-substitution grammars, the composition operation is substitution, so the linked nodes are substitution nodes.

We define a synchronous tree-adjoining grammar, then, as a quintuple $G = \langle \mathcal{F}_{in}, \mathcal{F}_{out}, P, S_{in}, S_{out} \rangle$, where

- $\mathcal{F}_{in}$ and $\mathcal{F}_{out}$ are the input and output ranked alphabets, respectively,

- $S_{in} \in \mathcal{F}_{in\downarrow}$ and $S_{out} \in \mathcal{F}_{out\downarrow}$ are the input and output initial symbols, and

- P is a set of elementary linked tree pairs, each of the form $\langle \gamma_{in}, \gamma_{out}, \frown \rangle$, where $\gamma_{in} \in \mathcal{T}(\mathcal{F}_{in} \cup \mathcal{F}_{in\downarrow} \cup \mathcal{F}_{in*})$ and $\gamma_{out} \in \mathcal{T}(\mathcal{F}_{in} \cup \mathcal{F}_{in\downarrow} \cup \mathcal{F}_{in*})$ are input and output trees and $\frown \subseteq \overline{\gamma_{in}} \times \overline{\gamma_{out}}$ is a bijection between operable sites from the two trees.

We define $G_{in} = \langle \mathcal{F}_{in}, P_{in}, S_{in} \rangle$ where $P_{in} = \{ \langle \gamma, \pi_{in} \rangle \mid \langle \gamma, \gamma', \frown \rangle \in P \}$; this is the left projection of the synchronous grammar onto a simple TAG. The right projection G_{out} is defined similarly. Recall that the elementary trees in this grammar need a permutation on their operable sites. In order to guarantee that derivations for the synchronized grammars are isomorphic, the permutations for the operable sites for paired trees should be consistent. We therefore choose an arbitrary permutation $\langle p_{in,1} \frown p_{out,1}, \ldots, p_{in,n} \frown p_{out,n} \rangle$ over the linked pairs, and take the permutations π_{in} for γ_{in} and π_{out} for γ_{out} to be defined as $\pi_{in} = \langle p_{in,1}, \ldots, p_{in,n} \rangle$ and $\pi_{out} = \langle p_{out,1}, \ldots, p_{out,n} \rangle$. Since $\frown$ is a bijection, these projections are permutations as required.

A synchronous derivation was originally defined (Shieber 1994) as a pair $\langle D_{in}, D_{out} \rangle$ where[6]

1. D_{in} is a well-formed derivation tree for G_{in}, and D_{out} is a well-formed derivation tree for G_{out}, and

2. D_{in} and D_{out} are isomorphic.[7]

The derived tree pair for derivation $\langle D_{in}, D_{out} \rangle$ is then $\langle \mathcal{D}(D_{in}), \mathcal{D}(D_{out}) \rangle$.

---

[6] In our earlier definition (Shieber 1994), a third condition required that the isomorphic operations be sanctioned by links in tree pairs. This condition can be dropped here, as it follows from the previous definitions. In particular, since the permutations for paired trees are chosen to be consistent, it follows that the isomorphic children of isomorphic nodes are substituted at linked paths.

[7] By "isomorphism" here, we mean the normal sense of isomorphism of rooted trees where the elementary-tree-pairing relation in P serves as the bijection witnessing the isomorphism.

Presentations of synchronous tree-adjoining grammars typically weaken the requirement that the linking relation be a bijection; multiple links are allowed to impinge on a single node. One of two interpretations is possible in this case. We might require that if multiple links impinge upon a node, only one of the links be used. Under this interpretation, the multiple links at a node can be thought of as abbreviatory for a set of trees, each of which contains only one of the links. (The abbreviated form allows for exponentially fewer trees, however.) Thus, the formalism is equivalent to the one described in this section in terms of bijective link relations. Alternatively, we might allow true multiple adjunction of nontrivial trees, which requires an extended notion of derivation tree and derivation relation. This interpretation, proposed by Schabes and Shieber (1994), is arguably better motivated. We defer discussion of multiple adjunction to Section 8, where we address the issue in detail.

6 THE BIMORPHISM CHARACTERIZATION OF STSG

The central result we provide relating STSG to tree transducers is this: STSG is weakly equivalent to $B(LC, LC)$, that is, equivalent in the characterized string relations. To show this, we must demonstrate that any STSG is reducible to a bimorphism, and vice versa.

6.1 *Reducing STSG to $B(LC, LC)$*

Given an STSG $G = \langle \mathcal{F}_{in}, \mathcal{F}_{out}, P, S_{in}, S_{out} \rangle$, we need to construct a bimorphism characterizing the same tree relation. All the parts are in place to do this. We start by defining a language $\mathbb{D}$ of synchronous derivation trees, which recasts synchronous derivations as single derivation trees from which the left and right derivation trees can be projected via homomorphisms. Rather than taking a synchronous derivation to be a pair of isomorphic trees D_{in} and D_{out}, we take it to be the single tree D isomorphic to both, whose element at address p is the elementary tree pair in P that includes $D_{in}@p$ and $D_{out}@p$. The two synchronized derivations D_{in} and D_{out} can be separately recovered by projecting this new derivation tree on its first and second elements via homomorphisms: h_{in} that projects on the first component and h_{out} that projects on the second, respectively. These homomorphisms are trivially linear and complete (indeed, they are mere delabelings).

We define the set $\mathbb{D}$ of well-formed synchronous derivation trees to be the set of trees $D \in \mathcal{T}(P)$ such that $h_{in}(D)$ and $h_{out}(D)$ are both well-formed derivation trees as per Section 4.3. Since tree automata are closed under inverse homomorphism and intersection, the set $\mathbb{D}$ is a regular tree language.

The fact that for any tree $D \in \mathbb{D}$, $h_{in}(D)$ and $h_{out}(D)$ are well-formed derivation trees for their respective TSGs is trivial by construction. It is also trivial to show that any paired derivation has a corresponding synchronous derivation tree in $\mathbb{D}$.

For a given derivation tree $D \in \mathbb{D}$, the paired derived trees can be constructed as $h_{\mathbb{D}}(h_{in}(D))$ and $h_{\mathbb{D}}(h_{out}(D))$, respectively. Thus the mappings from the derivation tree to the derived trees are the compositions of two linear complete homomorphisms, hence linear complete homomorphisms themselves. We take the bimorphism characterizing the STSG tree relation to be $\langle \mathbb{D}, h_{\mathbb{D}} \circ h_{in}, h_{\mathbb{D}} \circ h_{out} \rangle$. Thus, the tree relation defined by the STSG is in $B(LC, LC)$.

6.2   *Reducing $B(LC, LC)$ to STSG*

The other direction is somewhat trickier to prove. Given a bimorphism $\langle L, h_{in}, h_{out} \rangle$ over input and output alphabets $\mathcal{F}_{in}$ and $\mathcal{F}_{out}$, respectively, we construct a corresponding STSG $G = \langle \mathcal{F}'_{in}, \mathcal{F}'_{out}, P, S_{in}, S_{out} \rangle$. By "corresponding", we mean that the tree relation defined by the bimorphism is obtainable from the tree relation defined by the STSG via simple homomorphisms of the input and output that eliminate the nodes labeled in Q (as described below). The tree yields are unchanged by these homomorphisms; thus, the string relations defined by the bimorphism and the synchronous grammar are identical.

As the language L is a regular tree language, it is generable by a nondeterministic tree automaton $h_D = \langle Q, \mathcal{F}_d, \Delta, q_0 \rangle$. We use the states of this automaton in the input and output alphabets of the STSG. The input alphabet of the STSG is $\mathcal{F}'_{in} = \mathcal{F}_{in} \cup Q$, composed of the input symbols of the bimorphism, along with the states of the automaton (taken to be symbols of arity 1), and similarly for the output alphabet. The state symbols mark the places in the tree where substitutions occur, allowing control for appropriate substitutions. It is these state symbols that can be eliminated by a simple homomorphism.[8]

---

[8] In previous work (Shieber 2004), we used a construction that did not in-

The basic idea of the STSG construction is to construct an elementary tree pair corresponding to each compatible pair of transitions in the transducer $h_D \circ h_{in} = \langle Q_{in}, \mathcal{F}_d, \mathcal{F}_{in}, \Delta_{in}, q_{in,0} \rangle$ and $h_D \circ h_{out} = \langle Q_{out}, \mathcal{F}_d, \mathcal{F}_{out}, \Delta_{out}, q_{out,0} \rangle$. For each pair of transitions of the form

$$q_{in,i}(f(x_1, \ldots, x_n)) \doteq \tau_{in} \in \Delta_{in}$$

and

$$q_{out,j}(f(x_1, \ldots, x_n)) \doteq \tau_{out} \in \Delta_{out}$$

we construct a tree pair

$$\langle q_{in,i}(\lceil \tau_{in} \rceil), q_{out,j}(\lceil \tau_{out} \rceil) \rangle$$

where the following transformation is applied to the right-hand sides of the transitions to form the body of the synchronized trees:

$$\lceil f(t_1, \ldots, t_m) \rceil = f(\lceil t_1 \rceil, \ldots, \lceil t_m \rceil)$$
$$\lceil q_j(x_k) \rceil = \boxed{k} q_{j\downarrow}$$

Note that this transformation generates the tree along with a permutation of the operable sites (all substitution nodes) in the tree, and that there will be exactly n such sites in each element of the tree pair, since the transitions are linear and complete by hypothesis. Thus, the two permutations define an appropriate linking relation, which we take to be the synchronous grammar linking relation for the tree pair.

An example may clarify the construction. Take the language of the bimorphism to be defined by the following two-state automaton:

$$q(f(x, y)) \doteq f(q'(x), q'(y))$$
$$q(a) \doteq a$$
$$q'(g(x)) \doteq g(q(x))$$

troduce any extra tree structure in the STSG, so that the trees generated by the bimorphism relation could be recovered by a delabeling rather than a homomorphism deleting extra nodes. However, the proof of equivalence was considerably more subtle, and did not generalize as readily to the case of STAG. Nonetheless, it is useful to note that even more faithful STSG reconstructions of bimorphisms are possible.

Alternately, the definition of STSG (and similarly, STAG) can be modified to incorporate finite-state information explicitly at operable sites. By adding in this information, the bookkeeping done here can be folded into the states, allowing for a stricter strong-generative capacity equivalence. This elegant approach is pursued by Büchse *et al.* (2014).

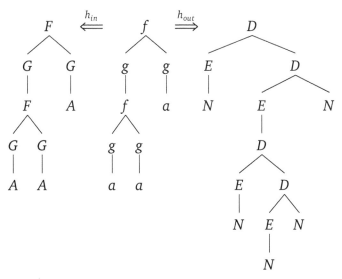

Figure 7: Example of bimorphism construction

This automaton uses the states to alternate g's with f's and a's level by level. For instance, it admits the middle tree in Figure 7. With input and output homomorphisms defined by

$$\hat{h}_{in}(f) \doteq F(x,y) \qquad \hat{h}_{out}(f) \doteq D(y, D(x, N))$$
$$\hat{h}_{in}(g) \doteq G(x) \qquad \hat{h}_{out}(g) \doteq E(x)$$
$$\hat{h}_{in}(a) \doteq A \qquad \hat{h}_{out}(a) \doteq N$$

the bimorphism so defined generates the tree relation instance exemplified in the figure.

The construction given above generates the elementary tree pairs in Figure 8 for this bimorphism. The reader can verify that the grammar generates a tree pair which corresponds to that shown in Figure 7 generated by the bimorphism after deletion of the state symbols.

By placing STSG in the class of bimorphisms, which have already been used to characterize tree transducers, we synthesize these two independently developed approaches to specifying tree relations. But the relation between a TAG derivation tree and its derived tree is not a mere homomorphism. The appropriate morphism generalizing linear complete homomorphisms to allow adjunction can be used to provide

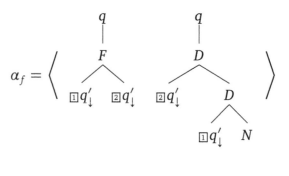

$$\alpha_f = \left\langle \quad \right\rangle$$

$$\alpha_g = \left\langle \quad \right\rangle$$

$$\alpha_a = \left\langle \begin{array}{cc} q & q \\ | & | \\ A & N \end{array} \right\rangle$$

Figure 8: Generated STSG for previous example of bimorphism construction (in Figure 7)

a bimorphism characterization of STAG as well, further unifying these strands of research. It is to this possibility that we now turn.

7   EMBEDDED TREE TRANSDUCERS

We have shown that the string relations defined by synchronous tree-substitution grammars were exactly the relations $B(LC, LC)$. Intuitively speaking, the tree language in such a bimorphism represents the set of derivation trees for the synchronous grammar, and each homomorphism represents the relation between the derivation tree and the derived tree for one of the projected tree-substitution grammars. The homomorphisms are linear and complete because the tree relation between a tree-substitution grammar derivation tree and its associated derived tree is exactly a linear complete tree homomorphism. To characterize the relations defined by synchronous tree-adjoining grammars, it similarly suffices to *find a simple homomorphism-like char-*

acterization of the tree relation between TAG derivation trees and derived trees. In Section 7.3 below, we show that linear complete embedded tree homomorphisms (which we introduce next) serve this purpose.

Embedded tree transducers are a generalization of tree transducers in which states are allowed to take a single additional argument in a restricted manner. They correspond to a restrictive subcase of macro tree transducers with one recursion variable. We use the term "embedded tree transducer" rather than the more cumbersome "monadic macro tree transducer" for brevity and by analogy with embedded pushdown automata (Schabes and Vijay-Shanker 1990), another automata-theoretic characterization of the tree-adjoining languages.

We modify the grammar of transducer equations to add an extra optional argument to each occurrence of a state q. To highlight the special nature of the extra argument, it is written in angle brackets before the input tree argument. We uniformly use the otherwise unused variable x_0 for this argument in the left-hand side, and add x_0 as a possible right-hand side itself. Finally, right-hand-side occurrences of states may be passed an arbitrary further right-hand-side tree in this argument. (The use of square brackets in the metanotation indicates optionality.)

$$
\begin{aligned}
q &\in Q \\
f^{(n)} &\in \mathcal{F}^{(n)} \\
x \in \mathcal{X} &::= x_0 \mid x_1 \mid x_2 \mid \cdots \\
Eqn &::= q\langle[x_0]\rangle(f^{(n)}(x_1,\ldots,x_n)) \doteq \tau^{(n)} \\
\tau^{(n)} \in \mathcal{R}^{(n)} &::= f^{(m)}(\tau^{(n)}{}_1,\ldots,\tau^{(n)}{}_m) \\
&\mid x_0 \\
&\mid q_j\langle[\tau^{(n)}{}_j]\rangle(x_i) \quad \text{where } 1 \le i \le n
\end{aligned}
\tag{7}
$$

Embedded transducers are strictly more expressive than traditional transducers, because the extra argument allows unbounded communication between positions unboundedly distant in depth in the output tree. For example, a simple embedded transducer can compute the reversal of a string, transducing $1(2(2(nil)))$ to $2(2(1(nil)))$, for instance. (This is not computable by a traditional tree transducer.) It is given by the following equations:

$$r\langle\rangle(nil) \doteq nil$$
$$r\langle\rangle(1(x)) \doteq s\langle 1(nil)\rangle(x)$$
$$r\langle\rangle(2(x)) \doteq s\langle 2(nil)\rangle(x)$$
$$s\langle x_0\rangle(nil) \doteq x_0 \tag{8}$$
$$s\langle x_0\rangle(1(x)) \doteq s\langle 1(x_0)\rangle(x)$$
$$s\langle x_0\rangle(2(x)) \doteq s\langle 2(x_0)\rangle(x)$$

This is, of course, just the normal accumulating reverse functional program, expressed as an embedded transducer.[9] The additional power of embedded transducers is exactly what is needed to characterize the additional power that TAGs represent over CFGs in describing tree languages, as we will demonstrate in this section. In particular, we show that the relation between a TAG derivation tree and derived tree is characterized by a deterministic linear complete embedded tree transducer (DLCETT).

The first direct presentation of the connection between the tree-adjoining languages and macro tree transducers – the basis for the presentation here – was given in an earlier paper (Shieber 2006). However, the connection may be implicit in a series of previous results in the formal-language theory literature.[10] For instance, Fujiyoshi and Kasai (2000) show that linear, complete monadic context-free tree grammars generate exactly the tree-adjoining languages via a normal form for spine grammars. Separately, the relation between context-free tree grammars and macro tree transducers has been described, where the relationship between the monadic variants of each is implicit. Thus, taken together, an equivalence between the tree-adjoining

---

[9] A simpler set of equations achieves the same end.

$$r\langle\rangle(x) \doteq s\langle nil\rangle(x)$$
$$s\langle x_0\rangle(nil) \doteq x_0$$
$$s\langle x_0\rangle(1(x)) \doteq s\langle 1(x_0)\rangle(x) \tag{9}$$
$$s\langle x_0\rangle(2(x)) \doteq s\langle 2(x_0)\rangle(x)$$

Unfortunately, this set of equations doesn't satisfy the structure of an embedded tree transducer given in Equation (7). Surprisingly, however, the compilation from equations to TAG presented in Section 7.2 applies to this set of equations as well, generating a TAG whose derived trees also reverse its derivation trees.

[10] We are indebted to Uwe Mönnich for this observation.

languages and the image languages of monadic macro tree transducers might be pieced together.

In the present work, we define the relation between tree-adjoining languages and linear complete embedded tree transducers directly, simply, and transparently, by giving explicit constructions in both directions. First, we show that for any TAG we can construct a DLCETT that specifies the tree relation between the derivation trees for the TAG and the derived trees. Then, we show that for any DLCETT we can construct a TAG such that the tree relation between the derivation trees and derived trees is related through a simple homomorphism to the DLCETT tree relation. Finally, we use these results to show that STAG and the bimorphism class $B(ELC, ELC)$ are weakly equivalent, where ELC stands for the class of linear complete embedded homomorphisms.

7.1   *From TAG to transducer*

As the first part of the task of characterizing TAG in terms of DLCETT, we show that for any TAG grammar $G = \langle \mathcal{F}, P, S \rangle$, there is a DLCETT $\langle \{h_{\mathcal{D}}\}, P, \mathcal{F}, \Delta, h_{\mathcal{D}} \rangle$ (in fact, an embedded homomorphism), that transduces the derivation trees for the grammar to the corresponding derived trees. This transducer plays the same role for TAG as the definition of $h_{\mathcal{D}}$ in Section 4.3 did for TSG. We define the components of the transducer as follows: The single state, evocatively named $h_{\mathcal{D}}$, is the initial state. The input alphabet is the set of elementary trees P in the grammar, since the input trees are to be the derivation trees of the grammar. The arity of a tree (qua symbol in the input alphabet) is as described in Section 4.3. The output alphabet is that used to define the trees in the TAG grammar, $\mathcal{F}$.

We now turn to the construction of the equations, one for each elementary tree $_\square\gamma \in P$. Suppose $_\square\gamma$ has a permutation $\pi = \langle \pi_1, \ldots, \pi_n \rangle$ on its operable sites. (We use this ordering by means of the diacritic representation below.) If γ is an auxiliary tree, construct the equation

$$h_{\mathcal{D}} \langle x_0 \rangle (_\square\gamma(x_1, \ldots, x_n)) \doteq \lfloor \gamma \rfloor$$

and if γ is an initial tree, construct the equation

$$h_{\mathcal{D}} \langle \rangle (_\square\gamma(x_1, \ldots, x_n)) \doteq \lfloor \gamma \rfloor$$

where the right-hand-side transformation $\lfloor \cdot \rfloor$ is defined by[11]

$$\lfloor f(t_1, \ldots, t_n) \rfloor = f(\lfloor t_1 \rfloor, \ldots, \lfloor t_n \rfloor)$$
$$\lfloor \boxed{k} f(t_1, \ldots, t_n) \rfloor = h_{\mathcal{D}} \langle \lfloor f(t_1, \ldots, t_n) \rfloor \rangle (x_k)$$
$$\lfloor f_* \rfloor = x_0 \tag{10}$$
$$\lfloor \boxed{k} f_\downarrow \rfloor = h_{\mathcal{D}} \langle \rangle (x_k) \quad .$$

Note that the equations so generated are linear and complete, because each variable x_i is generated once as the tree α is traversed, namely at position π_i in the traversal (marked with $\boxed{i}$), and the variable x_0 is generated at the foot node only. Thus, the generated embedded tree transducer is linear and complete. Because only one equation is generated per tree, the transducer is trivially deterministic. Because there is only one state, it is a kind of embedded homomorphism.

As noted for TSG in Section 4.3, by composing the automaton recognizing well-formed derivation trees from Section 4.3 with the embedded homomorphism above generating the derived tree, we can construct a single DLCETT doing the work of both. Where the construction of Section 4.3 would generate a transition of the form in Equation 2, repeated here as

$$q_{|N|}(_\square \gamma(x_1, \ldots, x_n)) \doteq {}_\square \gamma(q_{|\gamma @ \pi_1|}(x_1), \ldots, q_{|\gamma @ \pi_n|}(x_n))$$

we compose this transition with the corresponding transition from the previous section

$$h_{\mathcal{D}} \langle x_0 \rangle (_\square \gamma(x_1, \ldots, x_n)) \doteq \lfloor \gamma \rfloor$$

---

[11] It may seem like trickery to use the diacritics in this way, as they are not really components of the tree being traversed, but merely manifestations of an extrinsic ordering. But their use is benign. The same transformation can be defined, a bit more cumbersomely, keeping the permutation π separate, by tracking the permutation and the current address p in a revised transformation $\lfloor \cdot \rfloor_{\pi,p}$ defined as follows:

$$\lfloor f(t_1, \ldots, t_n) \rfloor_{\pi,p} = f(\lfloor t_1 \rfloor_{\pi, p \cdot 1}, \ldots, \lfloor t_n \rfloor_{\pi, p \cdot n})$$
$$\lfloor f(t_1, \ldots, t_n) \rfloor_{\pi,p} = h_{\mathcal{D}} \langle \lfloor f(t_1, \ldots, t_n) \rfloor_{\pi,p} \rangle (x_{\pi^{-1}(p)})$$
$$\lfloor f_* \rfloor_{\pi,p} = x_0$$
$$\lfloor f_\downarrow \rfloor_{\pi,p} = h_{\mathcal{D}} \langle \rangle (x_{\pi^{-1}(p)})$$

We then use $\lfloor \alpha \rfloor_{\pi, \epsilon}$ for the transformation of the tree α.

or

$$h_{\mathcal{D}}\langle\rangle(_{\square}\gamma(x_1,\ldots,x_n)) \doteq \lfloor\gamma\rfloor$$

for auxiliary and initial trees respectively. The composition construction generates a transducer with states in the cross-product of the states of the input transducers. In this case, since the latter transducer has a single state, we simply reuse the state set of the former, generating

$$q_{|N|}\langle x_0\rangle(_{\square}\gamma(x_1,\ldots,x_n)) \doteq \lfloor\gamma\rfloor$$

or

$$q_{|N|}\langle\rangle(_{\square}\gamma(x_1,\ldots,x_n)) \doteq \lfloor\gamma\rfloor$$

where

$$
\begin{aligned}
\lfloor f(t_1,\ldots,t_n)\rfloor &= f(\lfloor t_1\rfloor,\ldots,\lfloor t_n\rfloor) \\
\lfloor_{\boxed{k}}f(t_1,\ldots,t_n)\rfloor &= q_{|f|}\langle\lfloor f(t_1,\ldots,t_n)\rfloor\rangle(x_k) \\
\lfloor f_*\rfloor &= x_0 \\
\lfloor_{\boxed{k}}f_\downarrow\rfloor &= q_{|f_\downarrow|}\langle\rangle(x_k)
\end{aligned}
\tag{11}
$$

7.1.1   An example derivation

By way of example, we consider the tree-adjoining grammar given by the following trees:

$$
\begin{aligned}
\alpha: &\quad {}_{\boxed{1}}A(e) \\
\beta_A: &\quad A(_{\boxed{1}}B(a),_{\boxed{2}}C(_{\boxed{3}}D(A_*))) \\
\beta_B: &\quad {}_{\boxed{1}}B(b,B_*) \\
\text{NA}_B: &\quad B_* \\
\text{NA}_C: &\quad C_* \\
\text{NA}_D: &\quad D_*
\end{aligned}
$$

Starting with the auxiliary tree $\beta_A = A(_{\boxed{1}}B(a),_{\boxed{2}}C(_{\boxed{3}}D(A_*)))$, the adjunction sites, corresponding to the nodes labeled B, C, and D at addresses 1, 2, and 21, have been arbitrarily given a preorder permutation. We therefore construct the equation as follows:

$$
\begin{aligned}
h_{\mathcal{D}}\langle x_0\rangle(\beta_A(x_1,x_2,x_3)) &\doteq \lfloor A(\boxed{1}B(a),\boxed{2}C(\boxed{3}D(A_*)))\rfloor \\
&= A(\lfloor\boxed{1}B(a)\rfloor,\lfloor\boxed{2}C(\boxed{3}D(A_*))\rfloor) \\
&= A(h_{\mathcal{D}}\langle\lfloor B(a)\rfloor\rangle(x_1),\lfloor\boxed{2}C(\boxed{3}D(A_*))\rfloor) \\
&= A(h_{\mathcal{D}}\langle B(\lfloor a\rfloor)\rangle(x_1),\lfloor\boxed{2}C(\boxed{3}D(A_*))\rfloor) \\
&= \cdots \\
&= A(h_{\mathcal{D}}\langle B(a)\rangle(x_1),h_{\mathcal{D}}\langle C(h_{\mathcal{D}}\langle D(x_0)\rangle(x_3))\rangle(x_2))
\end{aligned}
$$

Similar derivations for the remaining trees yield the (deterministic linear complete) embedded tree transducer defined by the following set of equations:

$$
\begin{aligned}
h_{\mathcal{D}}\langle\rangle(\alpha(x_1)) &\doteq h_{\mathcal{D}}\langle A(e)\rangle(x_1) \\
h_{\mathcal{D}}\langle x_0\rangle(\beta_A(x_1,x_2,x_3)) &\doteq A(h_{\mathcal{D}}\langle B(a)\rangle(x_1),h_{\mathcal{D}}\langle C(h_{\mathcal{D}}\langle D(x_0)\rangle(x_3))\rangle(x_2)) \\
h_{\mathcal{D}}\langle x_0\rangle(\beta_B(x_1)) &\doteq h_{\mathcal{D}}\langle B(b,x_0)\rangle(x_1) \\
h_{\mathcal{D}}\langle x_0\rangle(\mathrm{NA}_B()) &\doteq x_0 \\
h_{\mathcal{D}}\langle x_0\rangle(\mathrm{NA}_C()) &\doteq x_0 \\
h_{\mathcal{D}}\langle x_0\rangle(\mathrm{NA}_D()) &\doteq x_0
\end{aligned}
$$

We can use this transducer to compute the derived tree for the derivation tree

$$
\alpha(\beta_A(\beta_B(\mathrm{NA}_B),\mathrm{NA}_C,\mathrm{NA}_D))
$$

as follows:

$$
\begin{aligned}
&h_{\mathcal{D}}\langle\rangle(\alpha(\beta_A(\beta_B(\mathrm{NA}_B),\mathrm{NA}_C,\mathrm{NA}_D))) \\
&\doteq h_{\mathcal{D}}\langle A(e)\rangle(\beta_A(\beta_B(\mathrm{NA}_B),\mathrm{NA}_C,\mathrm{NA}_D)) \\
&\doteq A(h_{\mathcal{D}}\langle B(a)\rangle(\beta_B(\mathrm{NA}_B)),h_{\mathcal{D}}\langle C(h_{\mathcal{D}}\langle D(A(e))\rangle(\mathrm{NA}_D))\rangle(\mathrm{NA}_C)) \\
&\doteq A(h_{\mathcal{D}}\langle B(b,B(a))\rangle(\mathrm{NA}_B),C(h_{\mathcal{D}}\langle D(A(e))\rangle(\mathrm{NA}_D))) \\
&\doteq A(B(b,B(a)),C(D(A(e))))
\end{aligned}
$$

7.1.2   Equivalence of $\mathcal{D}$ and $h_{\mathcal{D}}$

We can now show for TAG derivations, as we did for TSG derivations in Section 4.3, that the embedded homomorphism $h_{\mathcal{D}}$ constructed in this way computes the derivation relation $\mathcal{D}$.

In order to simplify the argument, we take advantage of the commutativity of operations (Equation 4), and assume without loss of generality that each permutation associated with the operable sites of an elementary tree is consistent with a postorder traversal of the nodes in the tree. We can then simplify Equation 3 to

$$\gamma[\text{OP}_{p_1} \gamma_1, \text{OP}_{p_2} \gamma_2, \ldots, \text{OP}_{p_n} \gamma_n] \equiv \gamma[\text{OP}_{p_1} \gamma_1][\text{OP}_{p_2} \gamma_2, \ldots, \text{OP}_{p_n} \gamma_n]$$

since in a postorder traversal, $p_i \not\prec p_{i+k}$.

It will also prove to be useful to have a single notation for the effect of both substitution and adjunction. Recall the definitions of substitution and adjunction:

$$\gamma[\text{SUBST}_p \alpha] \equiv \gamma[p \mapsto \alpha]$$
$$\gamma[\text{ADJ}_p \beta] \equiv \gamma[p \mapsto \beta[\text{foot}(\beta) \mapsto \gamma/p]]$$

Under the convention that mapping a (nonexistent) "foot" of an initial tree leaves the tree unchanged, that is,

$$\alpha[\text{foot}(\alpha) \mapsto \gamma] \equiv \alpha$$

the two operations collapse notationally, so that we can write

$$\gamma[\text{OP}_p \gamma'] \equiv \gamma[p \mapsto \gamma'[\text{foot}(\gamma') \mapsto \gamma/p]]$$

for both substitution and adjunction.

We prove that $\mathcal{D}(D) = h_{\mathcal{D}}\langle\rangle(D)$ for derivations D rooted in an initial tree, and $\mathcal{D}(D)[\text{foot}(\mathcal{D}(D)) \mapsto x] = h_{\mathcal{D}}\langle x\rangle(D)$ for derivations rooted in an auxiliary tree. The proof is again by induction on the height of the derivation D.

For the base case, the derivation consists of a single tree with no operable sites. If it is an initial tree α, then $\mathcal{D}(\alpha) = \alpha = h_{\mathcal{D}}\langle\rangle(\alpha)$ straightforwardly from the definition of $h_{\mathcal{D}}$, using only the first equation in Equation (10). Similarly, the base case for auxiliary trees,

$$\mathcal{D}(\beta)[\text{foot}(\beta) \mapsto x] = \beta[\text{foot}(\beta) \mapsto x] = h_{\mathcal{D}}\langle x\rangle(\beta)$$

requires only the first and third equations in (10).

For the recursive case,

$$h_{\mathcal{D}}\langle\rangle(\alpha(D_1,\ldots,D_n))$$
$$= \lfloor\alpha\rfloor[x_1 \mapsto D_1,\ldots,x_n \mapsto D_n]$$
$$= \alpha[\pi_1 \mapsto h_{\mathcal{D}}\langle\alpha/\pi_1\rangle(D_1)]\cdots[\pi_n \mapsto h_{\mathcal{D}}\langle\alpha/\pi_n\rangle(D_n)]$$
$$= \alpha[\pi_1 \mapsto \mathcal{D}(D_1)[\text{foot}(\mathcal{D}(D_1)) \mapsto \alpha/\pi_1]]$$
$$\cdots[\pi_1 \mapsto \mathcal{D}(D_n)[\text{foot}(\mathcal{D}(D_n)) \mapsto \alpha/\pi_n]] \qquad \Leftarrow$$
$$= \alpha[\text{OP}_{\pi_1} \mathcal{D}(D_1)]\cdots[\text{OP}_{\pi_n} \mathcal{D}(D_n)]$$
$$= \alpha[\text{OP}_{\pi_1} \mathcal{D}(D_1),\cdots,\text{OP}_{\pi_n} \mathcal{D}(D_n)]$$
$$= \mathcal{D}(\alpha(D_1,\ldots,D_n))$$

with the marked step appealing to the induction hypothesis.
Similarly, for derivations rooted in an auxiliary tree,

$$h_{\mathcal{D}}\langle x\rangle(\beta(D_1,\ldots,D_n))$$
$$= \lfloor\beta\rfloor[x_0 \mapsto x, x_1 \mapsto D_1,\ldots,x_n \mapsto D_n]$$
$$= \beta[\text{foot}(\beta) \mapsto x][\pi_1 \mapsto h_{\mathcal{D}}\langle\beta/\pi_1\rangle(D_1)]$$
$$\cdots[\pi_n \mapsto h_{\mathcal{D}}\langle\beta/\pi_n\rangle(D_n)]$$
$$= \beta[\text{foot}(\beta) \mapsto x][\pi_1 \mapsto \mathcal{D}(D_1)[\text{foot}(\mathcal{D}(D_1)) \mapsto \beta/\pi_1]]$$
$$\cdots[\pi_1 \mapsto \mathcal{D}(D_n)[\text{foot}(\mathcal{D}(D_n)) \mapsto \beta/\pi_n]]$$
$$= \beta[\text{foot}(\beta) \mapsto x][\text{OP}_{\pi_1} \mathcal{D}(D_1)]\cdots[\text{OP}_{\pi_n} \mathcal{D}(D_n)]$$
$$= \beta[\text{foot}(\beta) \mapsto x][\text{OP}_{\pi_1} \mathcal{D}(D_1),\ldots,\text{OP}_{\pi_n} \mathcal{D}(D_n)]$$
$$= \beta[\text{OP}_{\pi_1} \mathcal{D}(D_1),\cdots,\text{OP}_{\pi_n} \mathcal{D}(D_n)][\text{foot}(\mathcal{D}(\beta(D_1,\ldots,D_n))) \mapsto x]$$
$$= \mathcal{D}(\beta(D_1,\ldots,D_n))[\text{foot}(\mathcal{D}(\beta(D_1,\ldots,D_n))) \mapsto x] \qquad .$$

7.2 From transducer to TAG

Having shown how to construct a DLCETT that captures the relation
between derivation trees and derived trees of a TAG, we turn now to
showing how to construct a TAG that mimics in its derivation/derived
tree relation a DLCETT. Given a linear complete embedded tree trans-
ducer $\langle Q, \mathcal{F}, \mathcal{G}, \Delta, q_0 \rangle$, we construct a corresponding TAG $\langle \mathcal{G} \cup \dot{Q}, P, \dot{q}_0 \rangle$
where the alphabet consists of the output alphabet $\mathcal{G}$ of the transducer
together with the disjoint set of unary symbols $\dot{Q} = \{\dot{q}_1,\ldots,\dot{q}_{|Q|}\}$ cor-
responding to the states of the input transducer. The initial symbol of

the grammar is the symbol $\dot{q}_0$ corresponding to the initial state q_0 of the transducer.

The elementary trees of the grammar are constructed as follows. For each rule of the form

$$q\langle[x_0]\rangle(f^{(m)}(x_1,\ldots,x_m)) \doteq \tau$$

we build a tree named $\langle q, f, \tau \rangle$. Where this tree appears is determined solely by the state q, so we take the root node of the tree to be the corresponding symbol $\dot{q}$. Any foot node in the tree will also need to be marked with the same label, so we pass this information down as the tree is built inductively. The tree is therefore of the form $\dot{q}(\lceil \tau \rceil_q)$ where the right-hand-side transformation $\lceil \cdot \rceil_q$ constructs the remainder of the tree by the inductive walk of τ, with the subscript noting that the root is labeled by state q.

$$\lceil f^{(m)}(t_1,\ldots,t_m)\rceil_q = f(\lceil t_1 \rceil_q,\ldots,\lceil t_m \rceil_q)$$
$$\lceil q_j\langle\tau\rangle(x_k)\rceil_q = \boxed{k}\,\dot{q}_j(\lceil \tau \rceil_q)$$
$$\lceil q_j\langle\rangle(x_k)\rceil_q = \boxed{k}\,\dot{q}_{j\downarrow}$$
$$\lceil x_0 \rceil_q = \dot{q}_*$$

Note that at x_0, a foot node is generated of the proper label. (Because the equation is linear, only one foot node is generated, and it is labeled appropriately by construction.) Where recursive processing of the input tree occurs ($q_j\langle\tau\rangle(x_k)$), we generate a tree that admits adjunctions at $\dot{q}_j$. The role of the diacritic $\boxed{k}$ is merely to specify the permutation of operable sites for interpreting derivation trees; it says that the k-th child in a derivation tree rooted in the current elementary tree is taken to specify adjunctions at this node.

The trees generated by this TAG correspond to the outputs of the corresponding tree transducer. Because of the more severe constraints on TAG, in particular that all combinatorial limitations on putting subtrees together must be manifest in the labels in the trees themselves, the outputs actually contain more structure than the corresponding transducer output. In particular, the state-labeled nodes are merely for bookkeeping. A simple homomorphism removing these nodes gives the desired transducer output:[12]

$$rem(\dot{q}(x)) \doteq rem(x) \qquad\qquad\qquad\qquad \text{for } \dot{q} \in \dot{Q}$$
$$rem(f^{(n)}(x_1,\ldots,x_n)) \doteq f^{(n)}(rem(x_1),\ldots,rem(x_n)) \quad \text{for } f^{(n)} \in \mathcal{G}^{(n)}$$

An example may clarify the construction. Recall the reversal embedded transducer in (8) above. The construction above generates a TAG containing the following trees. We have given them indicative names rather than the cumbersome ones of the form $\langle q_i, f, \tau \rangle$.

$$
\begin{aligned}
\alpha_{nil} &: \quad \dot{r}(nil)\\
\alpha_1 &: \quad \dot{r}(\boxdot\dot{s}(1(nil)))\\
\alpha_2 &: \quad \dot{r}(\boxdot\dot{s}(2(nil)))\\
\beta_{nil} &: \quad \dot{s}(\dot{s}_*)\\
\beta_1 &: \quad \dot{s}(\boxdot\dot{s}(1(\dot{s}_*)))\\
\beta_2 &: \quad \dot{s}(\boxdot\dot{s}(2(\dot{s}_*)))
\end{aligned}
$$

It is simple to verify that the derivation tree

$$\alpha_1(\beta_2(\beta_2(\beta_{nil})))$$

derives the tree

$$\dot{r}(\dot{s}^4(2(\dot{s}(2(\dot{s}(1(nil)))))))) \qquad .$$

Simple homomorphisms that extract the input function symbols on the input and drop the bookkeeping states on the output (that is, the homomorphism rem provided above) reduce these trees to $1(2(2(nil)))$ and $2(2(1(nil)))$ respectively, just as for the corresponding tree transducer.

7.2.1   Equivalence of DLCETT and TAG

We demonstrate that the compilation from DLCETT to TAG generates a grammar with the same language as that of the DLCETT by appeal to the previous result of Section 7.1.2. Consider a DLCETT $T = \langle Q, \mathcal{F}, \mathcal{G}, \Delta, q_0 \rangle$ converted by the compilation above to a grammar $G = \langle \mathcal{G} \cup \dot{Q}, P, \dot{q}_0 \rangle$. That grammar may itself be compiled to a

---

[12] As noted in Footnote 8, a formalization of a modified form of TAG that directly incorporates state information at operable sites (Büchse *et al.* 2014) eliminates this need for bookkeeping through extra nodes in the tree structure, making the equivalence even stronger.

DLCETT using the compilation of Section 7.1.2, previously shown to be language-preserving. We show that this round-trip conversion preserves the language that is the range of the DLCETT by showing that each equation in the original grammar "round-trip" compiles to an equation that differs only in the tree structure. In particular, a rule of the form $q\langle x_0 \rangle(f(x_1, \ldots, x_m)) = \tau$ compiles to the equation $q\langle x_0 \rangle(f(x_1, \ldots, x_m)) = \tau'$ where $\tau = rem(\tau')$. We will write $\tau' \approx \tau$ when $\tau = rem(\tau')$.

For each rule in T of the form $q\langle x_0 \rangle(f(x_1, \ldots, x_m)) = \tau$, we generate a tree $\langle q, f, \tau \rangle$ in the grammar G of the form $\dot{q}(\lceil \tau \rceil_q)$. This tree, in turn, is compiled as in Section 7.1 to an equation in the output transducer T':

$$
\begin{aligned}
q\langle x_0 \rangle(\langle q, f, \tau \rangle(x_1, \ldots, x_m)) &= \lfloor \dot{q}(\lceil \tau \rceil_q) \rfloor \\
&= \dot{q}(\lfloor \lceil \tau \rceil_q \rfloor) \\
&\approx \lfloor \lceil \tau \rceil_q \rfloor
\end{aligned}
$$

(Here and in the following, we write q for $q_{|\dot{q}|}$ in the $\lfloor \cdot \rfloor$ construction, taking advantage of the bijection between the $\dot{Q}$ symbols and the corresponding states of the generated transducer.) Note that this is exactly of the required form, so long as $\lfloor \lceil \tau \rceil_q \rfloor \approx \tau$, which we now prove by induction on the structure of τ.

- If $\tau = x_0$, $\lfloor \lceil x_0 \rceil_q \rfloor = \lfloor \dot{q}_* \rfloor = x_0$.
- If $\tau = q_j \langle \rangle(x_k)$, $\lfloor \lceil q_j \langle \rangle(x_k) \rceil_q \rfloor = \lfloor \boxed{k} \dot{q}_{j\downarrow} \rfloor = q_j \langle \rangle(x_k)$.
- If $\tau = q_j \langle \tau_0 \rangle(x_k)$,

$$
\begin{aligned}
\lfloor \lceil q_j \langle \tau_0 \rangle(x_k) \rceil_q \rfloor &= \lfloor \boxed{k} \dot{q}_j(\lceil \tau_0 \rceil_q) \rfloor \\
&= q_j \langle \lfloor \dot{q}_j(\lceil \tau_0 \rceil_q) \rfloor \rangle(x_k) \\
&= q_j \langle \dot{q}_j(\lfloor \lceil \tau_0 \rceil_q \rfloor) \rangle(x_k) \\
&\approx q_j \langle \tau_0 \rangle(x_k).
\end{aligned}
$$

The last step follows from the induction hypothesis and the fact that rem removes the symbol $\dot{q}_j$.

- If $\tau = f^{(m)}(t_1, \ldots, t_m)$,

$$
\begin{aligned}
\lfloor \lceil f^{(m)}(t_1, \ldots, t_m) \rceil_q \rfloor &= \lfloor f^{(m)}(\lceil t_1 \rceil_q, \ldots, \lceil t_m \rceil_q) \rfloor \\
&= f^{(m)}(\lfloor \lceil t_1 \rceil_q \rfloor, \ldots, \lfloor \lceil t_m \rceil_q \rfloor) \\
&\approx f^{(m)}(t_1, \ldots, t_m).
\end{aligned}
$$

Again, the last step applies the induction hypothesis.

Writing $L(T)$ for the range string language of the transducer T, we have that $L(G) = L(T')$ and $L(T) = L(T')$. We conclude that $L(T) = L(G)$. In fact, by the above, the tree languages are identical up to the homomorphism *rem*. Most importantly, then, the weak generative capacity of TAGs and the range of DLCETTs are identical.

7.3   *The bimorphism characterization of STAG*

The major advantage of characterizing TAG derivation in terms of tree transducers (via the compilation (10)) is the integration of synchronous TAGs into the bimorphism framework, which follows directly.

In order to model a synchronous grammar formalism as a bimorphism, the well-formed derivations of the synchronous formalism must be characterizable as a regular tree language and the relation between such derivation trees and each of the paired derived trees as a homomorphism of some sort. As shown in Section 6, for synchronous tree-substitution grammars, derivation trees are regular tree languages, and the map from derivation to each of the paired derived trees is a linear complete tree homomorphism. Thus, synchronous tree-substitution grammars fall in the class of bimorphisms $B(LC, LC)$. The other direction holds as well; all bimorphisms in $B(LC, LC)$ define string relations expressible by an STSG.

A similar result follows for STAG. Crucially relying on the result above that the derivation relation is a DLCETT, we can use the same method directly to characterize the synchronous TAG string relations as just $B(ELC, ELC)$. We have thus integrated synchronous TAG with the other transducer and synchronous grammar formalisms falling under the bimorphism umbrella.

8   MULTIPLE ADJUNCTION

The discussion so far has assumed that derivations allow at most one operation to occur at any given node in an elementary tree (in fact, exactly one). This constraint inhered in the original formulations of TAG derivation (Vijay-Shanker 1987), and had the effect of removing systematic spurious ambiguities without reducing the range of definable languages. Schabes and Shieber (1994) point out the desirability of allowing multiple adjunctions at a single node, and provide various arguments for this generalization, most notably as needed for many applications of synchronous TAG, which is precisely the case that we are concerned with in this paper. It therefore behooves us to examine the effect of multiple adjunction on the analysis.

There are various ways in which multiple adjunction can be inserted. Most simply, one could specify that the set of operable nodes of a tree allows for a given node in the set a fixed number of times. (This could be graphically depicted by allowing more than one diacritic at a given node, with each diacritic to be used exactly once.) In theory, this would allow multiple nontrivial adjunctions to occur at a single node, inducing ambiguity as to the resulting derived tree, but we can eliminate this possibility by requiring that nontrivial (that is, non-NA) trees be adjoined at at most one site at a given node. We start by handling this kind of simple generalization of TAG derivation in Sections 8.1–8.2.

More generally, Schabes and Shieber (1994) call for allowing an arbitrary number of adjunctions at a given node. In particular, they call for distinguishing predicative and modifier auxiliary trees, and allowing any number of modifier trees and at most one predicative tree to adjoin at a given node. The derived tree is ambiguous as to the relative orderings of the modifier trees, but the predicative tree is required to fall above the modifier trees. We address this major generalization of TAG derivation in Section 8.3.

8.1   *Simple multiple adjunction*

We start with a simple generalization of TAG derivation in which operable nodes may be used a fixed number of times. Since the set of operable nodes may now include duplicates, adjunction nodes may occur more than once in the permutation π. To guarantee that at most one of these can be nontrivially adjoined, we need to revise the definition of derivation tree, that is, fix the tree automaton from Section 4.3 defining well-formed derivation trees, and to prove that the derivation relation $\mathcal{D}$ is still well-defined.

We present an alternative automaton defining the regular tree language of well-formed derivation trees now allowing the limited form of multiple adjunction. We double the number of states from the previous construction. The states of the automaton are the set $\{q_{N\triangle} \mid N \in \mathcal{F}\} \cup \{q_{N\bullet} \mid N \in \mathcal{F}\}$, two for each unranked vocabulary symbol in the derived tree language. The $\triangle$ diacritic indicates a nontrivial tree rooted in the given symbol; the $\bullet$ diacritic requires a nonadjunction NA tree rooted in that symbol. The start state is $q_{|S|\triangle}$.

For each nontrivial tree (that is, not an NA tree) $_\square\gamma = \langle \gamma, \pi \rangle$, of arity n and rooted with the symbol N, we construct all possible transitions of the form

$$q_{|N|\triangle}(\gamma(x_1, \ldots, x_n)) \doteq \gamma(q_1(x_1), \ldots, q_n(x_n))$$

where each q_i is either $q_{|\gamma@\pi_i|\bullet}$ or $q_{|\gamma@\pi_i|\triangle}$, subject to the constraint that for each node η in α, the sequence $\langle q_i \mid \pi_i = \eta \rangle$ contains at most one $\triangle$. Because there are many such ways of setting the q_i to satisfy this constraint, there are many (though still a finite number of) transitions for each γ.

In addition, for NA trees, there is a transition

$$q_{|N|\bullet}(\gamma) \doteq \gamma \qquad .$$

The set of well-formed derivation trees is thus still a regular tree set.

The only remaining issue is to verify that the limited form of multiple adjunction that we allow still yields a well-defined derived tree. In general, multiple adjunctions at the same site do not commute. However, the only cases of multiple adjunctions that we allow involve all but one of the auxiliary trees being vestigial nonadjunction trees. Such cases do commute. It suffices to show that $\gamma[\text{ADJ}_p \beta, \text{ADJ}_p \text{NA}] = \gamma[\text{ADJ}_p \text{NA}, \text{ADJ}_p \beta]$; we derive this as follows:

$$\begin{aligned}
\gamma[\text{ADJ}_p \beta, \text{ADJ}_p \text{NA}] &= \gamma[\text{ADJ}_p \beta][\text{ADJ}_{update(p,\beta,p)} \text{NA}] \\
&= \gamma[\text{ADJ}_p \beta][\text{ADJ}_p \text{NA}] \\
&= \gamma[\text{ADJ}_p \beta] \\
&= \gamma[\text{ADJ}_p \text{NA}][\text{ADJ}_p \beta] \\
&= \gamma[\text{ADJ}_p \text{NA}][\text{ADJ}_{update(p,\beta,p)} \beta] \\
&= \gamma[\text{ADJ}_p \text{NA}, \text{ADJ}_p \beta]
\end{aligned}$$

8.2   *Fixed multiple adjunction*

What if we allow more than one of the multiple (fixed) occurrences of a node to be operated on by a nontrivial auxiliary tree? At that point,

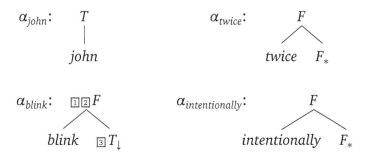

Figure 9: A fragment with multiple adjunction.

the definition of simultaneous operations no longer commutes, and which auxiliary tree is used at which position becomes important.

The definition of the derivation tree language given in Section 4.3 allows such derivations to be specified merely by relaxing the constraint that a node appears only once in the set of operable sites. If we move to a multiset of operable sites, with π a permutation over that multiset, the remaining definitions generalize properly.

We present (Figure 9) a fragment based on the semantic half of a synchronous TAG presented previously (Shieber 1994, Figure 1) to exemplify simultaneous adjunction. This grammar uses simultaneous adjunction at the root of the α_{blink} tree. That tree has three operable sites, two of which are the root node. We will take the permutation of operable sites for the tree to be $\langle \boxed{1}, \boxed{2}, \boxed{3} \rangle$.

We can examine what the compilation of Section 7.1 provides as the interpretation for this grammar. Applying it to the output trees in the grammar generates a DLCETT. We start with the problematic multiple adjunction tree α_{blink}.

$$
\begin{aligned}
q_F \langle\rangle(\alpha_{blink}(x_1, x_2, x_3)) &\doteq \lfloor \alpha_{blink} \rfloor \\
&= \lfloor \boxed{1}\boxed{2} F(blink, \boxed{3} T) \rfloor \\
&= q_F \langle \lfloor \boxed{2} F(blink, \boxed{3} T) \rfloor \rangle (x_1) \\
&= q_F \langle q_F \langle \lfloor F(blink, \boxed{3} T) \rfloor \rangle (x_1) \rangle (x_2) \\
&= q_F \langle q_F \langle F(blink, q_T \langle\rangle(x_3)) \rangle (x_1) \rangle (x_2)
\end{aligned}
$$

(Here, the second line uses the obvious generalization of the second equation of (10) to sets of diacritics, that is,

$$
\lfloor \boxed{k} \cdots f(t_1, \ldots, t_n) \rfloor = q_{|f|} \langle \lfloor \cdots f(t_1, \ldots, t_n) \rfloor \rangle (x_k) \quad ,
$$

the ellipses standing in for arbitrary further diacritics.)

The second and third steps are notable here, in that the choice of which of the two operable sites to use first was arbitrary. That is, one could just as well have chosen to process diacritic ② before ①, in which case the generated rule would have been

$$q_F \langle \rangle (\alpha_{blink}(x_1, x_2, x_3)) \doteq q_F \langle q_F \langle F(blink, q_T \langle \rangle(x_3)) \rangle (x_2) \rangle (x_1) \qquad .$$

This is, of course, just the consequence of the fact that multiple adjunctions at the same node do not commute. To manifest the ambiguity, we can just generate both transitions (and in general, all such transitions) in the transducer defining the derivation relation. The transducer naturally becomes nondeterministic. Alternatively, a particular order might be stipulated, regaining determinism, but giving up analyses that take advantage of the ambiguity.

Completing the compilation, we generate transitions for the other trees:

$$q_T \langle \rangle (\alpha_{john}) \doteq T(john)$$
$$q_F \langle x_0 \rangle (\beta_{twice}) \doteq F(twice, x_0)$$
$$q_F \langle x_0 \rangle (\beta_{intentionally}) \doteq F(intentionally, x_0)$$

The derivation tree $\alpha_{blink}(\beta_{intentionally}, \beta_{twice}, \alpha_{john})$ then derives trees as follows:

$$q_F \langle \rangle (\alpha_{blink}(\beta_{intentionally}, \beta_{twice}, \alpha_{john}))$$
$$\doteq q_F \langle q_F \langle F(blink, q_T \langle \rangle(\alpha_{john})) \rangle (\beta_{intentionally}) \rangle (\beta_{twice})$$
$$\doteq q_F \langle q_F \langle F(blink, T(john)) \rangle (\beta_{intentionally}) \rangle (\beta_{twice})$$
$$\doteq q_F \langle F(intentionally, F(blink, T(john))) \rangle (\beta_{twice})$$
$$\doteq F(twice, F(intentionally, F(blink, T(john))))$$

corresponding to the meaning $twice(intentionally(blink(john)))$. Alternatively, use of the other nondeterministic alternative transition yields

$$q_F \langle \rangle (\alpha_{blink}(\beta_{intentionally}, \beta_{twice}, \alpha_{john}))$$
$$\doteq q_F \langle q_F \langle F(blink, q_T \langle \rangle(\alpha_{john})) \rangle (\beta_{twice}) \rangle (\beta_{intentionally})$$
$$\doteq q_F \langle q_F \langle F(blink, T(john)) \rangle (\beta_{twice}) \rangle (\beta_{intentionally})$$
$$\doteq q_F \langle F(twice, F(blink, T(john))) \rangle (\beta_{intentionally})$$
$$\doteq F(intentionally, F(twice, F(blink, T(john))))$$

giving the alternative reading for the sentence.

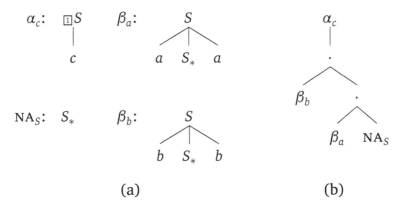

Figure 10: A grammar (a) for $\{wcw^R \mid w \in \{a \; b\}^*\}$, using general multiple adjunction, and (b) a derivation of the string $abba$.

8.3   *General multiple adjunction*

Finally, fully general multiple adjunction as described by Schabes and Shieber (1994) allows for one and the same operable site to be used an arbitrary number of times. To enable this interpretation of TAG derivations, major changes need to be made to the definitions of derivation tree and derivation relation.

Consider the sample grammar of Figure 10 where the two auxiliary trees β_a and β_b are modifier trees (in the terminology of Schabes and Shieber (1994)) and thus allowed to multiply adjoin at the two operable nodes in the initial tree. This grammar should generate the language $\{wcw^R \mid w \in \{a, b\}^*\}$.

Derivation trees must allow an arbitrary number of operations to occur at a given site. To represent this in a ranked tree, we can encode the sequence of trees adjoined at a given location with a recursive structure. In particular, we use a binary symbol $\cdot$ (which we write infix) to build a list of trees to be adjoined at the site, using a nonadjunction tree to mark the end of the list. Essentially, derivation trees now contain lists of auxiliary trees to operate at a site rather than a single tree, with the nonadjoining trees serving as the *nil* elements of the list and the binary $\cdot$ serving as the binary *constructor*. For example, a derivation for the grammar of Figure 10(a) can be represented by the tree in Figure 10(b).

The derivation tree language with lists instead of individual trees is still regular. In fact, the full specification of multiple adjunction given by Schabes and Shieber (1994) specifies that at a given operable site an arbitrary number of modifier trees but at most one predicative tree may be adjoined. Further, the predicative tree is to appear highest in the derived tree above the adjoined modifiers. This constraint can be specified by defining the derivation tree language appropriately, allowing at most one predicative tree, and placing it at the end of the list of nontrivial trees adjoining at a site. It is a simple exercise to show that the derivation tree language so restricted still falls within the regular tree languages.

Finally, we must provide a definition of the derivation relation for this generalized form of multiple adjunction. In particular, we need transitions for the new form of constructor node, which specifies the combination of two adjunctions at a single site. We handle this by stacking the rest of the adjunctions above the first. We add to the definition of the derivation transducer of Section 7.1 transitions of the following form for each symbol N that is the root of some auxiliary tree:

$$q_N\langle x_0\rangle(x_1 \cdot x_2) \doteq q_N\langle q_N\langle x_0\rangle(x_1)\rangle(x_2)$$

Note that the new transition is still linear and complete.

For the grammar of Figure 10(a) we would thus have the following transitions defining the derivation relation:

$$q_S\langle\rangle(\alpha(x)) \doteq q_S\langle S(c)\rangle(x)$$
$$q_S\langle x_0\rangle(NA_S) \doteq x_0$$
$$q_S\langle x_0\rangle(\beta_a) \doteq S(a, x_0, a)$$
$$q_S\langle x_0\rangle(\beta_b) \doteq S(b, x_0, b)$$
$$q_S\langle x_0\rangle(x_1 \cdot x_2) \doteq q_S\langle q_S\langle x_0\rangle(x_1)\rangle(x_2)$$

Using this derivation relation, the derived tree for the derivation tree of Figure 10(b) can be calculated as

$$q_S\langle\rangle(\alpha_c(\beta_b \cdot \beta_a \cdot NA_S)) \doteq q_S\langle S(c)\rangle(\beta_b \cdot \beta_a \cdot NA_S)$$
$$\doteq q_S\langle q_S\langle S(c)\rangle(\beta_b)\rangle(\beta_a \cdot NA_S)$$
$$\doteq q_S\langle S(b, S(c), b)\rangle(\beta_a \cdot NA_S)$$
$$\doteq q_S\langle q_S\langle S(b, S(c), b)\rangle(\beta_a)\rangle(NA_S)$$
$$\doteq q_S\langle S(a, S(b, S(c), b), a)\rangle(NA_S)$$
$$\doteq S(a, S(b, S(c), b), a)$$

corresponding to the string $abcba$ as expected.

9   CONCLUSION

Synchronous grammars and tree transducers – two approaches to the specification of language relations useful for a variety of formal and computational linguistics modeling of natural languages – are unified by means of the elegant construct of the bimorphism. This convergence synthesizes the approaches and allows a direct comparison among these and other potential systems for describing language relations through other bimorphisms. The examination of additional bimorphism classes may open up further possibilities for useful modeling tools for natural language.

ACKNOWLEDGEMENTS

This paper has been gestating for a long time. I thank the participants in my course on Transducers at the 2003 European Summer School on Logic, Language, and Information in Vienna, Austria, where some of these ideas were presented, and Mark Dras, Mark Johnson, Uwe Mönnich, Rani Nelken, Rebecca Nesson, James Rogers, and Ken Shan for helpful discussions on the topic of this paper and related topics. The extensive comments of the JLM reviewers were invaluable in improving the paper. This work was supported in part by grant IIS-0329089 from the National Science Foundation.

REFERENCES

Alfred V. AHO and Jeffrey D. ULLMAN (1969), Syntax Directed Translations and the Pushdown Assembler, *Journal of Computer and System Sciences*, 3(1):37–56, doi:10.1016/S0022-0000(69)80006-1.

Hiyan ALSHAWI, Srinivas BANGALORE, and Shona DOUGLAS (2000), Learning Dependency Translation Models as Collections of Finite State Head Transducers, *Computational Linguistics*, 26(1):45–60, doi:10.1162/089120100561629.

André ARNOLD and Max DAUCHET (1982), Morphismes et bimorphismes d'arbres [Morphisms and bimorphisms of trees], *Theoretical Computer Science*, 20(1):33–93, doi:10.1016/0304-3975(82)90098-6.

Matthias BÜCHSE, Andreas MALETTI, and Heiko VOGLER (2012), Unidirectional Derivation Semantics for Synchronous Tree-Adjoining Grammars, in *Developments in Language Theory*, volume 7410 of *Lecture Notes in Computer Science*, pp. 368–379, Springer, doi:10.1007/978-3-642-31653-1_33.

Matthias BÜCHSE, Heiko VOGLER, and Mark-Jan NEDERHOF (2014), Tree Parsing for Tree-Adjoining Machine Translation, *Journal of Logic and Computation*, 24(2):351–373, doi:10.1093/logcom/exs050.

Hubert COMON, Max DAUCHET, Remi GILLERON, Florent JACQUEMARD, Denis LUGIEZ, Sophie TISON, and Marc TOMMASI (2008), Tree Automata Techniques and Applications, http://tata.gforge.inria.fr/, release of November 18, 2008.

Steve DENEEFE and Kevin KNIGHT (2009), Synchronous Tree Adjoining Machine Translation, in *Proceedings of the 2009 Conference on Empirical Methods in Natural Language Processing*, pp. 727–736, Association for Computational Linguistics, Singapore, http://aclweb.org/anthology/D09-1076.

Akio FUJIYOSHI and Takumi KASAI (2000), Spinal-Formed Context-Free Tree Grammars, *Theory of Computing Systems*, 33:59–83, doi:10.1007/s002249910004.

Michel GALLEY, Mark HOPKINS, Kevin KNIGHT, and Daniel MARCU (2004), What's In a Translation Rule, in *Proceedings of the Human Language Technology Conference of the North American Chapter of the Association for Computational Linguistics: HLT-NAACL 2004*, pp. 273–280, Association for Computational Linguistics, Boston, Massachusetts, http://aclweb.org/anthology/N04-1035.

Jonathan GRAEHL and Kevin KNIGHT (2004), Training Tree Transducers, in *Proceedings of the Human Language Technology Conference of the North American Chapter of the Association for Computational Linguistics: HLT-NAACL 2004*, pp. 105–112, Association for Computational Linguistics, Boston, Massachusetts, http://aclweb.org/anthology/N04-1014.

Chung-Hye HAN and Nancy HEDBERG (2008), Syntax and Semantics of It-Clefts: A Tree Adjoining Grammar Analysis, *Journal of Semantics*, 25:345–380, doi:10.1093/jos/ffn007.

Aravind JOSHI and Yves SCHABES (1997), Tree-Adjoining Grammars, in G. ROZENBERG and A. SALOMAA, editors, *Handbook of Formal Languages*, volume 3, pp. 69–124, Springer, Berlin.

Alexander KOLLER and Marco KUHLMANN (2011), A Generalized View on Parsing and Translation, in *Proceedings of the 12th International Conference on Parsing Technologies*, IWPT '11, pp. 2–13, Association for Computational Linguistics, Stroudsburg, PA, USA, ISBN 978-1-932432-04-6, http://dl.acm.org/citation.cfm?id=2206329.2206331.

Philip M. LEWIS II and Richard E. STEARNS (1968), Syntax-Directed Transduction, *Journal of the Association for Computing Machinery*, 15(3):465–488, ISSN 0004-5411, doi:10.1145/321466.321477.

Andreas MALETTI (2008), Compositions of Extended Top-down Tree Transducers, *Information and Computation*, 206(9-10):1187–1196, doi:10.1016/j.ic.2008.03.019.

Andreas MALETTI, Jonathan GRAEHL, Mark HOPKINS, and Kevin KNIGHT (2009), The power of extended top-down tree transducers, *SIAM Journal on Computing*, 39:410–430, doi:10.1137/070699160.

I. Dan MELAMED (2003), Multitext Grammars and Synchronous Parsers, in *Proceedings of the 2003 Human Language Technology Conference of the North American Chapter of the Association for Computational Linguistics*, pp. 79–86, Association for Computational Linguistics, Edmonton, Canada, doi:10.3115/1073445.1073466.

I. Dan MELAMED (2004), Statistical Machine Translation by Parsing, in *Proceedings of the 42nd Annual Conference of the Association for Computational Linguistics*, pp. 653–660, Association for Computational Linguistics, Barcelona, Spain, doi:10.3115/1218955.1219038.

Mark-Jan NEDERHOF and Heiko VOGLER (2012), Synchronous Context-Free Tree Grammars, in *Proceedings of the 11th International Workshop on Tree Adjoining Grammars and Related Formalisms (TAG + 11)*, pp. 55–63, Paris, France.

Rebecca NESSON and Stuart M. SHIEBER (2006), Simpler TAG Semantics Through Synchronization, in *Proceedings of the 11th Conference on Formal Grammar*, pp. 129–142, Center for the Study of Language and Information, Malaga, Spain, http://nrs.harvard.edu/urn-3:HUL.InstRepos:2252595.

Rebecca NESSON, Stuart M. SHIEBER, and Alexander RUSH (2006), Induction of Probabilistic Synchronous Tree-Insertion Grammars for Machine Translation, in *Proceedings of the 7th Conference of the Association for Machine Translation in the Americas (AMTA 2006)*, pp. 128–137, Association for Machine Translation in the Americas, Cambridge, Massachusetts, http://nrs.harvard.edu/urn-3:HUL.InstRepos:2261232.

William C. ROUNDS (1970), Mappings and Grammars on Trees, *Mathematical Systems Theory*, 4(3):257–287, doi:10.1007/BF01695769.

Yves SCHABES and Stuart M. SHIEBER (1994), An Alternative Conception of Tree-Adjoining Derivation, *Computational Linguistics*, 20(1):91–124, http://aclweb.org/anthology/J94-1004.

Yves SCHABES and K. VIJAY-SHANKER (1990), Deterministic Left to Right Parsing of Tree Adjoining Languages, in *Proceedings of the 28th Annual Meeting of the Association for Computational Linguistics*, pp. 276–283, Association for Computational Linguistics, Pittsburgh, Pennsylvania, doi:10.3115/981823.981858.

Stuart M. SHIEBER (1994), Restricting the Weak-Generative Capacity of Synchronous Tree-Adjoining Grammars, *Computational Intelligence*, 10(4):371–385, doi:10.1111/j.1467-8640.1994.tb00003.x.

Stuart M. SHIEBER (2004), Synchronous Grammars as Tree Transducers, in *Proceedings of the Seventh International Workshop on Tree Adjoining Grammar and Related Formalisms (TAG + 7)*, pp. 88–95, Vancouver, Canada, http://nrs.harvard.edu/urn-3:HUL.InstRepos:2019322.

Stuart M. SHIEBER (2006), Unifying Synchronous Tree-Adjoining Grammars and Tree Transducers via Bimorphisms, in *Proceedings of the 11th Conference of the European Chapter of the Association for Computational Linguistics (EACL-06)*, pp. 377–384, European Chapter of the Association for Computational Linguistics, Trento, Italy, http://nrs.harvard.edu/urn-3:HUL.InstRepos:2252609.

Stuart M. SHIEBER and Yves SCHABES (1990), Synchronous Tree-Adjoining Grammars, in *Proceedings of the 13th International Conference on Computational Linguistics*, volume 3, pp. 253–258, International Committee on Computational Linguistics, Helsinki, Finland, doi:10.3115/991146.991191.

K. VIJAY-SHANKER (1987), *A Study of Tree Adjoining Grammars*, Ph.D. thesis, Department of Computer and Information Science, University of Pennsylvania, Philadelphia, Pennsylvania, http://repository.upenn.edu/dissertations/AAI8804974/.

Dekai WU (1996), A Polynomial-Time Algorithm for Statistical Machine Translation, in *Proceedings of the 34th Annual Meeting of the Association for Computational Linguistics*, pp. 152–158, Association for Computational Linguistics, Santa Cruz, California, doi:10.3115/981863.981884.

Dekai WU (1997), Stochastic Inversion Transduction Grammars and Bilingual Parsing of Parallel Corpora, *Computational Linguistics*, 23(3):377–404, http://aclweb.org/anthology/J97-3002.

Elif YAMANGIL and Stuart M. SHIEBER (2010), Bayesian Synchronous Tree-Substitution Grammar Induction and Its Application to Sentence Compression, in *Proceedings of the 48th Annual Meeting of the Association for Computational Linguistics*, pp. 937–947, Association for Computational Linguistics, Uppsala, Sweden, http://nrs.harvard.edu/urn-3:HUL.InstRepos:4733833.

2

A proof–theoretic approach to scope ambiguity in compositional vector space models

Gijs Jasper Wijnholds
School of Electronic Engineering and Computer Science,
Queen Mary University of London

Keywords: proof theory, scope ambiguity, compositional vector space models, bialgebra

ABSTRACT

We investigate the extent to which compositional vector space models can be used to account for scope ambiguity in quantified sentences (of the form *Every man loves some woman*). Such sentences containing two quantifiers introduce two readings, a direct scope reading and an inverse scope reading. This ambiguity has been treated in a vector space model using bialgebras by Hedges and Sadrzadeh (2016) and Sadrzadeh (2016), though without an explanation of the mechanism by which the ambiguity arises. We combine a polarised focussed sequent calculus for the non-associative Lambek calculus **NL**, as described in Moortgat and Moot (2011), with the vector-based approach to quantifier scope ambiguity. In particular, we establish a procedure for obtaining a vector space model for quantifier scope ambiguity in a derivational way.

1   INTRODUCTION

There is a long standing tradition in formal semantics on compositionality: in order to separate the meaning of basic elements (lexical semantics) from the construction of higher-level meaning (derivational semantics) one assigns a homomorphism from a *syntactic algebra* to a *semantic algebra*. Having been rigorously formalised by Montague in his seminal papers (Montague 1970, 1973), these ideas have been made concrete in the field of grammar, where syntactic types are mapped onto semantic types so that any derivation gives rise to a *meaning recipe*. Traditionally, meaning is taken to be a linear lambda term that evaluates to a truth value.

Ongoing research on distributional semantics, based on the idea that word meaning is defined relative to a word's context, has revealed an appealing way to incorporate type-logical grammar into distributional models (Coecke *et al.* 2010). This approach, also known as the DisCoCat approach (Distributional Compositional Categorical models), treats compositionality in the Montagovian style as a functorial passage from syntactic types and proofs to vectors and linear maps. Given that this line of research is still in its early phase, there is much to be done to formalise details of the model, give accounts for semantic phenomena, and evaluate the effectiveness of the chosen approach.

Though traditional categorial syntax and semantics go hand in hand, some aspects of the set-theoretic formal semantics get lost in the switch to a vector space model of meaning. First, the interpretation of constants that one can appeal to in formal semantics are not directly available in a vector-based setting; a logical word like "not" can be computed in the formal setting by taking set complement, but negating a vector or matrix is not trivial.[1] Similarly, for coordinators like "and" and "or" the standard set intersection and union are not available in a vectorial setting. One could replace intersection by vector multiplication and union by vector summation, but in the presence of concrete distributional vectors it is not clear that such operations indeed perform well in an experimental setting. Second, the DisCoCat approach assumes a tight categorical correspondence between a syntactic formalism and the concrete vector semantics: when we want to stay in the realm of finite dimensional vector spaces, we are dealing with a compact closed category; to model a categorial grammar as a category, one needs to fully explicate its proof-theoretic logical and structural rules, an exposition that is not trivially available for any categorial system.[2] Another issue with this categorical treatment is

---

[1] Although there is work on simulating negation in a tensor-based setting (Grefenstette 2013), it is not clear what negation really means in a distributional setting. For instance, an alternative view is to treat distributional negation as conversational (Kruszewski *et al.* 2016).

[2] For instance, the composition and type-raising combinators one finds in Combinatorial Categorial Grammar (Steedman 2000) don't easily translate into

that a simple vector-based model does not have the non-linearity that some models would assume. As an example, allowing a non-linearity in lexical lambda terms or as a syntactic mechanism means the copying of material which is not possible with all vectors. We discuss this issue in more detail in the rest of the paper.

Some of the above issues have been addressed in recent work by Sadrzadeh *et al.* (2013), Hedges and Sadrzadeh (2016), Sadrzadeh (2016), giving accounts of subject/object relativisation, generalised quantifiers, and quantifier scope. In Sadrzadeh *et al.* (2013), the meaning of pronoun relative clauses is explained by using Frobenius algebras in the lexicon, and assigning different pregroup grammar types to the subject relative pronoun "who" and the object relative pronoun "whom". Two different derivations then naturally arise, giving an intersectional meaning to subject relative clauses of the type "Men who like Mary", and object relative clauses such as "Men whom Mary likes". Such an approach does not lend itself to certain Germanic languages where the ambiguity has to be derivational: in Dutch, the subject relative and object relative interpretations above share the surface form "Mannen die Marie mogen".[3] To deal with this issue without specifying lexical alternatives, i.e. different possible typings of the relative pronoun "die", Moortgat and Wijnholds (2017) provide a derivational account that results in the same intersective vector space meaning as the ones of Sadrzadeh *et al.* (2013).

An element that lacks in the results obtained so far on quantifier scope ambiguity is a detailed discussion of the derivational process, giving rise to ambiguities. Quantifier scope ambiguity as opposed to pronoun relativisation is more pressing as the former exists in English and does not come from the lexicon, but rather from different ways of reading the same surface form. The account of Hedges and Sadrzadeh (2016) explores the use of bialgebras to represent quantifiers, using context free grammars as the syntactic engine; its follow up (Sadrzadeh 2016) discusses scope ambiguity but assumes the ambiguity to be given before detailing the direct scope and inverse scope readings of phrases of the shape "Every man loves some woman". In

---

a standard category, and the Displacement Calculus of Morrill *et al.* (2011) subsumes its structural rules in the rules of the system (Valentín 2014).

[3]"Die" can mean "who", "whom", "that", "mogen" is an inflection of "like".

order to explain how the ambiguity comes about, we need to detail the syntactic process, and integrate it with a vector-based semantics.

Our goal in this paper, then, is to pave the way to fully explain compositionality in vector space models of meaning while also taking into account the desirable mechanisms of e.g. Frobenius algebras and bialgebras. The contribution of this paper is to show how we can represent quantifier scope ambiguity in a derivational manner, fully determined by the syntactic process combined with a suitable lexical semantics.

We will make use of a polarised non-associative Lambek calculus, and use focussing as a technique to gain control over the space of sequent derivations. A *continuation-passing-style* translation from syntactic types into semantic objects then gives rise to the expected reading for quantifier scope ambiguity. This technique has been worked out by Moortgat and Moot (2011) (following Bernardi and Moortgat 2010 and Bastenhof 2012), but has not, until now, been put in the context of vector space models.

This paper is structured as follows: in Section 2, we briefly discuss quantifier scope ambiguity and its apparent non-linearity. Next, in Section 3 we define the basic, compositional DisCoCat model. We proceed to review quantifier scope ambiguity in vector space models in Section 4, and show in Section 5 how we can derive quantifier scope ambiguity in a compositional way using a polarised focussed sequent calculus that is interpreted in a vector space model. We conclude in Section 6 by explaining how our results can be further expanded and we introduce some potential new areas of investigation.

2   QUANTIFIER SCOPE AMBIGUITY

There seems to be an intrinsic non-linearity associated with quantifiers. Consider the word "all" in a phrase "all men sleep". One way of modelling the universal quantification in the phrase is to let "all" refer to an operation that decides whether the set of "men" is a subset of those entities that are sleeping, i.e. if "men" refers to some set A, and "sleep" to some set B, then "all men sleep" computes whether $A \subseteq B$. This can be given an alternative definition:

$$[all](A)(B) = \begin{cases} 1 & \text{if } A = A \cap B \\ 0 & \text{otherwise} \end{cases}$$

When one tries to give this interpretation in terms of a λ-term, the usual approach is to model both "men" and "sleep" as a *characteristic function* of a set of entities, where "all" is given a non-linear λ-term:

$$\llbracket all \rrbracket = \lambda P.\lambda Q.(\forall \; (\lambda x.(P \; x) \rightarrow (Q \; x)))$$

This λ-term will effectively decide whether $A \subseteq B$, or alternatively whether $A = A \cap B$. Both the modellings sacrifice linearity in a sense: where the first, relational interpretation needs to use A as an operand to the intersection operation and as an argument to decide equality, the second interpretation has to *copy* the variable x to decide whether everything in the universe satisfying the property P also satisfies Q. We argue that this required non-linearity that is introduced by allowing non-linear λ-terms to be inserted through the lexicon, is exactly the same kind of non-linearity that is introduced to vector space models by means of bialgebra operations. It has been argued before that modelling quantification in vector space models forces one to use non-linear maps (Grefenstette 2013). However, this issue has been partially resolved by Hedges and Sadrzadeh (2016) by admitting a powerset structure to the basis vectors of the model. The then obtained bialgebra operations are linear in the algebraic sense, but non-linear in terms of typing information. That is, they allow for copying a resource X into a resource $X \otimes X$ and deleting a resource in the opposite direction. That this kind of operation would jeopardize a Lambek-style grammar formalism is immediate as the bialgebra operations would correspond to contraction and expansion, respectively. Our argument will proceed by claiming that a continuation-passing-style translation that allows for lexical insertion of non-linear λ-terms can instead be interpreted by means of the bialgebra operations of Hedges and Sadrzadeh (2016).

3 COMPOSITIONAL DISTRIBUTIONAL SEMANTICS

Compositional distributional semantics in a categorical setting takes a mathematically rigorous approach to compositionality. Much like traditional Montagovian semantics, there is a syntactic algebra involved that provides grammaticality by means of a proof system, in this case it can be either a *pregroup grammar* or the *Lambek calculus* (Lambek 1958, 1997). The *semantic algebra* is, in the basic setup, the category of finite dimensional vector spaces, denoted **FVect**: content words are assigned a vector that represents its position in the space of word meanings, obtained through some method of co-occurrence extraction on a corpus. Whenever a sequence of words, annotated with their *syntactic types*, leads to a derivation that proves grammaticality, the proof term associated with that derivation provides a linear map on the vectors associated with basic words which, after evaluation, gives us the *phrase meaning* of that sequence of words.

3.1   *Lambek grammars*

We make the model sketched above concrete by giving the relevant definitions. These are based on work by Wijnholds (2014) in combination with the work of Coecke *et al.* (2013).

Definition 1 (Lambek types). *Given a set T of basic types, the set of Lambek types $F(T)$ is the smallest set such that:*

1. *If $p \in T$ then $p \in F(T)$,*
2. *If $A, B \in F(T)$ then $A \otimes B$, $A \backslash B$, $B/A \in F(T)$.*

We proceed to define a Lambek calculus in terms of a labelled deductive system, i.e. we use the notation of an inference system to show how proofs are derived:

Definition 2 (Non-associative Lambek calculus). *The (non-associative, non-unitary) Lambek calculus **NL** over T is given by the types in $F(T)$ and the proofs generated by the following (labelled) inference system:*

$$\frac{}{1_A : A \to A} \; Ax \qquad\qquad \frac{f : A \to B \quad g : B \to C}{g \circ f : A \to C} \; T$$

$$\frac{f : A \otimes B \to C}{\triangleright f : A \to C/B} \; R1 \qquad\qquad \frac{f : A \otimes B \to C}{\triangleleft f : B \to A \backslash C} \; R2$$

$$\frac{g : A \to C/B}{\triangleright^{-1} g : A \otimes B \to C} \; R1^{-1} \qquad\qquad \frac{g : B \to A \backslash C}{\triangleleft^{-1} g : A \otimes B \to C} \; R2^{-1}$$

One can show that monotonicity laws for each of the connectives are derived rules of inference:

$$\frac{f : A \to C \quad g : B \to D}{f \otimes g : A \otimes B \to C \otimes D} \; M_\otimes$$

$$\frac{f : A \to C \quad g : B \to D}{g/f : B/C \to D/A} \; M_/$$

$$\frac{f : A \to C \quad g : B \to D}{f\backslash g : C\backslash B \to A\backslash D} \; M_\backslash$$

where we have:

$$f \otimes g := \rhd^{-1}((\rhd\lhd^{-1}((\lhd 1_{C\otimes D}) \circ g)) \circ f)$$
$$g/f := \rhd(g \circ (\lhd^{-1}((\lhd\rhd^{-1} 1_{B\backslash C}) \circ f)))$$
$$f\backslash g := \lhd(g \circ (\rhd^{-1}((\rhd\lhd^{-1} 1_{C\backslash B}) \circ f)))$$

Leaving aside the issue of global associativity and its desirability from a linguistic perspective, we note how it can be added using two additional axioms:

$$\frac{}{a_{A,B,C} : (A \otimes B) \otimes C \to A \otimes (B \otimes C)} \; Ass$$

$$\frac{}{a^{-1}_{A,B,C} : A \otimes (B \otimes C) \to (A \otimes B) \otimes C} \; Ass^{-1}$$

The *categorical* version of the Lambek calculus can be obtained by imposing the relevant standard equivalences on proofs, amongst others stipulating that composing with the identity proof is a vacuous operation, and that all two-way inference rules are isomorphims. For more detail we refer the reader to Wijnholds (2014).

In order to make grammaticality judgments to sequences of words, we need a *lexicon* assigning types to words over an alphabet. For the sake of completeness we define the lexicon as a relation, but in the remainder of this paper we will freely abuse notation and treat the lexicon as if it were a function.

Definition 3 (Lexicon). *Let Σ be a finite, non-empty set of words (an alphabet). A lexicon over Σ is a relation $\delta \subseteq \Sigma \times F(T)$.*

Definition 4 (Lambek grammar). *Given a set of basic types T, a Lambek grammar over T is a triple (Σ, δ, S) where Σ is an alphabet, δ is a lexicon over T, and $S \in F(T)$ is a distinguished goal type.*

Definition 5 (Grammaticality). *Given a Lambek grammar (Σ, δ, S) over T, we say that a sequence of words $w_1...w_n$ over Σ is grammatical iff there is a merged sequence $W_1 \otimes W_2... \otimes W_n$ (where for each i we have $w_i \delta W_i$), and there exists a proof of $W_1 \otimes W_2... \otimes W_n \to S$ in the Lambek calculus.*

The presented definitions so far give a procedure to obtain a proof of sentencehood for a sequence of words. Moreover, there might be several proofs of the same sequence of words. This may be desirable (in cases of derivational ambiguity) or not (in the case proof-theoretic redundancy, e.g. the successive to and fro use of two-way rules). In the categorical variant of the Lambek calculus, we can simply take the proofs of sentencehood of a sequence to be the hom-set of morphisms $Hom(W_1 \otimes W_2 ... \otimes W_n, S)$. This produces fewer proofs as unnecessary ambiguity of the proof system is brought down by categorical equations. The structure of the (non-associative) Lambek calculus **NL** is that of a *biclosed magmatic category*.[4]

3.2   *Finite dimensional vector space models*

Lambek grammars are easily interpretable in vector space semantics, as vector spaces enjoy compact closure – a weaker variant of the biclosure of the Lambek calculus. We define the category **FVect** and show that it enjoys compact closure:

Definition 6 (Compact Closure). *A compact closed category is a monoidal category $\mathscr{C}$ with dual objects A^l, A^r for every object A in $\mathscr{C}$ and additional morphisms:*

$$A^l \otimes A \xrightarrow{\epsilon_A^l} I \xrightarrow{\eta_A^l} A \otimes A^l$$

$$A \otimes A^r \xrightarrow{\epsilon_A^r} I \xrightarrow{\eta_A^r} A^r \otimes A$$

that satisfy the yanking properties:[5]

$$(id_A \otimes \epsilon_A^l) \circ (\eta_A^l \otimes id_A) = id_A \qquad (\epsilon_A^r \otimes id_A) \circ (id_A \otimes \eta_A^r) = id_A$$

$$(\eta_A^l \otimes id_{A^l}) \circ (id_{A^l} \otimes \eta_A^l) = id_{A^l} \qquad (id_{A^r} \otimes \eta_A^r) \circ (\eta_A^r \otimes id_{A^r}) = id_{A^r}$$

In the category of finite dimensional vector spaces **FVect** we have that the dual space A^* is isomorphic to A when we fix a basis (which is the case for concrete models). The ϵ and η maps, now reduced to just two maps, are given by:

$$\epsilon := \sum_{ij} c_{ij}(v_i \otimes v_j) \mapsto \sum_{ij} c_{ij} \langle v_i \mid v_j \rangle$$

$$\eta := 1 \mapsto \sum_i (v_i \otimes v_i)$$

---

[4] A magmatic category is a weaker version of a monoidal category: the tensor has no unit and is not necessarily associative. See Wijnholds (2017).

[5] Note that we left out the hidden associativity morphism.

In concrete vector models, we will have vectors learnt for content words. For instance, the noun phrases "John" and "Mary" can be interpreted as vectors $\overrightarrow{n_1}, \overrightarrow{n_3} \in N$, respectively. This means that they are essentially single points in a vector space. Setting the sentence space to be the real numbers, a transitive verb such as "loves" would live in the vector space $N \otimes \mathbb{R} \otimes N$, and would carry information about the degree with which individuals love one another. In vector terms:

$$\sum_{ij} c_{ij} (\overrightarrow{n_i} \otimes 1 \otimes \overrightarrow{n_j})$$

The c_{ij} is the respective degree for any pair of individuals i, j. The meaning of the phrase "John loves Mary" should then reduce by taking the inner product of the noun phrases with the verbs to give:

$$\sum_{ij} c_{ij} \langle \overrightarrow{n_1} \mid \overrightarrow{n_i} \rangle \langle \overrightarrow{n_j} \mid \overrightarrow{n_3} \rangle$$

In the next section, we show how to relate derivations in a Lambek grammar to concrete computations in a vector space model.

3.3 *Interpretation*

Given that the compact closedness of **FVect** instantiates the closure of the Lambek calculus, we can easily interpret proofs in a Lambek grammar in a vector space model by passing from words and their lexical types to vectors in a homomorphically obtained vector space. Any proof of grammaticality will be interpreted through the η and ϵ maps:

Definition 7 (Interpretation). *Let (Σ, δ, S) be a Lambek grammar over T. An interpretation is a pair of maps $I_0 : F(T) \to \mathbf{FVect}, I_1 : \Sigma \to \delta(\Sigma)$, where $\delta(\Sigma)$ is the relational image of δ, such that I_0 respects typing and I_1 respects lexical type assignment. That is,*

$$I_0(A \otimes B) = I_0(A \backslash B) = I_0(A/B) = I_0(A) \otimes I_0(B)$$

$$\textit{and}$$

$$I_1(w) = \overrightarrow{v} \quad \textit{iff} \quad w \delta W \text{ and } \overrightarrow{v} \in I_0(W)$$

An interpretation map sends words to vectors that respect the syntactic types associated with those words. We need to give a vectorial interpretation of proofs as well, in order to know how to compute meanings of a tuple of vectors. The identity proof and transitivity of proofs carries over to the identity map on vector spaces and the composition of linear maps. The remaining rules of residuation are interpreted as shown below:

$$\frac{f' : I_0(A) \otimes I_0(B) \to I_0(C)}{\left(f' \otimes id_{I_0(B)}\right) \circ \left(id_{I_0(A)} \otimes \eta_{I_0(B)}\right) : I_0(A) \to I_0(C) \otimes I_0(B)} \; R1$$

$$\frac{f' : I_0(A) \otimes I_0(B) \to I_0(C)}{\left(id_{I_0(A)} \otimes f'\right) \circ \left(\eta_{I_0(A)} \otimes id_{I_0(B)}\right) : I_0(B) \to I_0(A) \otimes I_0(C)} \; R2$$

$$\frac{g' : I_0(A) \to I_0(C) \otimes I_0(B)}{\left(id_{I_0(C)} \otimes \epsilon_{I_0(B)}\right) \circ \left(g' \otimes id_{I_0(B)}\right) : I_0(A) \otimes I_0(B) \to I_0(C)} \; R1^{-1}$$

$$\frac{g' : I_0(B) \to I_0(A) \otimes I_0(C)}{\left(\epsilon_{I_0(A)} \otimes id_{I_0(C)}\right) \circ \left(id_{I_0(A)} \otimes g'\right) : I_0(A) \otimes I_0(B) \to I_0(C)} \; R2^{-1}$$

It is a nice puzzle for the reader to verify that by the yanking equations, we preserve isomorphicity of residuation, for example one can show that the interpretation of $\rhd^{-1}\rhd f$ is equal to the interpretation of f.

3.4   *Illustration*

Recall that we have vectors for "John", "Mary" and "loves" and we have an intended meaning of the phrase "John loves Mary". We take a Lambek grammar over the set of basic types $\{np, s\}$, where np will be interpreted as $\mathbf{N}$ and s will be mapped to $\mathbb{R}$. We define a lexicon as follows:

w	$\delta(w)$	$I_1(w)$	$I_0(\delta(w))$
"John"	np	n_1	$\mathbf{N}$
"Mary"	np	n_3	$\mathbf{N}$
"loves"	$(np\backslash s)/np$	$\sum_{ij} c_{ij}(\overrightarrow{n_i} \otimes 1 \otimes \overrightarrow{n_j})$	$\mathbf{N} \otimes \mathbb{R} \otimes \mathbf{N}$

Given that $\lhd^{-1}\rhd^{-1}(1_{(np\backslash s)/np})$ proves the grammaticality of "John loves Mary", the associated meaning computation will be:

$$(\epsilon_N \otimes id_\mathbb{R}) \circ (id_N \otimes ((id_{N \otimes \mathbb{R}} \otimes \epsilon_N) \circ (id_{N \otimes \mathbb{R} \otimes N} \otimes id_N)))$$

$$(\overrightarrow{n_1} \otimes \sum_{ij} c_{ij} (\overrightarrow{n_i} \otimes 1 \otimes \overrightarrow{n_j}) \otimes \overrightarrow{n_3})$$

$$= (\epsilon_N \otimes id_\mathbb{R}) \circ (id_{N \otimes N \otimes \mathbb{R}} \otimes \epsilon_N)(\overrightarrow{n_1} \otimes \sum_{ij} c_{ij} (\overrightarrow{n_i} \otimes 1 \otimes \overrightarrow{n_j}) \otimes \overrightarrow{n_3})$$

$$= (\epsilon_N \otimes id_\mathbb{R})(\overrightarrow{n_1} \otimes \sum_{ij} c_{ij} (\overrightarrow{n_i} \otimes \langle \overrightarrow{n_j} \mid \overrightarrow{n_3} \rangle)))$$

$$= \sum_{ij} c_{ij} \langle \overrightarrow{n_1} \mid \overrightarrow{n_i} \rangle \langle \overrightarrow{n_j} \mid \overrightarrow{n_3} \rangle$$

$$= c_{13}$$

This result is exactly the intended meaning we wanted to obtain. Note that the result of the computation relies on the fact that the content words in the vector space model are taken to be the basis vectors, hence they are orthogonal. The result c_{13} indicates the distributional strength of John loving Mary in a corpus that the vectors have been learnt from. Until now, we have neglected discussion about function words: logical words, relative pronouns, and quantifiers are not intuitively represented well by co-occurrence data. The logical word "and" may occur with many different words, but that statistic does not tell us much about the meaning of the word. So, although all the basic operations from a Lambek grammar are directly interpretable in vector space models, more advanced semantic phenomena lack an explanation in the simple models.

4   QUANTIFIER SCOPE AMBIGUITY IN VECTOR SPACE MODELS

In this section we review the use of bialgebras in vector space models as exhibited by Hedges and Sadrzadeh (2016) and Sadrzadeh (2016) and show how the two scope readings can be obtained. The treatment of quantifiers in vector space models relies on the use of powersets: as long as we can know of our vector space that its basis vectors are given by the powerset of some set A, we can perform additional operations on the vector space.

Definition 8 (Bialgebra). *Given a symmetric monoidal category* $(\mathscr{C}, \otimes, I, \sigma)$, *a bialgebra on an object* X *in* $\mathscr{C}$ *is a tuple of maps:*

$$X \xrightarrow{\delta_X} X \otimes X \xrightarrow{\mu_X} X$$

$$X \xrightarrow{\iota_X} I \xrightarrow{\zeta_X} X$$

that satisfy the conditions of a monoid for (X, μ, ζ) and a comonoid for (X, δ, ι) and furthermore satisfy the bialgebra axioms:

$$\iota \circ \mu = \iota \otimes \iota$$
$$\delta \circ \zeta = \zeta \otimes \zeta$$
$$\iota \circ \zeta = id_I$$
$$\delta \circ \mu = (\mu \otimes \mu) \circ (id_X \otimes \sigma \otimes id_X) \circ (\delta \otimes \delta)$$

The last of the four equations tells us that in a bialgebra, the order of copying and merging is irrelevant given that we can switch copies by means of the symmetry of the category. What is interesting to note is that any powerset $P(U)$ bears a bialgebra structure if we consider the Cartesian product to be the tensor and the singleton set $\{\star\}$ as the identity object. What follows is that any vector space over a powerset, denoted $V_{P(U)}$, carries a bialgebra structure. Both bialgebras are given below:

$$A \stackrel{\delta}{\Leftrightarrow} A \times A \qquad\qquad |A\rangle \stackrel{\delta}{\mapsto} |A\rangle \otimes |A\rangle$$
$$A \times B \stackrel{\mu}{\Leftrightarrow} A \cap B \qquad\qquad |A\rangle \otimes |B\rangle \stackrel{\mu}{\mapsto} |A \cap B\rangle$$
$$A \stackrel{\iota}{\Leftrightarrow} \{\star\} \qquad\qquad |A\rangle \stackrel{\iota}{\mapsto} 1$$
$$\{\star\} \stackrel{\zeta}{\Leftrightarrow} U \qquad\qquad 1 \stackrel{\zeta}{\mapsto} |U\rangle$$

The existence of a bialgebra on powerset vector spaces allows for a neat treatment of quantification. Given that nouns and noun phrases are represented as vectors on a powerset, universal quantification and existential quantification are treated as:

$$|A\rangle \stackrel{[\![all]\!]}{\mapsto} \sum_{A \subseteq B \subseteq U} |B\rangle$$

$$|A\rangle \stackrel{[\![some]\!]}{\mapsto} \sum_{\substack{B \text{ s.t.} \\ A \cap B \neq \emptyset}} |B\rangle$$

To get a feel for how the meaning of a quantified sentence should be computed according to Hedges and Sadrzadeh (2016), we show the example of "all men sleep", which gets assigned the meaning:

$$\epsilon_{V_{P(U)}} \circ ([\![all]\!] \otimes \mu_{V_{P(U)}}) \circ (\delta_{V_{P(U)}} \otimes id_{V_{P(U)}})(|[\![men]\!]\rangle \otimes |[\![sleep]\!]\rangle)$$

$$= \epsilon_{V_{P(U)}} \circ ([\![all]\!] \otimes \mu_{V_{P(U)}})(|[\![men]\!]\rangle \otimes |[\![men]\!]\rangle \otimes |[\![sleep]\!]\rangle)$$

$$= \epsilon_{V_{P(U)}} (\sum_{[\![men]\!] \subseteq B \subseteq U} |B\rangle \otimes |[\![men]\!] \cap [\![sleep]\!]\rangle)$$

$$= \sum_{[\![men]\!] \subseteq B \subseteq U} \langle B | [\![men]\!] \cap [\![sleep]\!]\rangle$$

$$= \langle [\![men]\!] | [\![men]\!] \cap [\![sleep]\!]\rangle$$

Although this approach works for statements with a single quantifier, it fails to deliver both readings for a doubly quantified statement such as "every student likes some teacher" as the computations for the subject and object quantifiers will be independent of each other. Hence, both readings will collapse to the same meaning. This lack of explanatory power of the model is amended in a subsequent paper (Sadrzadeh 2016), where the implicit quantified variable is passed on to the computation of the second quantifier. A transitive verb such as "likes" is modelled as an element:

$$\llbracket \text{likes} \rrbracket = \sum_{ij} c_{ij}(|A_i\rangle \otimes |A_j\rangle)$$

in $V_{P(U)} \otimes V_{P(U)}$, and we can model the forward image of an element in U as:

$$\llbracket \text{likes}_a \rrbracket = \sum_{ij} w_{ij}\langle\{a\} \mid A_i\rangle|A_j\rangle$$

The backward image is computed similarly by taking the inner product of $\overrightarrow{v_a}$ with $\overrightarrow{v_j}$. This construction now allows for both readings of "every student likes some teacher", though there is no procedure given to obtain these readings through a syntactic process.

5   QUANTIFIER SCOPE AMBIGUITY USING FOCUSSING AND POLARISATION

Focussing is a proof-theoretic technique stemming from the work of (Andreoli 2001) that aims to eliminate redundancy from regular sequent systems. Focussed proof search proceeds by distinguishing those formulas that enjoy invertible introduction rules (*asynchronous formulas*), and those that do not (*synchronous formulas*). Asynchronous formulas are decomposed in a backward chaining proof search until there is no more decomposition possible. Then, one of the synchronous formulas is selected to be put in focus, after which the process of decomposition continues. This implies that now only the number of synchronous formulas determines the number of distinct proofs. This approach has been applied to the Lambek-Grishin calculus, a symmetric extension of the Lambek calculus, by Bernardi and Moortgat (2010), and is worked out in more detail by Moortgat and Moot (2011).

In order to obtain a compositional Montagovian semantics from a display style presentation of focussed proofs for the Lambek-Grishin calculus, Bastenhof (2012) applies a polarisation technique, whereby formulas are assigned either positive or negative polarity. Atomic formulas are assigned an arbitrary polarity; the choice of this *bias* affects the set of proofs obtained. The polarity also influences semantics: under the continuation semantics of Bernardi and Moortgat (2010), a negative formula will be *negated* in its interpretation. Though the focussing and polarisation approaches are described by Bernardi and Moortgat (2010) and Bastenhof (2012), respectively, here we follow the focussed sequent presentation of Moortgat and Moot (2011).

We start by defining polarity of types:

Definition 9 (Polarity). *Given a set of basic types T, a polarity assignment on types is a map pol : $F(T) \rightarrow \{-, +\}$ that assigns to the types in T an arbitrary polarity but fixes the polarity for complex types:*

$$pol(A \otimes B) = +$$
$$pol(A \backslash B) = -$$
$$pol(B / A) = -$$

Given a Lambek grammar G over a set T, grammaticality is defined similarly to Definition 5, where the set of proofs is given by the underlying proof system. The only difference is that the final sequent should have the consequent formula in focus. Any proof is encoded by its abstract label, according to the abstract sequent system defined in Figure 1.

5.1   *CPS translation*

The translation of types and proofs given by Moortgat and Moot (2011) into a target semantic algebra is a two-step process:

$$\text{source} \quad \xrightarrow{I} \quad \begin{array}{c} \text{continuation} \\ \text{semantics} \end{array} \quad \xrightarrow{J} \quad \text{target}$$
$$\mathbf{NL}_{\otimes, \backslash, /} \quad\quad\quad \mathbf{LP}_{\otimes, \perp} \quad\quad\quad \mathbf{FVect}$$

Instead of considering a proof to be a simple transformation of values (the assumptions) to a value (the conclusion), we consider a proof to be a *continuation*, a function that awaits an evaluation context to compute a final value. The intermediate semantics is the Lambek calculus

Focused types are positive   Focused types are negative

$$\frac{}{Ax(A,x) \mid x : A \Rightarrow \boxed{A}} \; Ax \qquad\qquad \frac{}{CoAx(A,\alpha) \mid \boxed{A} \Rightarrow \alpha : A} \; CoAx$$

$$\frac{M \mid X[x : A] \Rightarrow Y}{\leftarrow (M,x,A) \mid X[\boxed{A}] \Rightarrow Y} \; \shortleftarrow \qquad\qquad \frac{M \mid X[\boxed{A}] \Rightarrow Y}{\leftarrow (M,x) \mid X[x : A] \Rightarrow Y} \; \shortleftarrow$$

$$\frac{M \mid X \Rightarrow \boxed{A}}{\rightarrow (M,\alpha) \mid X \Rightarrow \alpha : A} \; \shortrightarrow \qquad\qquad \frac{M \mid X \Rightarrow \alpha : A}{\rightarrow (M,\alpha) \mid X \Rightarrow \boxed{A}} \; \shortrightarrow$$

$$\frac{M \mid X[\boxed{A}] \Rightarrow Z \quad N \mid Y \Rightarrow \boxed{B}}{/L(M,N) \mid X[\boxed{A/B} \bullet Y] \Rightarrow Z} \; /L \qquad \frac{M \mid X \bullet x : B \Rightarrow \alpha : A}{/R(M,x,\alpha,\beta) \mid X \Rightarrow \beta : A/B} \; /R$$

$$\frac{M \mid X[x : A \bullet y : B] \Rightarrow Y}{\otimes L(M,x,y,z) \mid X[z : A \otimes B] \Rightarrow Y} \; \otimes L \qquad \frac{M \mid X \Rightarrow \boxed{A} \quad N \mid Y \Rightarrow \boxed{B}}{\otimes R(M,N) \mid X \bullet Y \Rightarrow \boxed{A \otimes B}} \; \otimes R$$

$$\frac{M \mid Y \Rightarrow \boxed{B} \quad N \mid X[\boxed{A}] \Rightarrow Z}{\backslash L(M,N) \mid X[Y \bullet \boxed{B\backslash A}] \Rightarrow Z} \; \backslash L \qquad \frac{M \mid x : B \bullet X \Rightarrow \alpha : A}{\backslash R(M,x,\alpha,\beta) \mid X \Rightarrow \beta : B\backslash A} \; \backslash R$$

Figure 1: Focussed labelled sequent system for **NL**

with permutation and negation, $\mathbf{LP}_{\otimes,\perp}$, a system that only uses a product operation but introduces a negation. Furthermore, permutation of resources is allowed to compensate for the lack of directionality without the $/, \backslash$ connectives. We will define a direct mapping from source to target, to skip the administrative details of the intermediate semantics.

In order to replicate the effect of the negation in $\mathbf{LP}_{\otimes,\perp}$, we use vector spaces over sets; given some type A, we define its interpretation to be a vector space over a set. In this way, we enjoy the bialgebras defined over those vector spaces. First, a type W is mapped to some set A, using the Cartesian product and powerset operations. Then, the final interpretation of a type will be the vector space over the given set, V_A. We get the intended tensor products on spaces due to the fact that $V_{A \times B} \cong V_A \otimes V_B$.

Definition 10 (Type interpretation). *Given a set of basic types T and a basic interpretation map $I_0 : T \to$ Set, the type interpretation is a map $I_1 : F(T) \to$ Set defined as follows:*

1. For basic types $p \in T$ we have:

$$I_1(p) = \begin{cases} I_0(p) & \text{if } pol(p) = + \\ P(I_0(p)) & \text{if } pol(p) = - \end{cases}$$

2. For complex types, the interpretation depends both on the polarity of subtypes and the connective involved:

A B	$I_1(A \otimes B)$	$I_1(A\backslash B)$	$I_1(B/A)$
$-$ $-$	$P(I_1(A)) \times P(I_1(B))$	$P(I_1(A)) \times I_1(B)$	$I_1(B) \times P(I_1(A))$
$-$ $+$	$P(I_1(A)) \times I_1(B)$	$P(I_1(A)) \times P(I_1(B))$	$I_1(B) \times I_1(A)$
$+$ $-$	$I_1(A) \times P(I_1(B))$	$I_1(A) \times I_1(B)$	$P(I_1(B)) \times P(I_1(A))$
$+$ $+$	$I_1(A) \times I_1(B)$	$I_1(A) \times P(I_1(B))$	$P(I_1(B)) \times I_1(A)$

3. We stipulate that for any type A, its interpretation $I_1(A)$ is lifted to the vector space spanned by its elements, that is we define the final interpretation $I_2 : F(T) \to$ FVect as $I_2(W) = V_{I_1(W)}$.

Definition 11 (Word interpretation). *Given a Lambek grammar (Σ, δ, S) over a set of basic types T and an interpretation map $I_2 : F(T) \to I_2(\delta(\Sigma))$, where $\delta(\Sigma)$ is the relational image of Σ under the lexicon, and $I_2(\delta(\Sigma))$ is the image under interpretation (i.e. vector spaces), the word interpretation is a map I_3 that respects the following:*

$$I_3(w) \in I_2(W) \qquad \textit{iff} \quad w \delta W \text{ and } pol(W) = +$$
$$I_3(w) \in I_2(W) \to \mathbb{R} \quad \textit{iff} \quad w \delta W \text{ and } pol(W) = -$$

That is, words with a positive type are translated as vectors, while words with a negative type are translated as linear maps.

As an example, if we define the associated vector space of the type np to be U and n to be $P(U)$, then the interpretation of a noun like "student" will be a constant $I_3(\text{"student"}) \in V_{P(U)}$, whereas a word like "all" that is typed np/n will be a linear map:

$$I_3(\text{"all"}) \in V_{P(U)} \otimes V_{P(U)} \to \mathbb{R}$$

We proceed to define how we interpret proof terms. The intuitive idea is that a proof term is translated into a linear map which will subsequently be applied to the word interpretations of its antecedents.

Though the proof system builds up terms with potentially unbound variables, we require for grammaticality (see above) that the conclusion formula be in focus; this means that the only unbound variables in the proof term are those of the antecedent formula, which will be substituted by word interpretations.

Definition 12 (Proof term interpretation). *Given a proof in the focussed sequent calculus for* **NL**, *there is a proof term that encodes the proof. We define the interpretation of a proof by giving the translation of proof terms into linear maps:*

$$Ax(A, x) \overset{I_4}{\Longrightarrow} x \in I_3(A)$$

$$CoAx(A, \alpha) \overset{I_4}{\Longrightarrow} \alpha \in I_3(A)$$

$$\leftharpoonup (M, x, A) \overset{I_4}{\Longrightarrow} |\{x \in I_3(A) | I_4(M) \neq 0\}\rangle$$

$$\leftharpoonup (M, x) \overset{I_4}{\Longrightarrow} x(I_4(M))$$

$$\rightharpoonup (M, \alpha) \overset{I_4}{\Longrightarrow} \alpha(I_4(M))$$

$$\rightharpoonup (M, \alpha) \overset{I_4}{\Longrightarrow} \alpha \mapsto I_4(M)$$

$$/L(M, N) \overset{I_4}{\Longrightarrow} I_4(M) \otimes I_4(N)$$

$$/R(M, x, \alpha, \beta) \overset{I_4}{\Longrightarrow} I_4(M)[\beta \to \alpha \otimes x]$$

$$\otimes L(M, x, y, z) \overset{I_4}{\Longrightarrow} I_4(M)[z \to x \otimes y]$$

$$\otimes R(M, N) \overset{I_4}{\Longrightarrow} I_4(M) \otimes I_4(N)$$

$$\backslash L(M, N) \overset{I_4}{\Longrightarrow} I_4(M) \otimes I_4(N)$$

$$\backslash R(M, x, \alpha, \beta) \overset{I_4}{\Longrightarrow} I_4(M)[\beta \to x \otimes \alpha]$$

Finally, as the interpretation is a continuation-passing-style translation, we will end up with a map that needs an evaluation context before finishing computation. So, given that a proof gives a linear map, we apply it to the identity map, and we instantiate the unbound variables with the relevant *word interpretations*.

5.2   *Deriving quantifier scope ambiguity*

Quantifier scope ambiguity as exemplified by the phrase "Every student likes some teacher", is already shown to be obtainable using the two-step translation process of Bernardi and Moortgat (2010) in a Lambek-Grishin grammar, and in a Lambek grammar (Moortgat and Moot 2011). Here, we alter the latter example given to translate into the vector space model as employed by Hedges and Sadrzadeh (2016) and Sadrzadeh (2016) to show that both readings (narrow/wide and wide/narrow) can be obtained and give exactly the kind of meaning we would expect from a vector space model. This means that we can obtain the intended meaning in a *derivational* way. What is more, given that we have both a grammar available and we have learned concrete vectors, the process can potentially be fully automated. Each word has to be associated with a syntactic type, and we have to give a word interpretation mapping the words to a vector or linear map. We assume a set of basic types $\{np, n, s\}$ where s is the distinguished goal type. Polarity assignment is handled by stipulating that np and n are positive, and s is negative. Basic types np and n are interpreted as U and $P(U)$, respectively, and s gets translated to $\mathbb{R}$. The syntactic types and the word interpretation are given by the following table:

w	$\delta(w)$	$\lceil w \rceil$
every	np/n	$\epsilon_{V_{P(U)}} \circ (\llbracket \text{all} \rrbracket \otimes \mu_{V_{P(U)}}) \circ (\delta_{V_{P(U)}} \otimes id_{V_{P(U)}}) \circ \sigma$
student	n	$\llbracket \text{student} \rrbracket$
likes	$(np\backslash s)/np$	$\vec{a} \otimes f \otimes \vec{b} \mapsto f(\llbracket (\text{likes}_b)_a \rrbracket)$
some	np/n	$\epsilon_{V_{P(U)}} \circ (\llbracket \text{some} \rrbracket \otimes \mu_{V_{P(U)}}) \circ (\delta_{V_{P(U)}} \otimes id_{V_{P(U)}}) \circ \sigma$
teacher	n	$\llbracket \text{teacher} \rrbracket$

As a reminder, we also note the vectorial interpretation of lexical constants in the word interpretation:

$$\llbracket \text{all} \rrbracket(|A\rangle) \quad = \quad \sum_{A \subseteq B \subseteq U} |B\rangle$$

$$\llbracket \text{some} \rrbracket(|A\rangle) \quad = \quad \sum_{\substack{B \subseteq U \text{ s.t.} \\ A \cap B \neq \emptyset}} |B\rangle$$

$$\llbracket \text{student} \rrbracket \quad = \quad |A\rangle \text{ for some } A \subseteq U$$

$$\llbracket \text{teacher} \rrbracket \quad = \quad |B\rangle \text{ for some } B \subseteq U$$

$$\llbracket \text{likes} \rrbracket \quad = \quad \sum_{ij} c_{ij}(|A_i\rangle \otimes 1 \otimes |A_j\rangle) \text{ for each } A_x \subseteq U$$

The two proofs that we get from the focussed sequent calculus are displayed in Figures 2 and 3 (without labelling).

$$\dfrac{\dfrac{\overline{a : np \Rightarrow \boxed{np}}\; Ax \quad \overline{\boxed{s} \Rightarrow \alpha : s}\; CoAx}{a : np \bullet \boxed{np\backslash s} \Rightarrow \alpha : s}\;\backslash L \quad \overline{b : np \Rightarrow \boxed{np}}\; Ax}{\dfrac{a : np \bullet (\boxed{(np\backslash s)/np} \bullet b : np) \Rightarrow \alpha : s}{\dfrac{a : np \bullet (z : (np\backslash s)/np \bullet b : np) \Rightarrow \alpha : s}{\dfrac{a : np \bullet (z : (np\backslash s)/np \bullet \boxed{np}) \Rightarrow \alpha : s \qquad \overline{\dfrac{teacher}{w : n \Rightarrow \boxed{n}}}\; Ax}{\dfrac{a : np \bullet (z : (np\backslash s)/np \bullet (\boxed{np/n} \bullet w : n)) \Rightarrow \alpha : s}{\dfrac{a : np \bullet (z : (np\backslash s)/np \bullet (u : np/n \bullet w : n)) \Rightarrow \alpha : s}{\dfrac{\boxed{np} \bullet (z : (np\backslash s)/np \bullet (u : np/n \bullet w : n)) \Rightarrow \alpha : s \qquad \overline{\dfrac{student}{y : n \Rightarrow \boxed{n}}}\; Ax}{\dfrac{(\boxed{np/n} \bullet y : n) \bullet (z : (np\backslash s)/np \bullet (u : np/n \bullet w : n)) \Rightarrow \alpha : s}{\dfrac{(x : np/n \bullet y : n) \bullet (z : (np\backslash s)/np \bullet (u : np/n \bullet w : n)) \Rightarrow \alpha : s}{(x : np/n \bullet y : n) \bullet (z : (np\backslash s)/np \bullet (u : np/n \bullet w : n)) \Rightarrow \boxed{s}}}}}}}}$$

$$\underset{every \qquad\quad student \qquad\quad likes \qquad\quad some \qquad\quad teacher}{}$$

Figure 2: Proof for wide over narrow scope

$$\dfrac{\dfrac{\overline{b : np \Rightarrow \boxed{np}}\; Ax \quad \overline{\boxed{s} \Rightarrow \alpha : s}\; CoAx}{b : np \bullet \boxed{np\backslash s} \Rightarrow \alpha : s}\;\backslash L \quad \overline{a : np \Rightarrow \boxed{np}}\; Ax}{\dfrac{b : np \bullet (\boxed{(np\backslash s)/np} \bullet a : np) \Rightarrow \alpha : s}{\dfrac{b : np \bullet (z : (np\backslash s)/np \bullet a : np) \Rightarrow \alpha : s}{\dfrac{\boxed{np} \bullet (z : (np\backslash s)/np \bullet a : np) \Rightarrow \alpha : s \qquad \overline{\dfrac{student}{y : n \Rightarrow \boxed{n}}}\; Ax}{\dfrac{(\boxed{np/n} \bullet y : n) \bullet (z : (np\backslash s)/np \bullet a : np) \Rightarrow \alpha : s}{\dfrac{(x : np/n \bullet y : n) \bullet (z : (np\backslash s)/np \bullet a : np) \Rightarrow \alpha : s}{\dfrac{(x : np/n \bullet y : n) \bullet (z : (np\backslash s)/np \bullet \boxed{np}) \Rightarrow \alpha : s \qquad \overline{\dfrac{teacher}{w : n \Rightarrow \boxed{n}}}\; Ax}{\dfrac{(x : np/n \bullet y : n) \bullet (z : (np\backslash s)/np \bullet (\boxed{np/n} \bullet w : n)) \Rightarrow \alpha : s}{\dfrac{(x : np/n \bullet y : n) \bullet (z : (np\backslash s)/np \bullet (u : np/n \bullet w : n)) \Rightarrow \alpha : s}{(x : np/n \bullet y : n) \bullet (z : (np\backslash s)/np \bullet (u : np/n \bullet w : n)) \Rightarrow \boxed{s}}}}}}}}$$

$$\underset{every \qquad\quad student \qquad\quad likes \qquad\quad some \qquad\quad teacher}{}$$

Figure 3: A proof for narrow over wide scope

If we take the proof term for the first proof and translate this into a vectorial map we get:

$$(1a)\ \alpha \mapsto x\ (\ |\{a \in U \mid u\ (\ |\{b \mid z\ (a \otimes \alpha \otimes b) \neq 0\}) \otimes w) \neq 0\}) \otimes y)$$

For the second proof term, we get a slightly different map:

$$(2a)\ \alpha \mapsto u\ (\ |\{a \in U \mid x\ (\ |\{b \mid z\ (b \otimes \alpha \otimes a) \neq 0\}) \otimes y) \neq 0\}) \otimes w)$$

The unfolded maps are quite intimidating so the complete computation is taken up in the Appendix. Here we just note that the two maps reduce to the readings shown below:

$$(1b)\ \langle [\![\text{student}]\!] \mid [\![\text{student}]\!] \cap \{a \in U \mid \sum_{\substack{B \subseteq U \text{ s.t.} \\ [\![\text{teacher}]\!] \cap B \neq \emptyset}} \langle B \mid [\![\text{teacher}]\!] \cap C \rangle\}\rangle$$

$$\text{where } C = \{b \in U \mid [\![(\text{likes}_b)_a]\!] \neq 0\}$$

$$(2b)\ \sum_{\substack{B \subseteq U \text{ s.t.} \\ [\![\text{teacher}]\!] \cap B \neq \emptyset}} \langle B \mid [\![\text{teacher}]\!] \cap \{a \in U \mid \langle [\![\text{student}]\!] \mid [\![\text{student}]\!] \cap D \rangle \neq 0\}\rangle$$

$$\text{where } D = \{b \in U \mid [\![(\text{likes}_a)_b]\!] \neq 0\}$$

We can see that these interpretations will give different results depending on the instantiation of the vectors. In fact, these interpretations correspond to the result of Sadrzadeh (2016). This effectively shows that quantifier scope ambiguity can be achieved in vector space models by the use of appropriate proof-theoretic notions.

6　　　　　CONCLUDING REMARKS

In this paper, we elaborated on quantifier scope ambiguity in compositional distributional models of meaning. In particular, the approach of Moortgat and Moot (2011) using a continuation-passing-style translation for a polarised and focussed proof system for the Lambek calculus was combined with the approach to generalised quantifiers of Hedges and Sadrzadeh (2016). The result is fully derivational and provides a fully worked out compositional way to obtain two readings for phrases of the type "Every student likes some teacher", thereby resolving the issue of manually assigning appropriate meaning vectors to such phrases.

Although we illustrate this with examples of two generalised quantifiers in a sentence, the approach works for a single quantifier, and since the applied strategy exploits the combinatorial choices of the proof system (focus on the first quantifier and then on the second one, or vice versa) we expect the approach to generalise to more quantifiers, though the possibility of overgeneration needs to be investigated.

As for experimental validation, since the writing of this paper, it has been recognised that using a powerset construction in vector spaces, to be able to make use of bialgebras, may not be very feasible in practical models: having a powerset as a basis may lead to an exponential blowup in vector space size, and could potentially give sparsity issues. One approach to deal with this could be to use fuzzy quantification (Zadeh 1983), which has already been explored by Dostal and Sadrzadeh (2016).

Another interesting avenue is to work out how several phenomena involving the copying of linguistic material can be analysed in a compositional distributional model. Coordination and pronoun relativisation have been given an account using Frobenius algebras over vector spaces (Kartsaklis 2016; Sadrzadeh *et al.* 2013), where the Frobenius operations allow one to express elementwise multiplication on arbitrary tensors. In future work we hope to analyse ellipsis, a phenomenon for which it can be argued that copying has to be part of the syntactic process. Rules of controlled copying, then, can be interpreted using the Frobenius or bialgebra operations. A first step has already been taken by Kartsaklis *et al.* (2016), and we wish to approach the problem from the type-logical perspective.

7   ACKNOWLEDGMENTS

I am grateful for a range of insightful discussions with Michael Moortgat on the focussing for the Lambek calculus, and various perspectives on (non-)linearity. Furthermore, I would like to thank Mehrnoosh Sadrzadeh and Dimitri Kartsaklis for the many short and long discussions on Frobenius algebras and bialgebras. Finally, I am grateful for technical comments from Paulo Oliva, and the anonymous reviewers of JLM. I was supported by a Queen Mary Principal Studentship during the writing of this paper. All remaining errors are my own.

APPENDIX

(1a) $\alpha \to x\,\big(\,|\{a \in U \mid u\,(\,|\{b \in U \mid z\,(a \otimes a \otimes b) \neq 0\}\} \otimes w) \neq 0\}\} \otimes y\big)$

Which, after lexical insertion gives

$$\alpha \to [\text{every}]\,\big(\,|\{a \in U \mid [\text{some}]\,(\,|\{b \in U \mid [\text{likes}]\,(a \otimes a \otimes b) \neq 0\}\} \otimes [\text{teacher}]) \neq 0\}\} \otimes [\text{student}]\big)$$

Unfolding the definition and inserting the identity map gives

$$\epsilon_{V_{P(U)}} \circ \big(\llbracket \text{all} \rrbracket \otimes \mu_{V_{P(U)}}\big) \circ \big(\delta_{V_{P(U)}} \otimes id_{V_{P(U)}}\big)$$

$$\circ\, \sigma\Big(\,|\{a \in U \mid \epsilon_{V_{P(U)}} \circ \big(\llbracket \text{some} \rrbracket \otimes \mu_{V_{P(U)}}\big) \circ \big(\delta_{V_{P(U)}} \otimes id_{V_{P(U)}}\big) \circ \sigma\big(\,|\{b \in U \mid \llbracket (\text{likes}_b)_a \rrbracket \neq 0\}\} \otimes \llbracket \text{teacher} \rrbracket\big) \neq 0\}\} \otimes \llbracket \text{student} \rrbracket\Big)$$

$$= \epsilon_{V_{P(U)}} \circ \big(\llbracket \text{all} \rrbracket \otimes \mu_{V_{P(U)}}\big) \circ \big(\delta_{V_{P(U)}} \otimes id_{V_{P(U)}}\big) \circ \sigma\Big(\,|\{a \in U \mid \sum_{\substack{B \subseteq U \text{ s.t.} \\ \llbracket \text{teacher} \rrbracket \cap B \neq \emptyset}} \langle B \mid \llbracket \text{teacher} \rrbracket \cap \{b \in U \mid \llbracket (\text{likes}_b)_a \rrbracket \neq 0\}\}\rangle\} \otimes \llbracket \text{student} \rrbracket\Big)$$

$$= \sum_{\llbracket \text{student} \rrbracket \subseteq C \subseteq U} \langle C \mid \llbracket \text{student} \rrbracket \cap \{a \in U \mid \sum_{\substack{B \subseteq U \text{ s.t.} \\ \llbracket \text{teacher} \rrbracket \cap B \neq \emptyset}} \langle B \mid \llbracket \text{teacher} \rrbracket \cap \{b \in U \mid \llbracket (\text{likes}_b)_a \rrbracket \neq 0\}\}\rangle\}\rangle$$

(2a) $\alpha \mapsto u\left(\,|\{a \in U \mid x\,(\,|\{b \in U \mid z\,(b \otimes \alpha \otimes a) \neq 0\}| \otimes y) \neq 0\}|\, \otimes w\right)$

Which, after lexical insertion gives

$$\alpha \mapsto \lceil \text{some} \rceil \left(\,|\{a \in U \mid \lceil \text{every} \rceil\,(\,|\{b \in U \mid \lceil \text{likes} \rceil\,(b \otimes \alpha \otimes a) \neq 0\}| \otimes \lceil \text{student} \rceil) \neq 0\}|\, \otimes \lceil \text{teacher} \rceil\right)$$

Unfolding the definition and inserting the identity map gives

$$\epsilon_{V_{P(U)}} \circ \left(\llbracket \text{some} \rrbracket \otimes \mu_{V_{P(U)}}\right) \circ \left(\delta_{V_{P(U)}} \otimes id_{V_{P(U)}}\right)$$

$$\circ\; \sigma\left(\,\Big|\Big\{a \in U \mid \epsilon_{V_{P(U)}} \circ \left(\llbracket \text{all} \rrbracket \otimes \mu_{V_{P(U)}}\right) \circ \left(\delta_{V_{P(U)}} \otimes id_{V_{P(U)}}\right) \circ \sigma\big(\,|\{b \in U \mid \llbracket (\text{likes}_a)_b \rrbracket \neq 0\}| \otimes \llbracket \text{student} \rrbracket\big) \neq 0\Big\}\Big| \otimes \llbracket \text{teacher} \rrbracket\right)$$

$$= \epsilon_{V_{P(U)}} \circ \left(\llbracket \text{some} \rrbracket \otimes \mu_{V_{P(U)}}\right) \circ \left(\delta_{V_{P(U)}} \otimes id_{V_{P(U)}}\right) \circ \sigma\left(\,\Big|\Big\{a \in U \mid \sum_{\llbracket \text{student} \rrbracket \subseteq B \subseteq U} \langle B \mid \llbracket \text{student} \rrbracket \cap \{b \in U \mid \llbracket (\text{likes}_a)_b \rrbracket \neq 0\} \rangle \neq 0\Big\}\Big| \otimes \llbracket \text{teacher} \rrbracket\right)$$

$$= \sum_{\substack{C \subseteq U \text{ s.t.} \\ \llbracket \text{teacher} \rrbracket \cap C \neq \emptyset}} \langle C \mid \llbracket \text{teacher} \rrbracket \cap \{a \in U \mid \sum_{\llbracket \text{student} \rrbracket \subseteq B \subseteq U} \langle B \mid \llbracket \text{student} \rrbracket \cap \{b \in U \mid \llbracket (\text{likes}_a)_b \rrbracket \neq 0\} \rangle \neq 0\}$$

REFERENCES

Jean-Marc ANDREOLI (2001), Focussing and proof construction, *Annals of Pure and Applied Logic*, 107(1):131–163, doi:https://doi.org/10.1016/S0168-0072(00)00032-4.

Arno BASTENHOF (2012), Polarized Montagovian semantics for the Lambek-Grishin calculus, in Philippe DE GROOTE and Mark-Jan NEDERHOF, editors, *15th and 16th International Conference on Formal Grammar*, volume 7395, pp. 1–16, Springer, Springer-Verlag Berlin Heidelberg, doi:http://dx.doi.org/10.1007/978-3-642-32024-8.

Raffaella BERNARDI and Michael MOORTGAT (2010), Continuation semantics for the Lambek–Grishin calculus, *Information and Computation*, 208(5):397–416, doi:https://doi.org/10.1016/j.ic.2009.11.005.

Bob COECKE, Edward GREFENSTETTE, and Mehrnoosh SADRZADEH (2013), Lambek vs. Lambek: Functorial vector space semantics and string diagrams for Lambek calculus, *Annals of Pure and Applied Logic*, 164(11):1079–1100, doi:https://doi.org/10.1016/j.apal.2013.05.009.

Bob COECKE, Mehrnoosh SADRZADEH, and Stephen CLARK (2010), Mathematical foundations for a compositional distributional model of meaning, *arXiv preprint arXiv:1003.4394*, https://arxiv.org/pdf/1003.4394.

Matej DOSTAL and Mehrnoosh SADRZADEH (2016), Many valued generalised quantifiers for natural language in the DisCoCat model, Technical report, Czech Technical University Prague and Queen Mary University of London, https://qmro.qmul.ac.uk/xmlui/bitstream/handle/123456789/17382/DisCoCat%20Maodel%20Paper%20M.Sadrzadeh.pdf.

Edward GREFENSTETTE (2013), Towards a formal distributional semantics: simulating logical calculi with tensors, in *Proceedings of the Second Joint Conference on Lexical and Computational Semantics*, pp. 1–10, Association for Computational Linguistics, http://aclweb.org/anthology/S13-1001.

Jules HEDGES and Mehrnoosh SADRZADEH (2016), A generalised quantifier theory of natural language in categorical compositional distributional semantics with bialgebras, *arXiv preprint arXiv:1602.01635*, https://arxiv.org/pdf/1602.01635.

Dimitri KARTSAKLIS (2016), Coordination in categorical compositional distributional semantics, *arXiv preprint arXiv:1606.01515*, https://arxiv.org/pdf/1606.01515.

Dimitri KARTSAKLIS, Matthew PURVER, and Mehrnoosh SADRZADEH (2016), Verb phrase ellipsis using Frobenius algebras in categorical compositional distributional semantics, *DSALT Workshop, European Summer School on Logic, Language and Information*, https://pdfs.semanticscholar.org/6c56/137ffb008ee5f94a482e0c74e494d7f7bc04.pdf.

German KRUSZEWSKI, Denis PAPERNO, Raffaella BERNARDI, and Marco BARONI (2016), There is no logical negation here, but there are alternatives: Modeling conversational negation with distributional semantics, *Computational Linguistics*, 42(4):637–660, doi:https://doi.org/10.1162/COLI_a_00262.

Joachim LAMBEK (1958), The mathematics of sentence structure, *The American Mathematical Monthly*, 65(3):154–170, doi:https://doi.org/10.1080/00029890.1958.11989160.

Joachim LAMBEK (1997), Type grammar revisited, in *International Conference on Logical Aspects of Computational Linguistics*, pp. 1–27, Springer, doi:https://doi.org/10.1007/3-540-48975-4_1.

Richard MONTAGUE (1970), English as a formal language, *Linguaggi nella Società e nella Tecnica*.

Richard MONTAGUE (1973), The proper treatment of quantification in ordinary English, in *Approaches to Natural Language*, pp. 221–242, Springer, doi:https://doi.org/10.1007/978-94-010-2506-5_10.

Michael MOORTGAT and Richard MOOT (2011), Proof nets for the Lambek-Grishin calculus, *arXiv preprint arXiv:1112.6384*, https://arxiv.org/pdf/1112.6384.

Michael MOORTGAT and Gijs WIJNHOLDS (2017), Lexical and derivational meaning in vector-based models of relativisation, *Proceedings of the 21st Amsterdam Colloquium*, pp. 55–64, https://semanticsarchive.net/Archive/jZiM2FhZ/AC2017-Proceedings.pdf.

Glyn MORRILL, Oriol VALENTÍN, and Mario FADDA (2011), The displacement calculus, *Journal of Logic, Language and Information*, 20(1):1–48, doi:https://doi.org/10.1007/s10849-010-9129-2.

Mehrnoosh SADRZADEH (2016), Quantifier scope in categorical compositional distributional semantics, *arXiv preprint arXiv:1608.01404*, https://arxiv.org/pdf/1608.01404.

Mehrnoosh SADRZADEH, Stephen CLARK, and Bob COECKE (2013), The Frobenius anatomy of word meanings I: subject and object relative pronouns, *Journal of Logic and Computation*, 23(6):1293–1317, doi:https://doi.org/10.1093/logcom/ext044.

Mark STEEDMAN (2000), *The Syntactic Process*, MIT Press.

Oriol VALENTÍN (2014), The hidden structural rules of the discontinuous Lambek calculus, in *Categories and Types in Logic, Language, and Physics*, pp. 402–420, Springer, doi:https://doi.org/10.1007/978-3-642-54789-8_23.

Gijs WIJNHOLDS (2014), *Categorical foundations for extended compositional distributional models of meaning*, Master's thesis, Universiteit van Amsterdam, https://www.illc.uva.nl/Research/Publications/Reports/reportlist/MoL-2014-22.text.pdf.

Gijs Jasper WIJNHOLDS (2017), Coherent diagrammatic reasoning in compositional distributional semantics, in *International Workshop on Logic, Language, Information, and Computation*, pp. 371–386, Springer, doi:https://doi.org/10.1007/978-3-662-55386-2_27.

Lotfi A. ZADEH (1983), A computational approach to fuzzy quantifiers in natural languages, *Computers & Mathematics with Applications*, 9(1):149–184, ISSN 0898-1221, doi:http://dx.doi.org/10.1016/0898-1221(83)90013-5.

3

Relative clauses as a benchmark for Minimalist parsing

Thomas Graf, James Monette, and Chong Zhang
Department of Linguistics, Stony Brook University, USA

Keywords: Parsing, sentence processing, Minimalist grammars,
memory usage, relative clauses, promotion analysis, English, East Asian

ABSTRACT

Minimalist grammars have been used recently in a series of papers to explain well-known contrasts in human sentence processing in terms of subtle structural differences. These proposals combine a top-down parser with complexity metrics that relate parsing difficulty to memory usage. So far, though, there has been no large-scale exploration of the space of viable metrics. Building on this earlier work, we compare the ability of 1,600 metrics to derive several processing effects observed with relative clauses, many of which have been proven difficult to unify. We show that among those 1,600 candidates, a few metrics (and only a few) can provide a unified account of all these contrasts. This is a welcome result for two reasons: First, it provides a novel account of extensively studied psycholinguistic data. Second, it significantly limits the number of viable metrics that may be applied to other phenomena, thus reducing theoretical indeterminacy.

1   INTRODUCTION

It is beyond doubt that the structural properties of a sentence influence how easily said sentence is processed by humans. For example, a sentence with multiple levels of center embedding is harder to parse than its counterpart with right embedding, and English subject relative clauses are processed more quickly than object relative clauses. There is large disagreement, however, on what the relevant structural properties are. This paper continues a recent series of investigations (Kobele *et al.* 2013; Graf and Marcinek 2014; Graf *et al.* 2015; Gerth

2015) that approach this question by combining Stabler's (2013) top-down parser for Minimalist grammars (MGs) with structurally rich analyses from Minimalist syntax, the most recent version of Chomsky's transformational grammar framework.

The works above are part of longer tradition applying computational formalisms to human sentence processing (Joshi 1990; Rambow and Joshi 1995; Steedman 2001; Hale 2011; Yun *et al.* 2014, among others). Common to all of them is a tripartite structure consisting of I) an articulated theory of syntax that has sufficient empirical coverage to be applicable to a wide range of constructions, II) a sound and complete parser for the syntactic formalism, and III) a complexity metric that acts as linking theory to derive psycholinguistic predictions from the previous two components. The allure of this approach is that all components are rigorously specified and mathematically worked out to a degree that allows for very fine-grained and detailed processing predictions. Not only does this provide insightful explanation of certain processing phenomena, it also makes it possible to distinguish between competing syntactic proposals based on their psycholinguistic predictions.

The decomposition into three distinct modules is intuitive and elegant, but it also highlights a worrying underspecification issue. With three components that by necessity have to make very detailed assumptions, it is to be expected that a large number of different combinations all replicate the same behavioral data. For instance, a syntactician whose analysis makes the wrong processing predictions may insist that the problem is not with the analysis but with the parser or the complexity metric. For the previous MG modeling work, the issue has already arisen with respect to the choice of complexity metrics, with Graf and Marcinek (2014) and Graf *et al.* (2015) arguing for slightly different metrics than Kobele *et al.* (2013) and Gerth (2015). The specificity of computational models – one of their biggest virtues – thus runs the risk of combinatorial explosion and empirical indeterminacy, which would severely weaken their appeal.

In order to address this issue, we define a total of 1,600 complexity metrics and evaluate whether they can account for the processing contrasts with relative clauses that were originally discussed in Kobele *et al.* (2013), Graf and Marcinek (2014), and Graf *et al.* (2016). We also use two different analyses of relative clauses from Minimalist syntax (promotion and wh) to determine whether the set of empirically viable metrics is still sufficiently structure-sensitive to distinguish between the accounts. Our findings show that the issues of indeterminacy and combinatorial explosion are much less severe in practice than one might expect – a handful of data points is sufficient to significantly reduce the space of empirically viable parsing models. Furthermore, this reduced set contains some very simple metrics that are capable of explaining a wide range of processing contrasts in an intuitively pleasing fashion. At the same time, the set of viable metrics varies with the posited analysis in an interesting way, which suggests that more data points will eventually allow us to rule out specific syntactic proposals.

The paper proceeds as follows. The next section introduces MGs (2.1) and explains how the behavior of Stabler's (2013) top-down parser for MGs can be represented at an abstract level with index/outdex annotated derivation trees. Section 3 then defines 1,600 complexity metrics that operate over these annotated derivation trees. This large number is obtained from just three basic metrics that are subsequently parameterized along various axes. In Section 4, we establish the empirical viability of only a few of these 1,600 metrics for the processing of relative clauses in English, Chinese, Korean, and Japanese. The paper concludes with a discussion of conceptual and methodological aspects of our finding.

2   MINIMALIST GRAMMARS FOR PROCESSING

The mathematical backbone of this paper is provided by MGs (Stabler 1997, 2011) and the top-down MG parser proposed by Stabler (2013). MGs were chosen because they present a rare combination of traits. On the one hand they incorporate ideas from Chomskyan syntax that have found wide adoption in syntactic processing. MGs are also flexible enough to implement even unusual proposals such as Late Merge (Lebeaux 1988; Takahashi and Hulsey 2009) and test their predictions. On the other hand they can be regarded as a simple variant of context-free grammars, which have been studied extensively in the computational parsing literature (Shieber *et al.* 1995; Sikkel 1997). MGs thus act as mathematical glue between formal parsing theory, psycholinguistics, and large areas of contemporary syntax.

After a brief introduction to MGs in Section 2.1, we discuss the central role of derivation trees (2.2) and how Kobele *et al.*'s (2013) system of annotating derivation trees acts as a high-level abstraction of Stabler's top-down parser (2.3). This provides us with a unified representational format that simultaneously describes the structure of a sentence and relevant parts of its parse history. When combined with the complexity metrics in Section 3, this simple system is sufficient to obtain concrete processing predictions.

2.1   *Non-technical introduction to Minimalist grammars*

MGs take inspiration from the most recent iteration of transformational grammar, known as *Minimalism* or *Minimalist syntax* (Chomsky 1995b, 2001). Like all iterations of transformational grammar, MGs furnish a mechanism for encoding basic head-argument relations which are then manipulated by a movement operation to produce the actual syntactic structure. In the case of MGs, these two modes of structure building are called *Merge* and *Move*, respectively. What differentiates MGs from standard Minimalism is their fully explicit feature calculus, which regulates when each operation has to be applied. This makes MGs a lexicalized formalism similar to CCG, LFG or HPSG in the sense that each grammar G is just a finite list of feature-annotated lexical items (LIs) – a structure is generated by G iff it can be assembled from LIs of G according to their feature specifications.

For the purposes of this paper, an intuitive understanding of MGs is sufficient, so we do not give a complete, rigorous definition here. The interested reader is referred to Stabler (2011), Graf (2013, Chapters 1 & 2), and Gerth (2015, Section 4.1) for detailed yet accessible introductions. Suppose that we want to generate the sentence *John, the girl likes*. While there are in principle infinitely many distinct ways to do so with MGs, only a few, marginally different ones are also entertained in Minimalist syntax. The most common analysis posits the syntactic structure shown in Figure 1, where dashed lines have been added to indicate which positions certain phrases were moved from. The basic idea is that the sentence starts out as *the girl likes John* and is subsequently transformed into *John, the girl likes* via Move. There are, however, several independently motivated factors that complicate this simple picture.

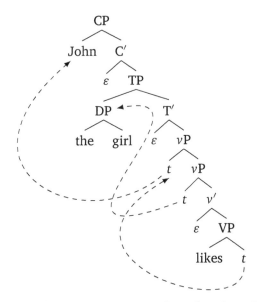

Figure 1: MG phrase structure tree for *John, the girl likes*; dashed arrows indicate movement

- Instead of the usual X′-structure, a more succinct Bare Phrase Structure tree (Chomsky 1995a) is assumed. The two are almost identical except that Bare Phrase Structure trees omit all unary branches (wherefore they are strictly binary branching). So an X′-structure like [DP [D′ [D *John*]]] reduces to simply *John*.

- A phrase can have multiple specifiers but only one complement. Heads are always linearized to the left of their complement and to the right of their specifiers (Kayne 1994).

- Sentences are allowed to contain unpronounced LIs, which are denoted ε.

- VPs are split into VP and *v*P (read "little VP") following ideas first formulated in Larson (1988). The *v*P phrase serves many purposes in the literature, but its relevance for this paper is limited to its role as the base position for subjects.

- Subjects in English (and all other languages discussed in this paper) move from the lowest specifier of *v*P to the canonical subject position, i.e. the lowest specifier of TP.

- For the sake of exposition, Figure 1 also incorporates the assumption that a phrase moving out of *v*P must intermittently land in a specifier of *v*P (Chomsky 2001). We omit this in the remainder of the paper as it has no effect on our results and thus would only add irrelevant complexity.

While many of these assumptions are not widely shared outside of Minimalist syntax and add a certain degree of verbosity, they rest on decades of syntactic research. Since a major goal of the MG parsing project is to determine to what extent different syntactic assumptions can affect processing predictions, we adapt these Minimalist analyses as faithfully as possible to MGs.

Let us then look more closely at how the phrase structure tree in Figure 1 is assembled by an MG. MGs combine LIs into trees via the structure-building operations *Merge* and *Move* based on the features carried by those LIs. We start out by applying Merge to *likes* and *John*, which marks *John* as an argument of *likes*. In order for this Merge step to be licensed, *likes* must have a feature that indicates that the verb takes a DP as its complement, whereas *John* must have the matching category feature D. The verb is then selected by the unpronounced head of *v*P, which also requires a DP as its specifier. In this particular case, the DP is obtained by merging *the* with *girl*. As before, all these instances of Merge must be licensed by suitable feature specifications on the LIs. We do not write out these features here as they will play no role in this paper beyond the fact that an MG parser needs to keep track of all features.

At this point we have assembled the tree depicted in Figure 2. This figure also shows the corresponding *derivation tree,* which records the structure-building steps taken to build the phrase structure tree. In a derivation tree, all leaves are lexical items, and all interior nodes are labeled by Merge and Move depending on which operation takes place at that point. The two trees in Figure 2 differ only in their interior node labels, but they will diverge more significantly once Move enters the picture.

So far each step has added new material to the tree via Merge. But now something different happens: the object DP *John* is displaced to a specifier of *v*P via Move. When exactly Move may take place and

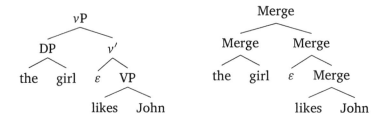

Figure 2: An intermediate state of the assembly of *John, the girl likes*; all feature specifications are omitted

which phrase it may displace is once again controlled by the feature calculus. In the case at hand, the vP-head must have a feature f that requires some phrase to move into a vP specifier. Similarly, *John* must have a feature that requires it to undergo f-movement. The result of Move is shown in Figure 3. Note that the phrase structure tree and the derivation tree now have different geometries, with *John* in a vP specifier in the former but still in its base position in the latter. Consequently, reading the leaves in a derivation tree from left to right thus may not produce the actual word order of the sentence, which will play an important role during the discussion of MG parsing in the next two sections.

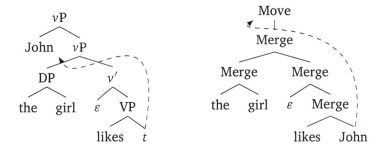

Figure 3: Phrase structure tree and derivation tree after the first movement step; dashed arrows are not part of the trees

The reader may also wonder why Move is represented as a unary branching node even though the operation seems to involve two arguments, a target position and the subtree that is to be displaced. The answer is that Move is a deterministic operation in MGs. The target position is always added at the root of the current tree, and from the feature specifications of LIs one can always infer which particular subtree is to be displaced. There simply is no need to explicitly specify the arguments of Move. However, in the derivation trees in this paper we omit the feature specifications for the sake of brevity and instead use dashed arrows to indicate what moves where.

Strictly speaking we could stop here as the current phrase structure tree already has *John, the girl likes* as its string yield. However, the tree is still incomplete according to Minimalist syntax and thus the derivation continues. After merging the tree with an unpronounced T-head, the subject *the girl* moves from its base position inside vP to the canonical subject position in the specifier of TP. Then the TP is merged with an unpronounced C-head, and *John* is topicalized by moving it to a CP specifier. By assumption, a tree is well-formed iff its root is

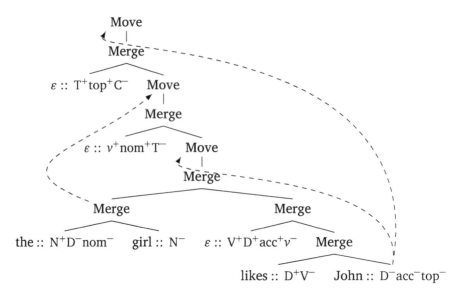

Figure 4:MG derivation tree for *John, the girl likes* with explicit feature specifications for all LIs

labeled CP and all feature requirements have been satisfied. Since this is the case for this tree, the derivation can stop here. The full deriva- tion is given in Figure 4 – to give the reader an idea of what the MG feature calculus looks like, we also list the feature specifications in this example.

2.2   *The central role of derivation trees*

Since derivation trees provide a record of how a given phrase struc- ture tree is to be assembled, they implicitly contain all the information encoded in the latter. In itself this is a rather unremarkable fact, but in the MG community a trend has developed in the last 10 years to treat derivation trees as the primary data structure of MGs (Kobele *et al.* 2007; Kobele 2011, 2015; Graf 2011, 2012a,b, 2013; Hunter 2011). That is to say, MGs are no longer viewed as generators of phrase struc- ture trees or strings but rather as a generator of derivation trees. A suit- able graph transduction then transforms the derivation trees into the desired output structure – strings, phrase structure trees, logical forms, dependency graphs, and so on. Similar ideas have been explored in a more general setting under the label of two-step approaches (Moraw- ietz 2003; Mönnich 2006), interpreted regular tree grammars (Koller and Kuhlmann 2011), and Abstract Categorial Grammar (de Groote 2001). This view of MGs has many technical advantages, but it also provides a unique perspective on parsing: if one assumes that the struc- tures to be produced by an MG parser are derivation trees rather than phrase structure trees, MG parsing turns out to be closely related to parsing of context-free grammars (CFGs).

It has been known for a while now that an MG's set of well-formed derivation trees forms a regular tree language (Michaelis 2001; Kobele *et al.* 2007; Salvati 2011; Graf 2012a).[1] Regular tree languages, in turn, can be directly linked to CFGs. For any CFG G, let $D(G)$ be the set of its derivation trees. Furthermore, a projection $\pi : \Sigma \to \Omega$ is a total function from alphabet Σ to alphabet Ω. Projections can be extended to trees in a point-wise fashion such that the image of tree t under π is the result of replacing each label in t by its image under π. A famous theorem by Thatcher (1967) states that a tree language L is regular iff there is a CFG G and projection π such that $L = \pi(D(G))$. In other words, every regular tree language can be generated by a CFG if one is willing to refine the node labels. For MGs, the refinement involves replacing all instances of Merge and Move with tuples of feature specifications. The details are of no particular interest here (see Michaelis 2001, Kobele *et al.* 2007 and section 2.1.1 of Graf 2013). The crucial point is that MGs have a close link to CFGs via their derivation trees, and this link can be exploited in parsing.

An MG parser can co-opt CFG parsing techniques as long as it has mechanisms to deal with the properties that separate MGs from CFGs. The use of Merge and Move as interior node labels instead of more fine-grained labels is rather trivial in this respect. The true challenge lies in the fact that the left-to-right order of leaves in the MG derivation tree does not correspond to the linear order in the string. The latter can be deduced from the former only if one keeps track of the structural alterations brought about by Move, which requires some ingenuity. At any rate, MGs can be regarded as CFGs with a more complex mapping

---

[1] This fact is not restricted to standard MGs as presented in the previous section. MGs have been extended and modified with numerous devices from the syntacticians' toolbox. Even the most truncated list includes adjunction (Frey and Gärtner 2002; Fowlie 2013; Hunter 2015a), new movement types (Kobele 2006; Stabler 2006; Gärtner and Michaelis 2010; Graf 2012b), and a variety of constraints (Gärtner and Michaelis 2007; Graf 2013). But these revised versions still preserve the regularity of the derivation tree language. The complexity of the string yield mapping is affected by new movement types, but stays within the restricted class of transductions that are definable in first-order logic with equality and proper dominance (Graf 2012b).

from trees to strings, and MG parsers are CFG parsers that have been augmented with a mechanism to handle this increased complexity.[2]

2.3   *Encoding parses with tree annotations*

Consider a standard recursive descent parser for CFGs, i.e. a parser that operates top-down, depth-first, and left-to-right. Following Kobele *et al.* (2013), the order in which a parser builds a given tree t for input string i can be represented by a specific annotation of the nodes of t as in Figure 5.

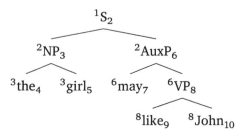

Figure 5: The annotations of the tree indicate in what order it is built by a recursive descent parser

Intuitively, the annotation indicates for each node in the tree when it is first conjectured by the parser and at what point it is considered completed and flushed from memory. So at the very first step, the parser conjectures S, which is expanded in step 2 to NP and AuxP. Assuming that NP and AuxP will eventually yield the desired string, S can be marked as done and removed from memory at step 2. After that the parser works on NP (because it operates left-to-right), adding *the* and *girl*. So those two are first conjectured at step 3 while NP is removed from memory at the same time. As the parser is depth-first, it now proceeds to work on *the* and *girl* rather than AuxP. First *the* is scanned at step 4. This means that the parser reads in the first word of

---

[2] The connection between MGs and CFGs does not emerge with phrase structure trees. MGs are known to be weakly equivalent to MCFGs (Harkema 2001; Michaelis 2001), from which it follows immediately that there are MGs whose set of well-formed phrase structure trees is supra-regular. But supra-regular tree languages cannot be made context-free via a simple relabeling as is the case for regular tree languages, wherefore CFG parsing techniques are not easily extended to Minimalist phrase structure trees. The technical gulf between phrase structure trees on the one hand and derivation trees on the other is significant, and it holds only because derivation trees need not directly encode the linear order of leaves in the string.

the input and verifies that it is indeed *the*. If so, the parser then scans *girl* at step 5, checking it against the second word in the string. Assuming that scanning succeeded, the parser then returns to AuxP, which it has held in memory since step 2. Now at step 6 it finally gets to flush AuxP from memory and replace it by *may* and VP. The remainder of the parse is straight-forward.

This is of course a highly abstracted view of the actual work done by a parser. For one thing, a parser operates with parse items rather than trees or tree nodes, and how such parse items are organized in memory depends on a lot on the specifics of the algorithm (for example, a chart-based parser would never remove an already constructed parse item from memory). More importantly, the problem of which rewrite rules must be chosen to derive the correct string is completely ignored. So this way of annotating trees is no substitute for a proper, rigorously defined parser. Crucially, though, these abstractions are immaterial for this paper's approach to modeling human sentence processing – the tree annotation is a sufficiently close representation of a parser's behavior to enable the kind of processing predictions we are interested in.

Now consider how a standard recursive descent parser would operate over an MG derivation tree. Consider first the derivation tree for *the girl likes John*, depicted in Figure 6. For the sake of clarity, we indicate unpronounced LIs by their category (C, T, *v*). As can be gleaned from the figure, the parser scans the leaf nodes in this derivation in the following order: C T *the girl v likes John*. But the actual order in the input string is C *the girl* T *v likes John*, with *the girl* preceding T rather than following it. In this particular case the slight difference does not matter because T is the empty string, so "T *the girl*" and "*the girl* T" are exactly the same string. However, this example already shows that a standard recursive descent parser is not guaranteed to scan the leaf nodes of an MG derivation in the order in which they appear in the input string. Problems arise whenever Move actually alters the precedence relations between leaf nodes, as is the case with *John, the girl likes* (also shown in Figure 6). The recursive descent parser will reach *the* and try to scan it. It subsequently aborts the parse because the scanned leaf node does not match the first word in the input, *John*. We see, then, that a CFG recursive descent parser does not operate correctly over MG derivation trees despite them being context-free.

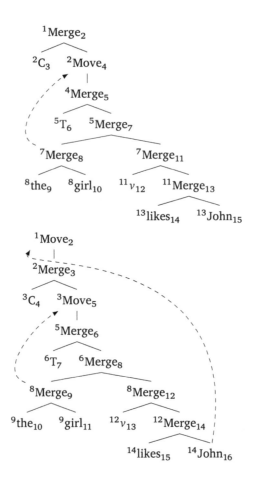

Figure 6: Standard recursive descent works for MG derivation trees only if Move does not alter the precedence relations in the string

The problem with the CFG recursive descent parser is its assumption that the left-to-right order in trees reflects the left-to-right order in the derived string. The core insight of Stabler (2013) (building on Mainguy 2010) is that the left-to-right order can instead be inferred from the MG feature calculus. At the level of abstraction used in this paper, the answer is even simpler. Given two sibling nodes m and n in an MG derivation, m is left of n iff m reflexively dominates a leaf node l such that every leaf node reflexively dominated by n is somewhere to the right of l in the derived string (where reflexive dominance is the reflexive, transitive closure of the mother-of relation). According to this definition, the recursive descent parser will choose a right branch instead of a left one whenever the right branch contains a mover and this mover appears to the left of all the material in the left branch.

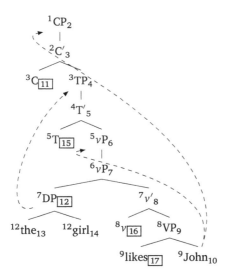

Figure 7: Modified recursive descent operates correctly over MG derivation trees

Figure 7 shows that this modified kind of recursive descent scans the leaf nodes in the correct order: *John* C *the girl* T *v* likes. To further increase the readability of derivation trees, this and all later figures replace the labels Merge and Move by the corresponding X′-labels in the phrase structure tree.

The annotations for MG derivation trees can be computed in a purely tree-geometric fashion (Graf *et al.* 2015). From here on out, we will refer to a node's superscript as its *index* and its subscript as its *outdex*. The terminology is intended to highlight that the index represents the step at which the parser first conjectures a node whereas the outdex records the point at which it has finished working on the node. Index and outdex thus provide information about the parser's memory usage. The greater the difference between the two, the longer an item has to be stored in memory. Since memory usage plays a central role in deriving processing predictions from these annotations, any outdex that is larger than the corresponding index by a non-trivial amount will be henceforth highlighted by a box (more on this in Section 3.2).

Definition 1 *Let s[urface]-precedence be the relation that holds between nodes m_d and n_d in a derivation tree iff their counterparts m_p and n_p in the corresponding phrase structure tree stand in the precedence relation. If m_d undergoes movement during the derivation, its counterpart m_p is the final landing site rather than its base position.*

Given a well-formed Minimalist derivation tree t, its index/outdex annotation is computed as follows:

1. *Every node of t has exactly one index and exactly one outdex.*
2. *The index of the root is 1. For every other node, its index is identical to the outdex of its mother.*
3. *If nodes n and n′ are distinct nodes with index i, and n reflexively dominates a node that is not s-preceded by any node reflexively dominated by n′, then n has outdex $i + 1$.*
4. *Otherwise, the outdex of node n with index i is $\max(i+1, j+1)$, where $j \geq 0$ is greatest among the outdices of all nodes that s-precede n but are not reflexively dominated by n.*

Throughout the rest of the paper we use these annotated derivation trees as abstract representations of the behavior of Stabler's (2013) recursive descent parser for MGs. This greatly simplifies the discussion by substituting easily interpreted derivation trees with indices and outdices for the complex mechanics of the parser. But it means that the difficulty of finding this derivation tree in the first place is completely ignored. The most demanding task of parsing – searching through a large space of structures in the search for the correct one – is taken out of the equation. This simplification is shared among all recent work that use Stabler's MG parser to model human processing (Kobele *et al.* 2013; Graf and Marcinek 2014; Graf *et al.* 2015; Gerth 2015). In the words of Graf *et al.* (2015, p.3):

> While psychologically implausible, this idealization is meant to stake out a specific research goal: processing effects must be explained purely in terms of the syntactic complexity of the involved structures, rather than the difficulty of finding these structures in a large space of alternatives. More pointedly, we assume that parsing difficulty *modulo* non-determinism is sufficient to account for the processing phenomena under discussion.

The aim of these MG processing models, then, is to see how much of human sentence processing can be explained by considering only the order of how the parts of the correct derivation are built. This does not deny that ambiguity has a large role to play, e.g. in garden path sentences, but it is taken out of the equation in order to determine the relevance of isolated structural factors. A simpler model has the advantage of being easier to reason about, and the focus on structure allows us to compare specific syntactic proposals according to their processing predictions.

3   COMPLEXITY METRICS FOR PROCESSING

The previous section recast Stabler's top-down parsing algorithm for MGs as a particular kind of tree annotation, but this raises the question how a simple annotation of derivation trees can be linked to psycholinguistic processing effects. This is accomplished via a linking theory, which takes the form of *complexity metrics*.[3] The next section discusses what we mean by complexity metrics and how all our metrics are rooted in notions of memory usage. Sections 3.2 and 3.3 then provide formal definitions of all the relevant metrics. The full set comprises 1,600 metrics, of which only a handful will prove able to account for all the data in Section 4.

3.1   *Complexity metrics and three notions of memory usage*

A complexity metric is any procedure that ranks strings according to processing difficulty. For instance, Kimball's (1973) principle that the human parser cannot work on more than two CPs at the same time provides a simple complexity metric that is computed over phrase structure trees. O'Grady (2011) suggests that the length of movement dependencies affects processing difficulty. The Derivational Theory of Complexity (Miller and Chomsky 1963; Miller and McKean 1964; see also Phillips 1996, Chapter 5) equates complexity with the number of syntactic operations that are required to build said sentence. Syntactic Prediction Locality Theory (Gibson 1998) and Dependency Locality Theory (Gibson 2000) instead operate directly over the string and measure the length and interaction of certain dependencies. There are also metrics that consider more than one isolated structure: surprisal and entropy reduction (Hale 2001, 2003, 2011; Levy 2013), for

---

[3] Following the advice of two reviewers, we refrain from using Graf *et al.*'s (2015) term *parsing metric*, which already has an established but distinct meaning in the formal parsing community.

instance, measure how the search space shrinks and grows during incremental processing.

The open-endedness of complexity metrics reflects the fact that the number of conceivable linking theories between the parser and the observed processing phenomena is dauntingly large. In the face of such an overabundance of choices, the methodologically soundest position is to explore simple metrics before moving on to more complicated ones. This is the stance we adopt throughout this paper. The MG parser has already been simplified to a degree where all ambiguity is abstracted away and parsing is reduced to index/outdex annotations of derivation trees. Sticking with our focus on derivation trees and maximal simplicity, we only consider complexity metrics that predict processing difficulty based on how the geometry of derivation trees affects memory usage.

That processing difficulty correlates with memory usage is a very common hypothesis in the psycholinguistic literature. The idea can be traced back to Kaplan (1974) and Wanner and Maratsos (1978),[4] with Joshi (1990), Gibson (1998, 2000) and many other as more recent examples (see Gerth (2015, Section 2.3.1) for a detailed discussion). Memory usage may be measured in many different ways, though, and as a result there is a myriad conceivable complexity metrics that differ only in minor details. This paper compares over a thousand memory-based complexity metrics, but fortunately they can be reduced to three basic concepts, which will be gradually refined and modified as we go along.

As we briefly remarked in Section 2.3, the MG parser does not actually hold nodes of the derivation tree in memory but rather *parse items* that encode various pieces of information about each node, in particular whether the node is the root of a subtree containing movers. For a parser that has to hold such parse items in memory, one can distinguish at least three kinds of memory usage:

Tenure How long is the item kept in memory?

Payload How many items are held in memory?

Size How many bits does the item consume in memory?

---

[4] We thank an anonymous reviewer for bringing these early works to our attention.

Each category is part of some complexity metric that has been invoked in previous work on MG parsing (Kobele *et al.* 2013; Graf and Marcinek 2014; Graf *et al.* 2015; Gerth 2015). In terms of annotated derivation trees, the three notions can be formalized as follows:

Definition 2 *Let t be some Minimalist derivation tree annotated with indices and outdices.*

- *For every node n with index i and outdex o ($i < o$), its tenure $\text{ten}(n)$ is $o - i$. A node's tenure is trivial iff $\text{ten}(n) \leq 2$.*
- *The payload of t is equal to the number of nodes in t with non-trivial tenure: $|\{n \mid \text{ten}(n) > 2\}|$.*
- *For every node n its size is identical to the number of phrases that are reflexively dominated by n, distinct from n, and are associated to a Move node that reflexively dominates n.*

For a concrete example, consider again the derivation tree in Figure 7. The tenure of the empty C-head is $11 - 3 = 8$, whereas the tenure of TP is just $4 - 3 = 1$. The derivation tree's payload is 5 as there are five nodes with non-trivial tenure (indicated by boxed outdices): the empty C-, T-, and v-heads, as well as DP and *likes*. The size of a parse item corresponding to node n is the same as the number of nodes below n that have a movement arrow pointing to somewhere above n. So the size of CP and v' is 1 and the size of T' is 2, whereas the size of DP and v is 0.

The definition of size may strike the reader as very stipulative. It derives from how information about movers is stored by Stabler's (2013) top-down parser. For a detailed discussion, the reader is referred to Graf *et al.* (2015). Similarly, readers may wonder why the threshold for payload is set to 2 rather than 1. Once again this is done for technical reasons, discussed in Graf and Marcinek (2014).

3.2   *From memory usage to complexity metrics*

Note that tenure, size and payload are not exactly on equal footing. While payload is a property of derivation trees, tenure and size are properties of individual nodes/parse items. Consequently, payload can already be used as a complexity metric for our simple purposes: given two derivation trees, the one with lower payload is predicted to be easier to process. Graf and Marcinek (2014) use the name **Box** to distinguish payload as a complexity metric over derivation trees from payload as general concept of memory usage. The name is motivated by the notational convention to draw a box around the outdices of nodes with non-trivial tenure, which we also adhere to in this paper. In contrast to payload, tenure and size can be applied to derivation trees in multiple ways.

Tenure was incorporated into three distinct complexity metrics by Kobele *et al.* (2013). Let T be the set of nodes of derivation tree t. Then

MaxT $\max(\{\text{ten}(n) \mid n \in T\})$

SumT $\sum_{n \in T, \text{ten}(n) > 2} \text{ten}(n)$

AvgT $\frac{\text{SumT}(t)}{\text{Box}(t)}$

So **MaxT** reports the maximum memory usage used by any single one node, **SumT** the total (non-trivial) tenure of the entire derivation tree, and **AvgT** the average memory usage of a node with non-trivial tenure. Recall that the derivation in Figure 1 has a payload of 5, which is also its **Box** value. Moreover we have **MaxT** $= 10$ (due to T), **SumT** $= 8 + 10 + 5 + 8 + 8 = 39$ (summing the tenure of all boxed nodes), and **AvgT** $= \frac{39}{5} = 7.8$.

Graf *et al.* (2015) furthermore generalize size to the complexity metric **Gap** in a fashion that mirrors **SumT** for tenure. To highlight this similarity, we call this metric **SumS** instead of **Gap** (the original name is motivated by the parallels to measuring the length of filler-gap dependencies). Let M be the set of all nodes of derivation tree t that are the root of a subtree undergoing movement. Also, for each $m \in M$, $i(m)$ is the index of m and $f(m)$ is the index of the highest Move node that m's subtree is moved to. With the visual aids in our derivation trees, M can be taken to consist of exactly those nodes that are the starting point of an arrow, while $f(m)$ is the target node of the highest arrow that starts in m. **SumS** sums the differences between these indices.

SumS $\sum_{m \in M} i(m) - f(m)$

Considering once more the derivation tree in Figure 1, we see that $M = \{\text{DP}, \text{John}\}$, $i(\text{DP}) - f(\text{DP}) = 7 - 3 = 4$, and $i(\text{John}) - f(\text{John}) = 9 - 1 = 8$. So the whole derivation tree has a **SumS** value of 12. The motivation behind **SumS** is again hard to convey without drilling deep into the bowels of the MG top-down parser. Intuitively, though, **SumS** expresses the idea (independently argued for in O'Grady 2011) that moving a subtree is computationally expensive – the longer it takes to actually get to the subtree that needs to be moved, the higher the resource cost.

Even though **SumS** is transparently a size-based analog of **SumT**, no complexity metrics have been previously proposed for size that operate similar to **Box**, **MaxT** or **AvgT**. We introduce these metrics here for the sake of completeness, even though they will eventually turn out to be inadequate for sentence processing.

Movers $|M|$, where M is the set of all nodes that are the root of a subtree undergoing movement

MaxS $\max(\{i(n) - f(n) \mid n \in T\})$, where T is the set of all nodes of the derivation tree

AvgS $\frac{\textbf{SumS}(t)}{\textbf{Movers}(t)}$

For the example in Figure 7, we have **Movers** $= 2$ (only subject and object move), **MaxS** $= 8$ (topicalization of *John*), and **AvgS** $= \frac{(9-1)+(7-3)}{2} = 6$.

3.3 *Further refinements*

3.3.1 Recursive application

Another metric briefly mentioned in Graf and Marcinek (2014) is **MaxT^R**, which applies **MaxT** recursively. With **MaxT**, two derivation trees may receive exactly the same score and would thus be predicted to be equally difficult. **MaxT^R** instead assigns each derivation tree a weight that enumerates in decreasing order the tenure of all nodes in the payload. Then derivation u is easier than derivation v iff their weights are identical up to position i, at which point u's weight contains a smaller number than v's weight. A similar strategy can also be used for size, yielding the complexity metric **MaxS^R**.

Our example derivation tree has the values **MaxT^R** $= [10,8,8,8,5]$ and **MaxS^R** $= [8,4]$. Therefore it would be harder than a competing derivation with **MaxT^R** $= [10,8,8,5]$, but easier than one with **MaxS^R** $= [8,3]$.

3.3.2   Restriction by node type

Graf and Marcinek (2014) refine the set of metrics even more by relativizing them to specific types of nodes. For each metric **M**, an additional four variants $\mathbf{M_I}$, $\mathbf{M_L}$, $\mathbf{M_P}$, and $\mathbf{M_U}$ are defined.

$\mathbf{M_I}$ restriction of metric **M** to interior nodes

$\mathbf{M_L}$ restriction of metric **M** to leaf nodes

$\mathbf{M_P}$ restriction of metric **M** to pronounced leaf nodes

$\mathbf{M_U}$ restriction of metric **M** to unpronounced leaf nodes

For instance, the unrestricted **MaxT** value of our derivation was 10, but the refined values are $\mathbf{MaxT_I} = 5$ (on DP), $\mathbf{MaxT_L} = 10$ (on T), $\mathbf{MaxT_P} = 8$ (on *likes*), and $\mathbf{MaxT_U} = 10$ (on T).

   Note that these restrictions make little sense for size-based metrics since moving subtrees usually contain pronounced material and the corresponding Move node is necessarily an interior node. Therefore we do not consider type-based restrictions of size metrics. At this point, then, the set of defined metrics includes **Box**, **MaxT**, **SumT**, **AvgT**, $\mathbf{MaxT^R}$, four restricted subtypes for each one of them, as well as the size-based metrics **Movers**, **MaxS**, **SumS**, **AvgS**, and $\mathbf{MaxS^R}$ (for a total of 30 metrics).

3.3.3   Time course of memory usage

The final metric to be considered refines payload so that it reflects maximum memory usage more faithfully. As we saw earlier, **Box** simply reports how many parse items had to be held in memory. However, a high **Box** value need not imply a heavy memory burden as long as one item is removed from memory before the next one is inserted. That is to say, if nodes u and v contribute to the payload of derivation t but the outdex of u is less than the index of v, then the two never reside in memory at the same time. In order to home in on this aspect, we define two metrics *convergence* **Con** and *divergence* **Div** that keep track of how many distinct nodes do or do not reside in memory at the same time.

Con $|\{\langle u, v \rangle \mid \text{ten}(u) \geq 2, \text{ten}(v) \geq 2, \text{index}(u) \leq \text{index}(v) \leq \text{outdex}(u)\}|$

Div $|\{\langle u, v \rangle \mid \text{ten}(u) \geq 2, \text{ten}(v) \geq 2, \text{outdex}(u) < \text{index}(v)\}|$

As before these metrics can be relativized to the four subtypes **I**, **L**, **P**, and **U**. Returning one final time to the derivation in Figure 7, we see that $\mathbf{Con_U} = |\{\langle C, T\rangle, \langle C, v\rangle, \langle T, v\rangle\}| = 3$ and $\mathbf{Div} = |\emptyset| = 0$.

3.3.4 Ranked complexity metrics

With just a handful of psycholinguistically plausible factors such as maximum and average memory usage and restrictions to specific types of nodes the number of metrics has quickly risen to a bewildering degree. But things do not stop here. Graf *et al.* (2015) argue in favor of a combined metric **MaxT** + **SumS** which uses **MaxT** to predict processing difficulty but relies on **SumS** whenever **MaxT** results in a tie. So given two derivation trees t_1 and t_2, t_1 is predicted to be easier than t_2 if either t_1 has a lower **MaxT** or t_1 and t_2 have the same **MaxT** value but t_1 has a lower **SumS** value. This is similar to constraint ranking in OT (Prince and Smolensky 2004), where a lower ranked constraint matters only if all higher ranked constraints have failed to pick out a unique winner. If complexity metrics are allowed to be ranked in such a way, their number quickly reaches an astronomical size. We have introduced 40 metrics, wherefore a ranked complexity metric can consist of up to 40 metrics. It follows that there are over 40 factorial (40!) distinct metrics that are ranked combinations of our 40 basic metrics – a truly astounding number. Even if one only allows pairs of our 40 complexity metrics, there are 1,600 distinct metrics (pairs of the form $\langle m, m\rangle$ are equivalent to just the metric m).

Ranked Metric Given a set C of complexity metrics, a ranked metric is an n-tuple $\langle c_1, \ldots, c_n\rangle$ such that for $1 \leq i, j \leq n$ it holds that $c_i \in C$ and that $i \neq j$ implies $c_i \neq c_j$. Given a ranked metric $\langle c_1, \ldots, c_n\rangle$ and two derivation trees t_1 and t_2, t_1 is predicted to be easier than t_2 iff there is some $j \leq n$ such that $c_i(t_1) = c_i(t_2)$ for all $i \leq j$ and c_j predicts t_1 to be easier than t_2.

3.4 *Discussion*

The large number of metrics poses a significant problem. Remember the promise of the MG parser and the psycholinguistic modeling work that builds on it: processing phenomena are explained in terms of the syntactic structures they involve, and in the other direction, syntactic analyses can be evaluated based on their processing predictions.

But the processing claims of these models arise from the interaction of three factors, which are the parser (represented via index/outdex annotation), the syntactic analysis (in the form of derivation trees), and the complexity metric.

There are few alternatives to the current top-down parser. Despite some suggestive evidence such as merely local syntactic coherence effects (Tabor *et al.* 2004; Konieczny 2005; Konieczny *et al.* 2009; Bicknell *et al.* 2009), there is still a large consensus among psycholinguists that if the human parser builds any kind of tree structures, it does not do so in a pure bottom-up fashion. The other prominent option is left-corner parsing. Unfortunately, no left-corner parser exists for MGs at this time because the notion *left corner* does not carry over neatly from CFGs (but see Hunter 2015b). Without a readily available alternative to top-down parsing, the two major parameters in the model are the choice of metric and the choice of syntactic analyses. But the larger the set of metrics, the higher the risk that just about any syntactic analysis will make the right predictions with some metric. This would significantly weaken the link between syntactic structure and processing effects, which is the very heart of the work carried out by Kobele *et al.* (2013), Graf and Marcinek (2014), Graf *et al.* (2015), and Gerth (2015).

Fortunately, this worst-case scenario does not seem to arise. It turns out that a few constructions involving relative clauses are sufficient to rule out the vast majority of these metrics. We have no principled explanation as to why this is the case – it is far from a logical necessity. But this result, established in the next section, strengthens the viability of the enterprise started by Kobele *et al.* (2013) to model processing phenomena with MGs and use these findings to distinguish competing Minimalist analyses. It demonstrates that I) a very simplified processing model can still account for a noteworthy range of challenging processing phenomena, and II) the set of workable complexity metrics is small enough to give the model discriminative power with respect to syntactic analyses.

4   TESTING METRICS WITH RELATIVE CLAUSES

Now that we have a precisely defined parsing model (abstractly represented in terms of annotated derivation trees) as well as a collection of complexity metrics that link the parser's behavior to processing predictions, we are finally in a position to investigate how well these tools model a collection of phenomena from human sentence processing. All these phenomena, which will be presented in detail in Section 4.1, involve relative clauses (RCs) to some extent and have been studied separately in Kobele *et al.* (2013), Graf and Marcinek (2014), and Graf *et al.* (2015).[5] In contrast, we consider the full data set and test our much bigger collection of metrics against each one of them. We furthermore compare two competing analyses of RCs (4.2) using a fairly simple methodology of automated comparisons (4.3). We conclude that this small set of data points is highly discriminative in that it rules out a large number of metrics for each analysis (4.4) while still allowing for linguistically natural explanations of the observed patterns (4.5).

4.1   *Overview of relative clause constructions*

Our testing data for the comparison of metrics and syntactic proposals relies on several well-known processing contrasts involving RCs. RCs are a promising test case because they are complex enough to allow for syntactically interesting structures while factoring out aspects that aren't purely structural in nature such as co-reference resolution. The general idea is to take a pair of constructions A and B such that A is easier to process than B. This result then has to be replicated by the complexity metrics given a specific analysis of RCs.

The specific behavioral contrasts to be accounted for were chosen according to several criteria. First, the processing effects must be well-documented in the psycholinguistic research. Second, the phenomenon should involve a clear structural contrast, rather than just a meaning contrast (e.g. pronoun resolution). Third, ambiguity should not be a major factor, which rules out garden path effects.

1. **SC/RC < RC/SC**

   A sentence with a relative clause embedded inside a sentential complement (SC/RC) is easier to parse than a sentence with a

---

[5] Gerth (2015) investigates some additional phenomena which were not included in our data sample as we were not aware of her findings until recently, unfortunately.

sentential complement embedded inside a relative clause (RC/SC; Gibson 1998, 2000).

2. **SRC < ORC**

- Subject relative clauses (SRCs) are easier to parse than object relative clauses (ORCs) in languages like English, where relative clauses are post-nominal and therefore follow their head noun (Mecklinger *et al.* 1995; Gibson 1998, 2000; Mak *et al.* 2002, 2006; Gordon *et al.* 2006).
- SRCs are also easier to parse than ORCs in Chinese, Korean, and Japanese, where relative clauses are pre-nominal, that is to say, they precede their head noun (Miyamoto and Nakamura 2003, 2013; Lin and Bever 2006; Ueno and Garnsey 2008; Kwon *et al.* 2010; Gibson and Wu 2013).

3. **Right < Center**
Right embedding is easier than center embedding.

These generalizations have been carefully established in the literature via self-paced reading experiments and ERP studies with minimal pairs such as the ones listed in (1)–(6).

(1)   **SC/RC < RC/SC**

a. The fact [$_{SC}$ that the employee$_i$ [$_{RC}$ who the manager hired t_i] stole office supplies] worried the executive.

b. The executive$_i$ [$_{RC}$ who the fact [$_{SC}$ that the employee stole offices supplies] worried t_i] hired the manager.

(2)   **SRC < ORC in English**

a. The reporter$_i$ [$_{RC}$ who t_i attacked the senator] admitted the error.

b. The reporter$_i$ [$_{RC}$ who the senator attacked t_i] admitted the error.

(3)   **SRC < ORC in Chinese**

a. [$_{RC}$ t_i gongji yiyuan] de   jizhe   chengren-le cuowu
              attack senator REL reporter admit-PRF   error

b. [$_{RC}$ yiyuan gongji t_i] de   jizhe   chengren-le cuowu
              senator attack   REL reporter admit-PRF   error

(4)   **SRC < ORC in Korean**

   a. [$_{RC}$ t_i uywon-ul   kongkyekha-n] kica$_i$-ka
            senator-ACC attacked-REL   reporter-NOM
      silswu-lul siinhayssta
      error-ACC admitted

   b. [$_{RC}$ uywon-i t_i kongkyekha-n] kica$_i$-ka
            senator-NOM   attacked-REL   reporter-NOM
      silswu-lul siinhayssta
      error-ACC admitted

(5) **SRC < ORC in Japanese**

   a. [$_{RC}$ t_i giin-ga   hinanshita] kisha$_i$-ga   ayamari-o
            senator-ACC attacked   reporter-NOM error-ACC
      mitometa
      admitted

   b. [$_{RC}$ giin-ga t_i hinanshita] kisha$_i$-ga   ayamari-o
            senator-NOM   attacked   reporter-NOM error-ACC
      mitometa
      admitted

(6) **Right < Center**

   a. The boy disappeared [$_{RC}$ who the man saw [$_{RC}$ who the woman praised]].

   b. The boy [$_{RC}$ who the man [$_{RC}$ who the woman praised] saw] disappeared.

It should be pointed out that the SRC preference is less robust in Chinese than Korean or Japanese. This has been attributed to structural ambiguities (Gibson and Wu 2013), which is corroborated by Yun *et al.* (2014) and their ambiguity-based account rooted in entropy reduction. Recall from Section 2.3, though, that we deliberately ignore ambiguity in this paper so that only tree-geometric aspects of the derivation can derive processing effects. For this reason, we assume that Chinese would also exhibit a uniform preference for SRCs over ORCs if it were not for the confound of structural ambiguity.

Some of the contrasts above have previously proven difficult to account for. While the preference for SC/RC and SRC in English can be explained by string-based models such as the Dependency Locality Theory (Gibson 1998) or the Active-Filler strategy (Frazier 1987), these models erroneously derive an ORC preference for East Asian languages with their pre-nominal RCs. This is because the head noun is closer to the object than the subject position of the RC in this case. A functional account like Keenan and Comrie's (1977) accessibility hierarchy, on the other hand, derives the SRC preference across languages but has little to say about the ease of SC/RC in comparison to RC/SC. That right embeddings are much easier than center embeddings has an elegant explanation in terms of left-corner parsing (Resnik 1992), but this account in turn does not generalize to the other configurations. Overall, then, the data points above have been accounted for individually, but their unification is challenging.

4.2   *Promotion and wh-analysis of relative clauses*

As one of the promises of the MG processing model is the ability to distinguish syntactic analyses based on their processing predictions, our evaluation uses two popular proposals for the structure of RCs: the *wh-movement* analysis (Chomsky 1965, 1977; Montague 1970; Heim and Kratzer 1998), and the *promotion* analysis (Vergnaud 1974; Kayne 1994). Graf *et al.* (2015) did the same in their investigation of the SRC preference in East Asian, whereas Kobele *et al.* (2013) and Graf and Marcinek (2014) only used a promotion analysis.

Both the promotion analysis and the wh-analysis posit that the gap inside the RC is initially filled by some element, but disagree on what this element is and where it moves. In the promotion analysis, it is the head noun itself that starts from the gap position. The wh-analysis has two variants. Either the relative pronoun[6] moves from the gap position, or it acts as the C-head of the RC while a silent operator undergoes movement from the base position. For the purposes of this paper the two variants of the wh-movement analysis are fully equivalent.

---

[6] The use of "relative pronoun" is slightly misleading here in that the relative clause markers in Chinese and Korean are not pronouns (as is rightfully noted by an anonymous reviewer). But since the syntactic category of LIs is ignored by all complexity metrics, we freely change between the terms relative pronoun and RC marker in the discussion. We also represent the East Asian RC markers with *who* in the derivation trees in an attempt to ease the comparison to the English derivation trees.

Notably absent are proposals that do not involve any movement at all. This is because in the absence of movement, the MG parser behaves exactly like a recursive descent parser for CFGs and thus would have little new to offer. In addition, the comparison and detailed analysis of the complexity metrics already involves a multitude of factors, so that increasing the number of analyses would run the risk of rendering the discussion (even more) impenetrable.

With both the promotion analysis and the wh-analysis, the target of movement depends on whether RCs are post-nominal or pre-nominal in the language under investigation. Let us consider languages with post-nominal RCs like English, French, and German. All these languages also have overt complementizers, although they may optionally remain unpronounced, as is the case in English. The general template is [$_{DP}$ Det head-noun [$_{RC}$ complementizer subject verb object]], with either the subject or the object unrealized. The position of the verb depends on language-specific word order constraints, but we can safely ignore this aspect because English is the only language with post-nominal RCs in our data set. Figures 8 and 9 show the promotion analysis and the wh-analysis, respectively, for the SRC *The reporter who attacked the senator admitted the error*. In both derivation trees the element that fills the gap in the SRC moves to the CP specifier (Spec,CP), i.e. the left edge of the relative clause. But note that the head noun is outside the RC in the wh-movement analysis, whereas it is in Spec,CP (and thus inside the RC) in the promotion analysis.

The only difference between SRC and ORC under these analyses is the position that the mover occupies initially. In the SRC, the mover fills the base position of subjects (equated with Spec,vP here), whereas the ORC requires the mover to start out in object position (i.e. as the VP complement). This is illustrated in Figure 10, which depicts an ORC with an embedded sentential complement.

Languages with pre-nominal RCs, such as Chinese, Japanese, and Korean, can also be accommodated, but the word order differences render both analyses more complex. Below is an example of pseudo-English SRCs and ORCs with Chinese word order.

(7)   a.   [$_{DP}$ [$_{RC}$ _ invited the tycoon who] the mayor] likes wine.

        b.   [$_{DP}$ [$_{RC}$ the tycoon invited _ who] the mayor] likes wine.

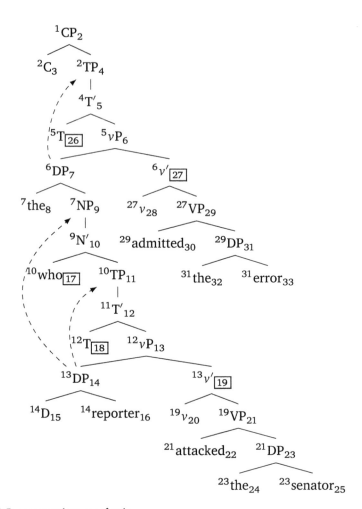

Figure 8: English SRC, promotion analysis

Since standard MGs do not provide a headedness parameter to determine the linearization of arguments (following the received view in
Minimalist syntax), the pre-nominal word order must be derived from
the post-nominal one via movement. This causes the wh-movement
analysis and the promotion analysis to diverge more noticeably.

In the promotion analysis, the RC is no longer a CP, but rather
a RelP that contains a CP (see also Yun *et al.* 2014). The head noun
still moves from within the RC to Spec,CP, but this is followed by the
TP moving to Spec,RelP. This creates the desired word order with the
complementizer between the rest of the RC in Spec,RelP and the head
noun in Spec,CP. In the wh-movement analysis, on the other hand,
the head noun is once again outside the RC, which is just a CP instead
of a RelP. The complementizer starts out in subject or object position

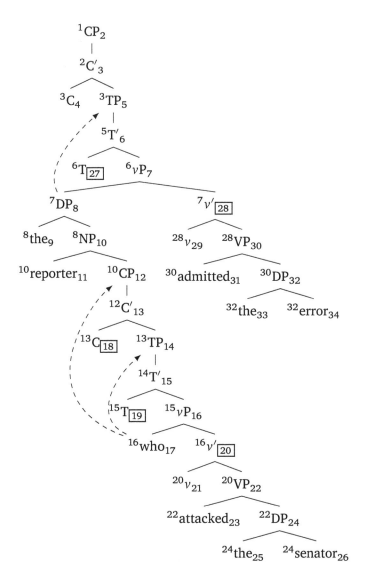

Figure 9: English SRC, wh-movement analysis

depending on the type of RC, and then moves into a right specifier of the CP (rightward movement is not part of Stabler's (2013) MG parser, but we can easily add it without modifying the annotation rules from Definition 1 as they are defined in terms of s-precedence). The CP subsequently moves to the specifier of the DP of the head noun, once again yielding the desired word order with the complementizer between the RC and the head noun. In sum, the promotion analysis needs to posit a new phrase RelP but all movement is leftward and takes place within this phrase. This contrasts with the wh-movement

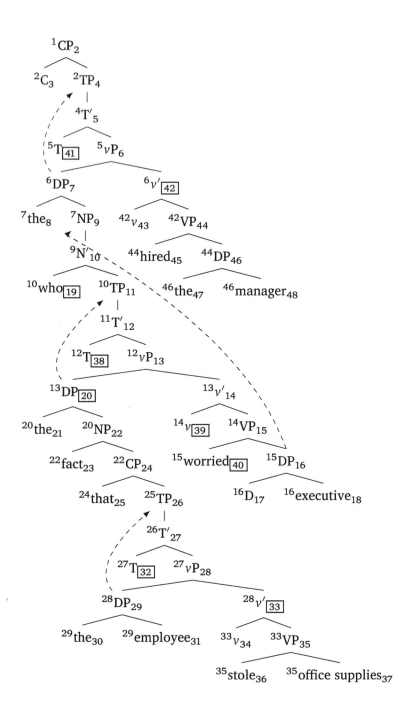

Figure 10: ORC containing a sentential complement, promotion analysis

analysis, which sticks with a single CP but invokes one instance of rightward movement and moves the RC into Spec,DP, a higher position than Spec,RelP. Examples of the two derivation trees for a Chinese SRC are given in Figures 11 and 12, where dotted arrows are used instead of dashed ones for rightward movement.

Among the three East Asian languages, Chinese still has the simpler analysis thanks to its SVO word order, whereas Japanese and Korean are SOV languages. As was the case with the linear order of RCs relative to their head noun, Minimalist syntax assumes that the SOV word order is derived via Move rather than simply linearizing the complement of the verb to its left. The standard assumption is that SOV

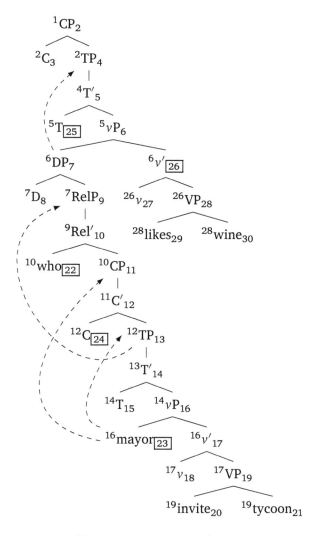

Figure 11: SRC in Chinese, promotion analysis

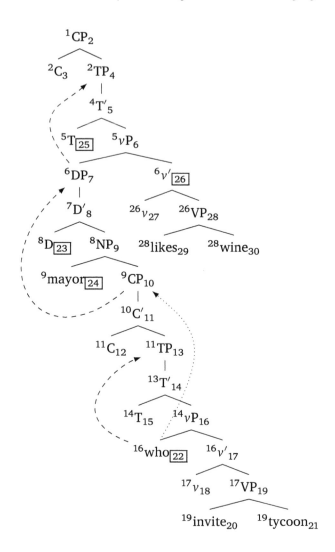

Figure 12: SRC in Chinese, wh-movement analysis

languages require the object to move from the VP-complement position to a specifier of vP as exemplified in Figure 13. While this might seem like a minor complication, we will see in the next section that it actually causes many metrics to incorrectly prefer ORCs over SRCs. Korean and Japanese thus show that the complexity metrics are indeed exquisitely sensitive to minor structural alterations.

We also use rightward movement in right embedding constructions (Figure 14), as embedding without additional movement yields center embedding structures. Whether these instances of extraposition are best analyzed as rightward movement has been called into question in recent research (Hunter and Frank 2014), but it is the best

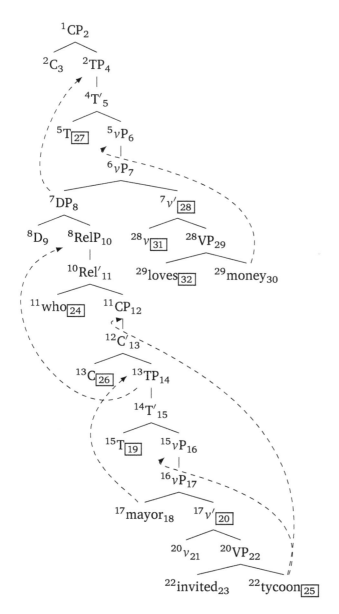

Figure 13: ORC in Korean, promotion analysis

choice here to maintain analytical consistency across the different constructions.

For a full listing of all the analyses with annotated derivation trees, the reader is referred to the supplementary material for this article. Derivation trees for Japanese are omitted since they are identical to the Korean ones except that the RC complementizer remains unpronounced.

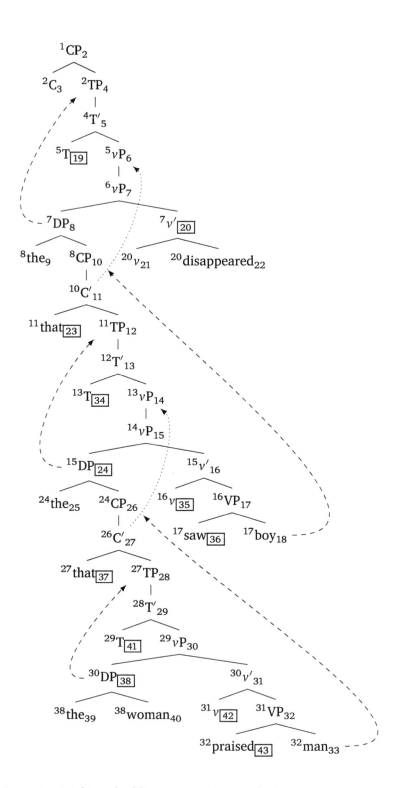

Figure 14: Right embedding, promotion analysis

4.3 *Methodological remarks*

As 1,600 metrics cannot be accurately compared by hand, we rely on a collection of Python scripts, available in the Github repository of the Stony Brook Computational Linguistics lab: https://github.com/ CompLab-StonyBrook. For each basic metric, these scripts perform pairwise comparisons of minimally different derivation trees, e.g. the English SRC in Figure 8 and its ORC counterpart. Whichever one receives a better (= lower) score has a lower memory burden is thus predicted to be easier to process. From the relative rankings that are obtained this way one can then automatically compute all the metrics – including combinations of multiple metrics – that correctly predict all processing contrasts.

Note that the difficulty metric only has to account for overall sentence difficulty. This is different from more ambitious approaches such as Hale (2001) and Yun *et al.* (2014), which seek to predict online difficulty, i.e. how difficulty increases or decreases with each word in the input. Modeling online processing is feasible with certain complexity metrics like **MaxT** (see Kobele *et al.* 2013 and Gerth 2015), but it is hard to automatically compare metrics at this level of granularity. Finally, we reiterate that all ambiguity is factored out – we only consider how the parser builds a specific derivation tree, rather than how it finds this tree among many alternatives.

4.4 *Quantitative evaluation of complexity metrics*

The performance of the basic metrics with the respective syntactic analyses is summarized in Tables 1 and 2. A checkmark ($\checkmark$) indicates that the metric correctly predicts structure A to be easier than structure B, a tie that they are expected to be equally difficult, and a cross ($\times$) that the complexity metric incorrectly reverses difficulty, making B easier than A. Consequently, all basic metrics that contain a cross in at least one column can be discarded. This leaves only one metric for the promotion analysis – $\mathbf{MaxT^R_U}$ – and one for the wh-movement analysis – $\mathbf{AvgT_P}$.

Many inadequate basic metrics, though, may still occur as the second component in a ranked metric. As the second component is only invoked to handle ties for the first component, wrong predictions for a given contrast have no effect unless the first component could not conclusively resolve this contrast. When ranked metrics are also taken

Table 1: Predictions of complexity metrics with promotion analysis

| | SC/RC < RC/SC | SRC < ORC | | | | Right < Center |
		Eng	Chi	Kor	Jap	
Box	tie	✓	✓	tie	tie	✗
Box$_I$	tie	tie	✓	✓	✓	✗
Box$_L$	tie	✓	✓	✗	✗	tie
Box$_P$	tie	✓	tie	✗	✗	✓
Box$_U$	✓	✓	✓	tie	tie	✗
AvgT	✓	✓	✗	✗	✗	✓
AvgT$_I$	✗	✓	✗	✗	✗	✗
AvgT$_L$	✓	✓	✗	✓	✓	✓
AvgT$_P$	✓	✓	✗	✗	✗	✓
AvgT$_U$	✓	✓	✗	✓	✓	✓
MaxT	tie	tie	tie	tie	tie	✓
MaxT$_I$	tie	tie	tie	tie	tie	✗
MaxT$_L$	tie	tie	tie	tie	tie	✓
MaxT$_P$	✓	✓	tie	tie	✗	✓
MaxT$_U$	tie	tie	tie	tie	tie	✓
MaxT^R	✓	✓	✗	✗	✗	✓
MaxT$_I^R$	✗	✓	✓	✓	✓	✗
MaxT$_L^R$	✓	✓	✗	✗	✗	✓
MaxT$_P^R$	✓	✓	✗	✗	✗	✓
MaxT$_U^R$	✓	✓	✓	✓	✓	✓
SumT	✓	✓	✓	✗	✗	✗
SumT$_I$	✗	✓	✓	✓	✓	✗
SumT$_L$	✓	✓	✗	✗	✗	✓
SumT$_P$	✓	✓	✗	✗	✗	✓
SumT$_U$	✓	✓	✓	✓	✓	✗
AvgS	✗	✓	✓	✓	✓	✗
Movers	tie	✓	✓	tie	tie	✗
MaxS	tie	✓	✓	tie	tie	✗
MaxS^R	✗	✓	✓	✓	✓	✗
SumS	✗	✓	✓	✓	✓	✗
Con	✗	✓	✓	✗	✗	✗
Con$_I$	✗	tie	✓	✓	✓	✗
Con$_L$	✗	✓	✓	✗	✗	✓
Con$_P$	tie	✓	tie	✗	✗	✓
Con$_U$	tie	✓	✓	tie	tie	✗
Div	✓	tie	✓	✓	✓	✗
Div$_I$	✓	tie	tie	tie	tie	✗
Div$_L$	✓	tie	✓	✗	✗	✗
Div$_P$	tie	tie	tie	✗	✗	tie
Div$_U$	tie	tie	tie	tie	tie	✗

Table 2: Predictions of complexity metrics with wh-movement analysis

	SC/RC < RC/SC	SRC < ORC				Right < Center
		Eng	Chi	Kor	Jap	
Box	tie	✓	✓	✗	✗	✗
Box$_I$	tie	tie	✓	✓	✓	✗
Box$_L$	tie	✓	tie	✗	✗	✗
Box$_P$	tie	✓	✗	✗	✗	tie
Box$_U$	tie	✓	✓	tie	✗	✗
AvgT	✓	✓	✗	✓	✓	✓
AvgT$_I$	✗	✓	✗	✗	✗	✗
AvgT$_L$	✓	✓	✗	✓	✓	✓
AvgT$_P$	✓	✓	✓	✓	✓	✓
AvgT$_U$	✓	✓	✗	✓	✓	✓
MaxT	tie	tie	tie	tie	tie	✓
MaxT$_I$	tie	tie	tie	tie	tie	✗
MaxT$_L$	tie	tie	tie	tie	tie	✓
MaxT$_P$	✓	✓	tie	tie	tie	✓
MaxT$_U$	tie	tie	tie	tie	tie	✓
MaxT^R	✓	✓	✗	✗	✗	✓
MaxT$_I^R$	✗	✓	✓	✓	✓	✗
MaxT$_L^R$	✓	✓	✗	✗	✗	✓
MaxT$_P^R$	✓	✓	✗	✗	✗	✓
MaxT$_U^R$	✓	✓	✓	✓	✗	✓
SumT	✓	✓	tie	✗	✗	✓
SumT$_I$	✗	✓	✓	✓	✓	✗
SumT$_L$	✓	✓	✗	✗	✗	✓
SumT$_P$	✓	✓	✗	✗	✗	✓
SumT$_U$	✓	✓	✓	✓	✗	✓
AvgS	✗	tie	✓	✓	✓	✗
Movers	tie	✓	✓	tie	tie	✗
MaxS	tie	✓	✓	tie	tie	✗
MaxS^R	✗	✓	✓	✓	✓	✗
SumS	✗	✓	✓	✓	✓	✗
Con	✗	✓	✗	✗	✗	✓
Con$_I$	✗	tie	✗	✓	✓	tie
Con$_L$	✗	✓	tie	✗	✗	✓
Con$_P$	tie	tie	✓	✗	✗	✓
Con$_U$	✗	✓	✗	tie	✗	✓
Div	✓	tie	tie	✗	✗	✗
Div$_I$	✓	tie	tie	tie	tie	✗
Div$_L$	✓	tie	tie	✗	✗	✗
Div$_P$	tie	tie	tie	✗	✗	✗
Div$_U$	✓	tie	tie	tie	✗	✗

Table 3: List of empirically viable complexity metrics

	Promotion	*Wh-Movement*
Basic	$\mathbf{MaxT_U^R}$	$\mathbf{AvgT_P}$
Ranked	$\langle \mathbf{MaxT}, \mathbf{SumT_U} \rangle$	$\langle \mathbf{MaxT_P}, \mathbf{AvgS} \rangle$
	$\langle \mathbf{MaxT_L}, \mathbf{SumT_U} \rangle$	$\langle \mathbf{MaxT_P}, \mathbf{Box_I} \rangle$
	$\langle \mathbf{MaxT_U}, \mathbf{SumT_U} \rangle$	$\langle \mathbf{MaxT_P}, \mathbf{Con_I} \rangle$
		$\langle \mathbf{MaxT_P}, \mathbf{MaxS^R} \rangle$
		$\langle \mathbf{MaxT_P}, \mathbf{MaxT_I^R} \rangle$
		$\langle \mathbf{MaxT_P}, \mathbf{SumS} \rangle$
		$\langle \mathbf{MaxT_P}, \mathbf{SumT_I} \rangle$

into consideration, the number of metrics increases from 40 to 1,600. The number of empirically adequate metrics, on the other hand, does not increase by the same factor and grows from 1 to 4 (promotion) and 8 (wh-movement), respectively. No metric is a viable candidate for both analyses (see Table 3). Note that these numbers do not include ranked metrics whose first component is an empirically adequate basic metric ($\mathbf{MaxT_U^R}$ or $\mathbf{AvgT_P}$) because the second metric would never be used in those cases. If those pair metrics are included, the respective numbers grow to $4 + 39 = 43$ and $8 + 39 = 47$. Depending on how one counts, then, between $\frac{4}{1600-39} = 0.2\%$ and $\frac{47}{1600} = 2.9\%$ of the full space of complexity metrics can account for the five observed processing contrasts with relative clauses. In addition, all the remaining ranked metrics have some variant of $\mathbf{MaxT}$ as their first component. This shows that the underspecification problem is not nearly as bad as one might expect, with a few contrasts ruling out the great majority of metrics.

In fact, the five constructions differ in their discriminatory power in a manner that roughly reflects how difficult they are to account for. For example, the preference for SRCs over ORCs in English requires no structure at all and can be explained purely in terms of string distance (Gibson 1998, 2000), and no metric reverses difficulty for this construction. Even the number of ties is comparatively low. The same contrast is much harder to account for in East Asian languages with their pre-nominal RCs. String-based explanations fail in this case, and so do more than half of all the basic metrics. The processing difference between right embedding and center embedding is interesting in this case because there are a variety of explanations in the psycholinguistic literature, and except for the size- or diversion-based metrics, all the core metrics have some variant that captures the contrast. The failure of size-based metrics is not surprising in this case. Recall that right embedded RCs induce additional syntactic complexity because they start out as center embedded RCs that have to undergo rightward movement. The additional movement steps inevitable cause size-based metrics to make the wrong predictions. Crucially, though, not all metrics fall into this trap, which proves that well-chosen complexity metrics can factor out irrelevant aspects of structural complexity.

4.5   *Qualitative evaluation of complexity metrics*

Since the connection between complexity metrics and the structure of derivation trees is very subtle and sensitive to even minor differences, determining why a complexity metric fails to capture a specific contrast while succeeding at another can be difficult. An exhaustive discussion of all the patterns reported in Table 1–3 is not feasible within the confines of a single paper. Instead, we present a few general observations on the role of **MaxT**, which has been a prominent metric in all previous work on MG parsing and is a component of almost all successful metrics.

First it is instructive, though, to consider why $\mathbf{AvgT_P}$ works for the wh-analysis but fails for the promotion analysis. The problematic constructions are the East-Asian RCs. Recall that in the promotion analysis, it is the head noun that moves from the gap, whereas in the wh-movement analysis it is the RC marker (simply transcribed as *who* in our derivation trees). Since RCs in East-Asian languages are prenominal and have the RC marker at their very end, the wh-movement analysis has

1. high tenure on the head noun outside the RC (which is encountered before the RC but cannot be finished until the latter is complete),

2. medium tenure on the RC marker in SRCs (as it occupies the structurally prominent subject position, which means that it is hypothesized early by the parser but must wait until the rest of the RC is completed),

3. low tenure on the verb in Korean and Japanese (which is introduced at the same time as the object but only finished after it due
   to object movement to the left).

In an ORC, the object moves to the right of the RC, so the low tenure
on the RC marker disappears, and since it is an ORC the verb does not
have any tenure either. But $\mathbf{AvgT_p}$ divides the sum of tenure of pronounced nodes by the number of pronounced nodes with non-trivial
tenure. Removing two entries with low tenure ends up increasing the
$\mathbf{AvgT_p}$ value for ORCs. The final numbers are $\frac{16+6+3}{3} = 8.3$ for SRCs in
contrast to $\frac{16}{1} = 16$ for an ORC.

The structural differences in the promotion analysis, on the other
hand, mean that although the switch from SRC to ORC reduces the
tenure on the mover (the head noun, rather than the relative pronoun)
it does not completely eliminate it. Hence the mover still counts towards the payload and thus greatly lowers the $\mathbf{AvgT_p}$ value for ORCs:
$\frac{13+7+3}{2} = 11.5$ in contrast to $\frac{13+3}{2} = 8$. The success of $\mathbf{AvgT_p}$ with the
wh-movement thus relies on completely eliminating non-trivial tenure
on some nodes in ORCs, rather than just reducing it. The counterin-
tuitive prediction of $\mathbf{AvgT}$ and its variants – if a derivation contains a
node with high tenure, it will become easier the more nodes have low
tenure instead of no tenure – accidentally makes the right prediction
for SRCs and ORCs.

Let us now turn to $\mathbf{MaxT}$, which strikes us as a more insightful
and overall more robust choice of metric. The non-recursive variants
of $\mathbf{MaxT}$ are a good choice for ranked metrics because they rarely
make a completely wrong prediction but instead produce many ties.
This is the reason why all successful ranked metrics contain them as
their first component: a complexity metric with a cross in at least one
column cannot be the first component of a ranked metric, which rules
out all basic metrics except the "tie-heavy" $\mathbf{MaxT}$ variants (and the
basic metrics that capture all the data, for which we do not list any
ranked metrics).

The high frequency of ties with $\mathbf{MaxT}$ variants is a natural consequence of our focus on embedding constructions. All embedding constructions follow a template where different subtrees are inserted into
a fixed main clause. For instance, the English SRC and ORC sentences
differ only in the shape of their RCs; the main clause always has the

same structure. The overall number of steps it takes to parse an RC is independent of whether it is an SRC or an ORC. But this, in turn, implies that I) the nodes in the main clause that are introduced before the RC but cannot be worked on until the RC is finished (e.g. T and v' in Figure 8) have very large tenures exceeding that of any node inside the RC, and II) the tenure of these nodes is independent of whether the RC is an SRC or an ORC. As **MaxT** metrics only pay attention to the largest tenure in a tree, the differences between SRCs and ORCs get drowned out by the high tenure on nodes in the main clause.

This accidental flattening of contrasts does not occur in the case of right and center embedded RCs because the movement of an RC in right embedding directly interacts with the nodes in the clause containing the RC. In particular, moving an RC to the right of an LI l means that l can be worked on before the RC is explored by the parser, thus reducing its tenure. With center embedding, the parser would first have to explore the full RC, so the sister node of the RC would wind up with very high tenure. The overall generalization, then, is that **MaxT** metrics flatten contrasts where the differences between constructions are restricted to nodes within the embedded subtree.

MaxT_p is an exception because its restriction to pronounced nodes filters out the tenure of interior nodes like v' and unpronounced lexical heads like T. This improves its performance for the SC/RC versus RC/SC contrast as well as English SRC and ORC constructions. If our analysis had treated T as a pronounced head (e.g. for *do* support, or as the carrier of inflection that affix hops onto the verb), MaxT_p would also produce ties in these cases. But even in this case the behavior of MaxT_p could still be replicated by a metric that ignores interior nodes and functional heads, irrespective of whether they are pronounced.

While MaxT_p improves on other variants in some respects, it is also the only non-recursive **MaxT** version to incorrectly derive an ORC advantage in Japanese with the promotion analysis. This is due to the RC marker being unpronounced in Japanese, so that the only pronounced nodes with tenure are the head noun and the embedded verb. The head noun has the same tenure for SRC and ORC, but the embedded verb has non-trivial tenure in the SRC as it is introduced at the same time as the object but must wait for it to move leftward to Spec,vP. In the ORC, on the other hand, the object moves to a position to the right of the embedded verb, so that the latter can be completed as soon as it is introduced. The ORC advantage thus is due to object extraction negating the inherent disadvantage of object movement.

In sum, it seems that any variant of **MaxT** that does not restrict itself to just pronounced nodes provides a solid baseline for a ranked metric with a suitably chosen ancillary metric to resolve ties. **MaxT** has previously been studied by Kobele *et al.* (2013), Graf and Marcinek (2014) and Gerth (2015), and it can even be traced back to Kaplan (1974) and Wanner and Maratsos (1978). It also plays a role in the TAG processing models of Joshi (1990) – in fact, Joshi (1990) ignores the memory usage of empty nodes and thus uses what amounts to our **MaxT$_P$**, which is part of the majority of viable metrics. That three very different processing models home in on the same kind of memory usage as a benchmark for processing difficulty is very suggestive.

From the perspective of Minimalist syntax, $\langle$**MaxT**, **SumS**$\rangle$ and $\langle$**MaxT**, **MaxS^R**$\rangle$ are arguably the most elegant metric as they, intuitively speaking, combine maximum memory load with the total resource demand of all movement dependencies. In the generative literature, O'Grady (2011) has independently argued for the impact of movement dependencies on sentence processing, supporting a size-based metric. Our study confirms that these conceptually pleasing metrics have a lot of explanatory power to offer, although there are still some viable alternatives.

5   FURTHER OBSERVATIONS AND DISCUSSION

While the present study considers a much wider range of constructions and metrics than previous work on MG processing, it is still more limited in its scope than is desirable. The set of syntactic analyses, processing phenomena, and MG parsing algorithms all need to be extended to get a fuller picture of the empirical feasibility of this approach.

Our syntactic analyses still fix a plethora of parameters that need to be carefully modulated. For example, the low starting position of subjects and the movement of objects to Spec,vP cause tenure on T and v, respectively, which affects certain metrics. Replacing rightward movement by sequences of leftward movement (also known as remnant movement) will also be picked up on by some metrics, as would the introduction of a general headedness parameter to do away with certain movement steps. Since the derivation trees using these alternative proposals need to be carefully constructed by hand, a piecewise comparison that alters only one parameter at a time is a very laborious process.

A reviewer raises similar concerns and asks how useful these results are considering that the structure of East Asian languages is not nearly as well understood as that of English, wherefore their Minimalist analyses are much more likely to be fatally flawed. We agree that if push comes to shove, a metric's failure to account for the East Asian processing patterns has less weight than its performance on English data. However, the English data that is available and easily tested in this framework lacks some discriminatory power that the East Asian RC data provides. In science, we have to work with the data that is available, even if that data is sometimes sub-optimal.

But suppose that the structure of East Asian RCs does indeed need to be reanalyzed. We do not believe that this would lead to completely different metrics being chosen. We did some tests with an analysis of Korean and Japanese that simply linearizes the object to the left of the verb rather than moving it to Spec,vP. This made the processing predictions for them more similar to Chinese, and as a result widened the set of feasible metrics to also include ranked metrics whose first component is **SumT** for the wh-movement analysis or a variant of **Box** for the promotion analysis. Crucially, though, all the previously successful metrics were still available.

In the other direction, we also experimented with adding the preference for crossing dependencies over nested dependencies (Bach *et al.* 1986) to our data set. This preference was already shown in Kobele *et al.* (2013) to be predicted by **MaxT**. So it comes as little surprise that this contrast has no discriminative power relative to our current data set. All of our successful metrics correctly predict the contrast. Preliminary work on attachment preferences for dative arguments in Korean and quantifier scope preferences in English suggest that these, too, can be accounted for with the metrics identified in this paper. Overall, then, it seems that the class of complexity metrics carved out in this paper is fairly robust and more than just an accident.

CONCLUSION

We defined a large set of reasonably simple complexity metrics that make predictions about processing behavior based on the shape of index/outdex annotated MG derivation trees that closely mimic well-known analyses from Minimalist syntax. Only a few metrics could cover the full range of relative clause constructions, suggesting that the choice of metric is much more restricted than one might initially expect, and that underspecification is not too much of an issue in practice. In addition, the fact that it was at all possible to give a unified explanation of relative clause processing effects, which have proven challenging to deal with in the psycholinguistic literature, is encouraging. The MG processing model we advocate deliberately abstracts away from many aspects of sentence processing in order to clearly bring out the role that might be played by syntactic factors. It seems that at least in the case of relative clauses, structural considerations go a long way.

ACKNOWLEDGMENTS

We are grateful to the three anonymous reviewers, whose feedback has led to several changes in the presentation of the material (for the better, we like to believe). This research project would not exist if it were not for the continued encouragement by John Drury and the unique atmosphere created by the participants of the Fall 2014 parsing seminar at Stony Brook University.

REFERENCES

Emmon BACH, Colin BROWN, and William MARSLEN-WILSON (1986), Crossed and Nested Dependencies in German and Dutch: A Psycholinguistic Study, *Language and Cognitive Processes*, 1:249–262.

Klinton BICKNELL, Roger LEVY, and Vera DEMBERG (2009), Correcting the Incorrect: Local Coherence Effects Modeled with Prior Belief Update, in *Proceedings of the 35th Annual Meeting of the Berkeley Linguistics Society*, pp. 13–24, doi:10.3765/bls.v35i1.3594.

Noam CHOMSKY (1965), *Aspects of the Theory of Syntax*, MIT Press, Cambridge, MA.

Noam CHOMSKY (1977), *Essays on Form and Interpretation*, New York, North Holland.

Noam CHOMSKY (1995a), Bare Phrase Structure, in Gert WEBELHUTH, editor, *Government and Binding Theory and the Minimalist Program*, pp. 383–440, Blackwell, Oxford.

Noam CHOMSKY (1995b), *The Minimalist Program*, MIT Press, Cambridge, MA, doi:10.7551/mitpress/9780262527347.003.0003.

Noam CHOMSKY (2001), Derivation by Phase, in Michael J. KENSTOWICZ, editor, *Ken Hale: A Life in Language*, pp. 1–52, MIT Press, Cambridge, MA.

Philippe DE GROOTE (2001), Towards Abstract Categorial Grammars, in *Association for Computational Linguistics, 39th Annual Meeting and 10th Conference of the European Chapter*, pp. 148–155.

Meaghan FOWLIE (2013), Order and Optionality: Minimalist Grammars with Adjunction, in András KORNAI and Marco KUHLMANN, editors, *Proceedings of the 13th Meeting on the Mathematics of Language (MoL 13)*, pp. 12–20.

Lyn FRAZIER (1987), Sentence Processing: A Tutorial Review, in M. COLTHEART, editor, *Attention and Performance XII: The Psychology of Reading*, pp. 559–586, Lawrence Erlbaum Associates, Inc.

Werner FREY and Hans-Martin GÄRTNER (2002), On the Treatment of Scrambling and Adjunction in Minimalist grammars, in Gerhard JÄGER, Paola MONACHESI, Gerald PENN, and Shuly WINTNER, editors, *Proceedings of the Conference on Formal Grammar*, pp. 41–52.

Hans-Martin GÄRTNER and Jens MICHAELIS (2007), Some Remarks on Locality Conditions and Minimalist Grammars, in Uli SAUERLAND and Hans-Martin GÄRTNER, editors, *Interfaces + Recursion = Language? Chomsky's Minimalism and the View from Syntax-Semantics*, pp. 161–196, Mouton de Gruyter, Berlin.

Hans-Martin GÄRTNER and Jens MICHAELIS (2010), On the Treatment of Multiple-Wh-Interrogatives in Minimalist Grammars, in Thomas HANNEFORTH and Gisbert FANSELOW, editors, *Language and Logos*, pp. 339–366, Akademie Verlag, Berlin.

Sabrina GERTH (2015), *Memory Limitations in Sentence Comprehension. A Structure-Based Complexity Metric of Processing Difficulty*, Ph.D. thesis, University of Potsdam.

Edward GIBSON (1998), Linguistic Complexity: Locality of Syntactic Dependencies, *Cognition*, 68:1–76.

Edward GIBSON (2000), The Dependency Locality Theory: A Distance-Based Theory of Linguistic Complexity, in Y. MIYASHITA, Alec MARANTZ, and W. O'NEIL, editors, *Image, Language, Brain*, pp. 95–126, MIT Press, Cambridge, MA.

Edward GIBSON and H.-H. Iris WU (2013), Processing Chinese Relative Clauses in Context, *Language and Cognitive Processes*, 28(1-2):125–155.

Peter C. GORDON, Randall HENDRICK, Marcus JOHNSON, and Yoonhyoung LEE (2006), Similarity-Based Interference During Language Comprehension: Evidence From Eye Tracking During Reading, *Journal of Experimental Psychology: Learning, Memory, and Cognition*, 32(6):1304.

Thomas GRAF (2011), Closure Properties of Minimalist Derivation Tree Languages, in Sylvain POGODALLA and Jean-Philippe PROST, editors, *LACL 2011*, volume 6736 of *Lecture Notes in Artificial Intelligence*, pp. 96–111, Springer, Heidelberg, doi:10.1007/978-3-642-22221-4_7.

Thomas GRAF (2012a), Locality and the Complexity of Minimalist Derivation Tree Languages, in Philippe DE GROOT and Mark-Jan NEDERHOF, editors, *Formal Grammar 2010/2011*, volume 7395 of *Lecture Notes in Computer Science*, pp. 208–227, Springer, Heidelberg, doi:10.1007/978-3-642-32024-8_14.

Thomas GRAF (2012b), Movement-Generalized Minimalist Grammars, in Denis BÉCHET and Alexander J. DIKOVSKY, editors, *LACL 2012*, volume 7351 of *Lecture Notes in Computer Science*, pp. 58–73, doi:10.1007/978-3-642-31262-5_4.

Thomas GRAF (2013), *Local and Transderivational Constraints in Syntax and Semantics*, Ph.D. thesis, UCLA.

Thomas GRAF, Alëna AKSËNOVA, and Aniello DE SANTO (2016), A Single Movement Normal Form for Minimalist Grammars, in Annie FORET, Glyn MORRILL, Reinhard MUSKENS, Rainer OSSWALD, and Sylvain POGODALLA, editors, *Formal Grammar: 20th and 21st International Conferences*, pp. 200–215, doi:10.1007/978-3-662-53042-9_12.

Thomas GRAF, Brigitta FODOR, James MONETTE, Gianpaul RACHIELE, Aunika WARREN, and Chong ZHANG (2015), A Refined Notion of Memory Usage for Minimalist Parsing, in *Proceedings of the 14th Meeting on the Mathematics of Language (MoL 2015)*, pp. 1–14, Association for Computational Linguistics, Chicago, USA.

Thomas GRAF and Bradley MARCINEK (2014), Evaluating Evaluation Metrics for Minimalist Parsing, in *Proceedings of the 2014 ACL Workshop on Cognitive Modeling and Computational Linguistics*, pp. 28–36.

John HALE (2001), A Probabilistic Earley Parser as a Psycholinguistic Model, in *Proceedings of the Second Meeting of the North American Chapter of the Association for Computational Linguistics*, pp. 1–8.

John HALE (2011), What a Rational Parser Would Do, *Cognitive Science*, 35:399–443.

John T. HALE (2003), *Grammar, Uncertainty and Sentence Processing*, Ph.D. thesis, John Hopkins University.

Henk HARKEMA (2001), A Characterization of Minimalist Languages, in Philippe DE GROOTE, Glyn MORRILL, and Christian RETORÉ, editors, *Logical*

Aspects of Computational Linguistics (LACL'01), volume 2099 of *Lecture Notes in Artificial Intelligence*, pp. 193–211, Springer, Berlin.

Irene HEIM and Angelika KRATZER (1998), *Semantics in Generative Grammar*, Blackwell, Oxford.

Tim HUNTER (2011), Insertion Minimalist Grammars: Eliminating Redundancies between Merge and Move, in Makoto KANAZAWA, András KORNAI, Marcus KRACHT, and Hiroyuki SEKI, editors, *The Mathematics of Language: 12th Biennial Conference*, pp. 90–107, Springer, Berlin, Heidelberg, ISBN 978-3-642-23211-4, doi:10.1007/978-3-642-23211-4_6.

Tim HUNTER (2015a), Deconstructing Merge and Move to Make Room for Adjunction, *Syntax*, 18:266–319, doi:10.1111/synt.12033.

Tim HUNTER (2015b), Left-Corner Parsing of Minimalist Grammars, slides of a talk presented at the First Workshop on Minimalist Parsing, October 10–11 2015, MIT.

Tim HUNTER and Robert FRANK (2014), Eliminating Rightward Movement: Extraposition as Flexible Linearization of Adjuncts, *Linguistic Inquiry*, 45:227–267.

Aravind JOSHI (1990), Processing Crossed and Nested Dependencies: An Automaton Perspective on the Psycholinguistic Results, *Language and Cognitive Processes*, 5:1–27.

Ronald M. KAPLAN (1974), *Transient Processing Load in Relative Clauses*, Ph.D. thesis, Harvard University.

Richard S. KAYNE (1994), *The Antisymmetry of Syntax*, MIT Press, Cambridge, MA.

Edward L. KEENAN and Bernard COMRIE (1977), Noun Phrase Accessiblity and Universal Grammar, *Linguistic Inquiry*, 8:63–99.

John KIMBALL (1973), Seven Principles of Surface Structure Parsing in Natural Language, *Cognition*, 2:15–47.

Gregory M. KOBELE (2006), *Generating Copies: An Investigation into Structural Identity in Language and Grammar*, Ph.D. thesis, UCLA.

Gregory M. KOBELE (2011), Minimalist Tree Languages are Closed Under Intersection with Recognizable Tree Languages, in Sylvain POGODALLA and Jean-Philippe PROST, editors, *LACL 2011*, volume 6736 of *Lecture Notes in Artificial Intelligence*, pp. 129–144, doi:10.1007/978-3-642-22221-4_9.

Gregory M. KOBELE (2015), LF-Copying Without LF, *Lingua*, 166:236–259, doi:10.1016/j.lingua.2014.08.006.

Gregory M. KOBELE, Sabrina GERTH, and John T. HALE (2013), Memory Resource Allocation in Top-Down Minimalist Parsing, in Glyn MORRILL and Mark-Jan NEDERHOF, editors, *Formal Grammar: 17th and 18th International Conferences*, pp. 32–51, doi:10.1007/978-3-642-39998-5_3.

Gregory M. KOBELE, Christian RETORÉ, and Sylvain SALVATI (2007), An Automata-Theoretic Approach to Minimalism, in James ROGERS and Stephan KEPSER, editors, *Model Theoretic Syntax at 10*, pp. 71–80.

Alexander KOLLER and Marco KUHLMANN (2011), A Generalized View on Parsing and Translation, in *Proceedings of the 12th International Conference on Parsing Technologies*, pp. 2–13, Association for Computational Linguistics, Stroudsburg, PA.

Lars KONIECZNY (2005), The Psychological Reality of Local Coherences in Sentence Processing, in *Proceedings of the 27th Annual Conference of the Cognitive Science Society*.

Lars KONIECZNY, Daniel MÜLLER, Wibke HACHMANN, Sarah SCHWARZKOPF, and Sascha WOLFER (2009), Local Syntactic Coherence Interpretation. Evidence from a Visual World Study, in *Proceedings of the 31st Annual Conference of the Cognitive Science Society*, pp. 1133–1138.

Nayoung KWON, Peter C. GORDON, Yoonhyoung LEE, Robert KLUENDER, and Maria POLINSKY (2010), Cognitive and Linguistic Factors Affecting Subject/Object Asymmetry: An Eye-Tracking Study of Prenominal Relative Clauses in Korean, *Language*, 86(3):546–582.

Richard LARSON (1988), On the Double Object Construction, *Linguistic Inquiry*, 19(3):335–391.

David LEBEAUX (1988), *Language Acquisition and the Form of the Grammar*, Ph.D. thesis, University of Massachusetts, Amherst, doi:10.1075/z.97, reprinted in 2000 by John Benjamins.

Roger LEVY (2013), Memory and Surprisal in Human Sentence Comprehension, in Roger P. G. VAN GOMPEL, editor, *Sentence Processing*, pp. 78–114, Psychology Press, Hove.

Chien-Jer Charles LIN and Thomas G. BEVER (2006), Subject Preference in the Processing of Relative Clauses in Chinese, in *Proceedings of the 25th West Coast Conference on Formal Linguistics*, pp. 254–260, Cascadilla Proceedings Project Somerville, MA.

Thomas MAINGUY (2010), A Probabilistic Top-Down Parser for Minimalist Grammars, arXiv:1010.1826v1.

Willem M. MAK, Wietske VONK, and Herbert SCHRIEFERS (2002), The Influence of Animacy on Relative Clause Processing, *Journal of Memory and Language*, 47(1):50–68.

Willem M. MAK, Wietske VONK, and Herbert SCHRIEFERS (2006), Animacy in Processing Relative Clauses: The Hikers That Rocks Crush, *Journal of Memory and Language*, 54(4):466–490.

Axel MECKLINGER, Herbert SCHRIEFERS, Karsten STEINHAUER, and Angela D. FRIEDERICI (1995), Processing Relative Clauses Varying on Syntactic and

Semantic Dimensions: An Analysis with Event-Related Potentials, *Memory & Cognition*, 23(4):477–494.

Jens MICHAELIS (2001), Transforming Linear Context-Free Rewriting Systems into Minimalist Grammars, *Lecture Notes in Artificial Intelligence*, 2099:228–244.

George A. MILLER and Noam CHOMSKY (1963), Finitary Models of Language Users, in R. LUCE, R. BUSH, and E. GALANTER, editors, *Handbook of Mathematical Psychology*, volume 2, pp. 419–491, John Wiley, New York.

George A. MILLER and Kathryn Ojemann MCKEAN (1964), A Chronometric Study of Some Relations Between Sentences, *Quarterly Journal of Experimental Psychology*, 16:297–308.

Edson T. MIYAMOTO and Michiko NAKAMURA (2003), Subject/Object Asymmetries in the Processing of Relative Clauses in Japanese, in *Proceedings of WCCFL*, volume 22, pp. 342–355.

Edson T. MIYAMOTO and Michiko NAKAMURA (2013), Unmet Expectations in the Comprehension of Relative Clauses in Japanese, in *Proceedings of the 35th Annual Meeting of the Cognitive Science Society*, pp. 3074–3079.

Uwe MÖNNICH (2006), Grammar Morphisms, ms. University of Tübingen.

Richard MONTAGUE (1970), English as a Formal Language, in Bruno VISENTINI and ET AL., editors, *Linguaggi nella Società e nella Tecnica*, pp. 189–224, Edizioni di Comunità, Milan.

Frank MORAWIETZ (2003), *Two-Step Approaches to Natural Language Formalisms*, Walter de Gruyter, Berlin, doi:10.1515/9783110197259.

William O'GRADY (2011), Relative Clauses. Processing and Acquisition, in Evan KIDD, editor, *Processing, Typology, and Function*, pp. 13–38, John Benjamins, Amsterdam.

Colin PHILLIPS (1996), *Order and Structure*, Ph.D. thesis, MIT.

Alan PRINCE and Paul SMOLENSKY (2004), *Optimality Theory: Constraint Interaction in Generative Grammar*, Blackwell, Oxford.

Owen RAMBOW and Aravind JOSHI (1995), A Processing Model for Free Word Order Languages, Technical Report IRCS-95-13, University of Pennsylvania.

Philip RESNIK (1992), Left-Corner Parsing and Psychological Plausibility, in *Proceedings of COLING-92*, pp. 191–197.

Sylvain SALVATI (2011), Minimalist Grammars in the Light of Logic, in Sylvain POGODALLA, Myriam QUATRINI, and Christian RETORÉ, editors, *Logic and Grammar — Essays Dedicated to Alain Lecomte on the Occasion of His 60th Birthday*, number 6700 in Lecture Notes in Computer Science, pp. 81–117, Springer, Berlin, doi:10.1007/978-3-642-21490-5_5.

Stuart M. SHIEBER, Yves SCHABES, and Fernando C. PEREIRA (1995), Principles and Implementations of Deductive Parsing, *Journal of Logic Programming*, 24:3–36.

Klaas SIKKEL (1997), *Parsing Schemata*, Texts in Theoretical Computer Science, Springer, Berlin.

Edward P. STABLER (1997), Derivational Minimalism, in Christian RETORÉ, editor, *Logical Aspects of Computational Linguistics*, volume 1328 of *Lecture Notes in Computer Science*, pp. 68–95, Springer, Berlin, doi:10.1007/BFb0052152.

Edward P. STABLER (2006), Sidewards Without Copying, in Gerald PENN, Giorgio SATTA, and Shuly WINTNER, editors, *Formal Grammar '06, Proceedings of the Conference*, pp. 133–146, CSLI, Stanford.

Edward P. STABLER (2011), Computational Perspectives on Minimalism, in Cedric BOECKX, editor, *Oxford Handbook of Linguistic Minimalism*, pp. 617–643, Oxford University Press, Oxford, doi:10.1093/oxfordhb/9780199549368.013.0027.

Edward P. STABLER (2013), Two Models of Minimalist, Incremental Syntactic Analysis, *Topics in Cognitive Science*, 5:611–633, doi:10.1111/tops.12031.

Mark STEEDMAN (2001), *The Syntactic Process*, MIT Press, Cambridge, MA.

Whitney TABOR, Bruno GALANTUCCI, and Daniel RICHARDSON (2004), Effects of Merely Local Syntactic Coherence on Sentence Processing, *Journal of Memory and Language*, 50:355–370.

Shoichi TAKAHASHI and Sarah HULSEY (2009), Wholesale Late Merger: Beyond the A/Ā Distinction, *Linguistc Inquiry*, 40:387–426.

James W. THATCHER (1967), Characterizing Derivation Trees for Context-Free Grammars Through a Generalization of Finite Automata Theory, *Journal of Computer and System Sciences*, 1:317–322.

Mieko UENO and Susan M GARNSEY (2008), An ERP Study of the Processing of Subject and Object Relative Clauses in Japanese, *Language and Cognitive Processes*, 23(5):646–688.

Jean-Roger VERGNAUD (1974), *French Relative Clauses*, Ph.D. thesis, MIT.

Eric WANNER and Michael MARATSOS (1978), An ATN Approach to Comprehension, in Morris HALLE, Joan BRESNAN, and George A. MILLER, editors, *Linguistic Theory and Psychological Reality*, pp. 119–161, MIT Press, Cambridge, MA.

Jiwon YUN, Zhong CHEN, Tim HUNTER, John WHITMAN, and John HALE (2014), Uncertainty in Processing Relative Clauses Across East Asian Languages, *Journal of East Asian Linguistics*, pp. 1–36.

4

Factivity and presupposition in Dependent Type Semantics

Ribeka Tanaka[1], Koji Mineshima[1,2], and Daisuke Bekki[1,2]

[1] Ochanomizu University

[2] CREST, Japan Science and Technology Agency

Keywords: dependent type, anaphora, presupposition, proof object, factive verb

ABSTRACT

Dependent type theory has been applied to natural language semantics to provide a formally precise and computationally adequate account of dynamic aspects of meaning. One of the frameworks of natural language semantics based on dependent type theory is Dependent Type Semantics (DTS), which focuses on the compositional interpretations of anaphoric expressions. In this paper, we extend the framework of DTS with a mechanism to handle logical entailment and presupposition associated with factive verbs such as *know*. Using the notion of proof objects as first-class objects, we provide a compositional account of presuppositional inferences triggered by factive verbs. The proposal also gives a formal reconstruction of the type-distinction between propositions and facts, and thereby accounts for the lexical semantic differences between factive and non-factive verbs in a type-theoretical setting.

1   INTRODUCTION

Dependent Type Semantics (DTS, Bekki 2014) is a framework of natural language semantics based on dependent type theory (Martin-Löf 1984; Nordström *et al.* 1990). In contrast to traditional model-theoretic semantics, DTS is a proof-theoretic semantics, where inference relations between sentences are characterized as provability relations between semantic representations. One of the distinctive features of DTS, as compared to other type-theoretical frameworks, is that it is augmented with underspecified terms, so as to provide a unified analysis of inference, anaphora and presupposition from a logical/computational perspective. In contrast to previous work on anaphora in dependent type theory (cf. Ranta 1994), DTS gives a fully compositional account of inferences involving anaphora. It is also extended to the analysis of modal subordination (Tanaka *et al.* 2015).

In this paper, we provide the framework of DTS with a mechanism to handle logical entailment and presupposition associated with factive verbs. We will mostly focus on the epistemic verb *know*. Although there are numerous studies on factive verbs in natural language semantics, they are usually based on model-theoretic approaches; it seems fair to say that there has been little attempt to formalize inferences with factivity from a proof-theoretical perspective. On the other hand, various proof systems for knowledge and belief have been studied in the context of epistemic logic (cf. Meyer and van der Hoek 2004). However, such systems are mainly concerned with knowledge and belief themselves, not with how they are expressed in natural languages, nor with linguistic phenomena such as factivity presuppositions. Our study aims to fill this gap by providing a framework that explains logical entailment and presuppositions with factive verbs in dependent type theory.

2   DEPENDENT TYPE SEMANTICS

This section introduces the framework of DTS and explains how presuppositions are handled in this framework. In Section 2.1, we provide some necessary background on DTS, including the basics of dependent type theory and the analysis of anaphora within this approach. One of the important problems in the application of dependent type theory to natural language semantics is how to represent common nouns using the machinery of dependent types. Section 2.2 is devoted to discussing this problem. We give several reasons for preferring the view that common nouns are represented as *predicates* rather than as *types*. Given this background, Section 2.3 provides a compositional analysis of presupposition in DTS.

2.1   *Dependent type theory*

In dependent type theory, there are two type constructors, Σ and Π, which play a crucial role in forming the semantic representations for natural language sentences. The type constructor Σ is a generalized form of the product type and behaves as an existential quantifier. An object of type $(\Sigma x : A)B(x)$ is a pair (m, n) such that m is of type A and n is of type $B(m)$. Conjunction $A \wedge B$ is a degenerate form of $(\Sigma x : A)B$ if x does not occur free in B. The Σ-types are associated with projection functions π_1 and π_2 that are computed with the rules $\pi_1(m, n) = m$ and $\pi_2(m, n) = n$, respectively. The type constructor Π is a generalized form of the functional type and behaves as a universal quantifier. An object of type $(\Pi x : A)B(x)$ is a function f such that for any object a of type A, $f\,a$ is an object of type $B(a)$. Implication $A \to B$ is a degenerate form of $(\Pi x : A)B$ if x does not occur free in B. The inference rules for Π-types and Σ-types are shown in the Appendix.[1] Throughout the paper, we will make use of the DTS-notation for Π-types and Σ-types as shown in Figure 1.

	Π-types	Σ-types
Standard notation	$(\Pi x : A)B(x)$	$(\Sigma x : A)B(x)$
Notation in DTS	$(x{:}A) \to B(x)$	$\begin{bmatrix} x : A \\ B(x) \end{bmatrix}$
When $x \notin fv(B)$	$A \to B$	$\begin{bmatrix} A \\ B \end{bmatrix}$

Figure 1: Notation for Π-types and Σ-types in DTS ($fv(B)$ means the set of free variables in B)

Based on the Curry-Howard correspondence (Howard 1980), a type can be regarded as a proposition and a term can be regarded as a proof. Thus the judgement $a : A$ can be read as "a is a proof of proposition A", as well as "a is a term of type A". In this setting, the truth of a proposition A is defined as the existence of a term of type A. The term that serves as a proof of a proposition is called a *proof term* and plays an important role in representing natural language sentences in dependent type theory.

Since the work of Sundholm (1986) and Ranta (1994), dependent type theory has been applied to the analysis of various dynamic discourse phenomena, providing a type-theoretic alternative to model-theoretic frameworks such as Discourse Representation Theory (van der Sandt 1992; Kamp *et al.* 2011), Dynamic Predicate Logic (Groenendijk and Stokhof 1991), and Dynamic Semantics (Heim

---

[1] For more details, readers can refer to Martin-Löf (1984) and Ranta (1994).

1983). For instance, according to the analysis presented in Sundholm (1986) and Ranta (1994), a semantic representation for the donkey sentence in (1) can be given as (2) in terms of dependent types.

(1)   Every farmer who owns a donkey beats it.

(2) $\left(u \colon \begin{bmatrix} x \colon \textbf{farmer} \\ \begin{bmatrix} y \colon \textbf{donkey} \\ \textbf{own}(x,y) \end{bmatrix} \end{bmatrix} \right) \to \textbf{beat}(\pi_1 u, \pi_1 \pi_2 u)$

The sentence (1) as a whole is a universal sentence, which is represented as a Π-type. The restrictor *farmer who owns a donkey* is analyzed as a Σ-type. A term u having this Σ-type would be a tuple $(f, (d, o))$, where f is a term of type **farmer**, d is a term of type **donkey**, and o is a proof-term of the proposition **own**(f, d). Recall that π_1 and π_2 are projection functions that take a pair and return the first and the second element, respectively. Thus the terms $\pi_1 u$ and $\pi_1 \pi_2 u$ appearing in the consequent of (2) pick up from u the term f of type **farmer** and the term d of type **donkey**, respectively. In this way, via the proof term u associated with the Σ-type, the discourse referents introduced in the antecedent in (2) can be successfully passed to the subsequent discourse. An advantage of dependent type theory over previous dynamic theories is that such an externally dynamic character of quantification can be captured without any further stipulation; Σ-types and Π-types, which are natural generalizations of existential and universal quantifiers in predicate logic, are equipped with the mechanism to handle dynamic aspects of discourse interpretations.

The work by Sundholm and Ranta[2] provides a foundation for applying the expressiveness of dependent types to problems in natural language discourse interpretation such as donkey anaphora. However, a problem remains: how can the semantic representation in (2) be systematically obtained from the sentence in (1)? From the viewpoint of standard compositional semantics, the problem can be divided into two tasks. The first is to deterministically map the sentence (1) into an

---

[2] Sundholm (1986) and Ranta (1994) only consider the so-called strong reading of donkey sentences. There are some later works using dependent types that treat other phenomena discussed in the dynamic semantics literature, in particular, Sundholm (1989) for the proportion problem. See also Tanaka *et al.* (2014) and Tanaka (2014) for discussion of Sundholm's analysis of donkey anaphora and treatment of weak and strong readings within the framework of DTS.

underspecified representation, a semantic representation that contains an underspecified element corresponding to the pronoun in question. The second task is to resolve anaphora. In our example, the underspecified element needs to be resolved to $\pi_1 \pi_2 u$. The semantics satisfying the requirement of compositionality must provide an explicit procedure for these two tasks.

Dependent Type Semantics (Bekki 2014) provides such a procedure. To give an explicit compositional mapping from sentences to semantic representations, we adopt Combinatory Categorial Grammar (CCG, Steedman 2000) as a syntactic framework. Note that, as emphasized in Bekki (2014), DTS can be combined with other categorial grammars; see Kubota and Levine (2017) for a concrete proposal that combines DTS with a type-logical grammar. In compositional mapping, an anaphoric expression is mapped on to an underspecified element. The process of resolving underspecification is formulated as the process of *type checking*. Using the machinery of underspecified semantics in DTS, we will give an analysis of presuppositions in Section 2.3.

2.2   *Common nouns: types or predicates?*

There are two possible approaches to representing basic sentences like *A man entered* in dependent type theory. One is the approach proposed in Ranta (1994) and Luo (2012a,b), according to which common nouns like *man* are interpreted as *types* so that the sentence is represented as (3) in our notation.

(3) $\begin{bmatrix} x : \textbf{man} \\ \textbf{enter}(x) \end{bmatrix}$

One problem with this approach is that it is not straightforward to analyze *predicational* sentences, i.e., sentences containing *predicate nominals*, such as (4a, b).[3]

(4)   a.   John is *a man*.

      b.   Bob considers Mary *a genius*.

One might analyze (4a) as a judgement **john** : **man**. However, a judgement itself can neither be negated nor embedded under a log-

---

[3] See Mikkelsen (2011) for a useful overview of the syntax and semantics of predicational sentences.

ical operator. Accordingly, it is not clear how to account for the fact that a predicational sentence can be negated, as in (5a), or appear in the antecedent of a conditional, as in (5b).

(5)   a. John is not a man.

       b. If John is a man, ….

Nor is it clear how to analyze a construction embedding a predicational sentence as in (4b).

One might try to analyze *be*-verbs as the so-called "*is*-of identity" along Russell-Montague lines (Russell 1919; Montague 1973). This enables us to represent (4a) as a *proposition*, as in (6), rather than as a judgement.

(6) $\begin{bmatrix} x : \mathbf{man} \\ \mathbf{john} =_{\mathrm{man}} x \end{bmatrix}$

Then, (5a) and (5b) can be represented as follows:

(7)   a. $\neg \begin{bmatrix} x : \mathbf{man} \\ \mathbf{john} =_{\mathrm{man}} x \end{bmatrix}$

       b. $\begin{bmatrix} x : \mathbf{man} \\ \mathbf{john} =_{\mathrm{man}} x \end{bmatrix} \rightarrow \cdots$

There are two problems with this approach, however. First, this analysis predicts that the predicate nominal *a man* introduces a discourse referent in terms of Σ-types. Contrary to this prediction, a predicate nominal cannot serve as an antecedent of an anaphoric pronoun such as *he* or *she* (Kuno 1970; Mikkelsen 2005); hence it does not introduce an individual discourse referent.[4]

The second problem is the interpretation of equality. In dependent type theory, equality is relativised to some type A and the formation rule requires the arguments of equality symbols to have type A:

---

[4] The form of the pronoun anaphoric on a predicate nominal in (i) must be *it*, rather than *him*; the relative pronoun in (ii) must be *which*, not *who* (Kuno 1970; Mikkelsen 2005).

(i)   He is a fool, although he doesn't look { it /*him }.

(ii)   He is a gentleman, {which / *who} his brother is not.

See Fara (2001) for more discussion of the problems of the Russell-Montague analysis of predicate nominals.

(8) $\dfrac{A:\textbf{type} \quad t:A \quad u:A}{t =_A u : \textbf{type}} = F$

Accordingly, the proposition **john** $=_{\text{man}} x$ is well-formed only if **john** : **man** is provable. This is also the case if the proposition is embedded under a logical operator. It thus follows that under the Russell-Montague analysis combined with the equality rule (8), not only the positive sentence (6), but also the negation (7a) and the conditional (7b) presuppose that John is a man. To rescue the common-nouns-as-types view from this problem, one has to provide a more complex analysis of logical operators such as negation and implication.[5] However, the resulting theory would then become more complicated.

As an alternative approach, we interpret a common noun as a predicate. Common nouns in argument position and in predicate position are both analyzed as predicates of type **entity** → **type**.

(9) A man walks.
$$\left[u : \left[\begin{array}{l} x : \textbf{entity} \\ \textbf{man}(x) \end{array} \right] \\ \textbf{walk}(\pi_1 u) \right]$$

(10) John is a man. **man**(**john**)

This approach is in line with the traditional analysis of common nouns, so we can integrate standard assumptions in formal semantics into our framework. Moreover, since predicates do not introduce discourse referents, we can explain the impossibility of referential anaphora to predicate nominals.

Retoré (2014) suggests that common nouns can be interpreted both as types and as predicates; for instance, using type **entity**, the common noun *animal* interpreted as a type **animal** could be related to a predicate **animal**[*] of type **entity** → **type**, via some suitably defined mapping (·)[*] from one to another. The question of whether a type system for natural language semantics needs to be enriched with the structures of common nouns would ultimately depend on the treatment of the lexical semantic phenomena it attempts to capture, such as coercion and selectional restriction – phenomena that have been widely discussed in the recent literature on type-theoretical semantics (Asher 2011; Asher and Luo 2012; Bekki and Asher 2013; Retoré

---

[5] Some discussion of the treatment of negation in the context of dependent type theory can be found in Chatzikyriakidis and Luo (2014).

2014; Kinoshita *et al.* 2016). But investigating this matter further is beyond the scope of the present paper and we leave it to a future study.

2.3   *Analysis of presupposition in DTS*

To handle anaphora and presupposition in a compositional setting, DTS extends dependent type theory with a mechanism of context passing and underspecified terms.

Dependent Type Semantics distinguishes two kinds of propositions: *static* and *dynamic* propositions. Following the Curry-Howard correspondence, we call an object of type **type** (i.e., the type of types) a *static* proposition. A *dynamic* proposition is a function which maps a proof term of the static proposition representing the preceding discourse to a static proposition. The basic idea is that for each (static) proposition P, the information obtained up to that point is passed to P as a proof term. Such a proof term is called a *local context*.

Dependent Type Semantics extends the syntax of dependent type theory with an underspecified term $@_i$, which is used to represent anaphora and presupposition triggers.[6] We show how it can provide a compositional account of anaphora and presupposition. We take the existence presupposition triggered by a definite description as a representative example. Consider the following example.

(11)   The book arrived.

The definite description *the book* here triggers the presupposition that there is a book.[7] We analyze the determiner *the* appearing in the subject position as having the CCG category $(S/(S\backslash NP))/N$, and give a semantic representation by using an underspecified term. The lexical

---

[6] Bekki (2014) provides an overview and comparison of previous approaches to representing underspecification in the context of dependent type theory (Dávila-Pérez 1995; Krahmer and Piwek 1999; Piwek and Krahmer 2000).

[7] Here we take it that the uniqueness presupposition is not part of the conventional meaning of a definite description but can be derived on pragmatic considerations along the lines of Heim (1982). Although it is technically possible to take the uniqueness implication as part of presupposition, the proof-search procedure to find the antecedent of an underspecified term would then become much more complicated.

$$N^\bullet = \textbf{entity} \to \delta \to \textbf{type} \qquad N^\bullet_{+c} = \textbf{type} \to \delta \to \textbf{type}$$

$$NP^\bullet = \textbf{entity} \qquad\qquad NP^\bullet_{+c} = \delta \to \textbf{type}$$

$$S^\bullet = \delta \to \textbf{type} \qquad\qquad \overline{S}^\bullet = \delta \to \textbf{type}$$

$$(C_1/C_2)^\bullet = (C_1\backslash C_2)^\bullet = C_2^\bullet \to C_1^\bullet$$

Figure 2: Mapping syntactic categories to semantic types[9]

entry for *the* can be specified as follows (a mapping $(\cdot)^\bullet$ from syntactic categories to semantic types can be defined as in Figure 2).[8]

(12)   the; $(S/(S\backslash NP))/N$; $\lambda n.\lambda v.\lambda c. v\left(\pi_1\left(@_i c :: \begin{bmatrix} x : \textbf{entity} \\ nxc \end{bmatrix}\right)\right)c$

Determiner *the* denotes a function that takes a predicate n denoted by a restrictor and a predicate v denoted by a verb and returns a dynamic proposition, which is in turn a function from a local context c to a (static) proposition. The local context c is passed to the underspecified term $@_i$ as an argument. It is also sent to the predicates n and v as an extra argument, because n and v may contain underspecified terms.

The form $M :: A$ is called *type annotation* and specifies that the term M has type A. When an underspecified term $@_i$ is annotated with a type A, that is, when we have $@_i :: A$, the annotated type A represents the presupposition triggered by this underspecified term. In (12), the underspecified term with a local context, $@_i c$, is annotated with a Σ-type. This means that the underspecified term $@_i$ is a function that takes a local context c as an argument and returns a term having the annotated Σ-type. Given this type annotation, we see that $@_i c$ is a pair of an entity x and a proof term for the proposition that x satisfies

---

[8] For the purpose of concreteness, we use a type-raised form of semantic representations for determiners. The entry for the determiner *the* in the object position can be given as follows:

the; $((S\backslash NP)\backslash((S\backslash NP)/NP))/N$; $\lambda n.\lambda v.\lambda x.\lambda c. v\left(\pi_1\left(@_i c :: \begin{bmatrix} y : \textbf{entity} \\ nyc \end{bmatrix}\right)\right)xc$

Although there are other possible syntactic analyses of determiners in object position (cf. Bekki 2014), this entry would ensure a concise derivation tree for semantic composition.

[9] Subscripted $+c$ is a syntactic feature for content noun. We represent N_{-c} and NP_{-c} simply as N and NP, respectively. We also abbreviate other syntactic features, which are not relevant to the discussion in this paper.

the predicate n given a local context c. In other words, the annotated type represents the existence presupposition triggered by the definite article. What is applied to the main predicate appearing in v is the first projection of the obtained pair, i.e., a term of type **entity**.

The semantic representation for (11) is derived as follows.[10]

(13)

$$
\cfrac{
\cfrac{\text{The}}{\cfrac{(S/(S\backslash NP))/N}{\lambda n.\lambda v.\lambda c.\, v\left(\pi_1\left(@_1 c :: \left[\begin{array}{l} x : \textbf{entity} \\ nxc \end{array}\right]\right)\right)c}}
\quad
\cfrac{\text{book}}{\cfrac{N}{\lambda x.\lambda c.\,\textbf{book}(x)}}
}{
\cfrac{S/(S\backslash NP)}{\lambda v.\lambda c.\, v\left(\pi_1\left(@_1 c :: \left[\begin{array}{l} x : \textbf{entity} \\ \textbf{book}(x) \end{array}\right]\right)\right)c} \;>
\qquad
\cfrac{\text{arrived}}{\cfrac{S\backslash NP}{\lambda x.\lambda c.\,\textbf{arrive}(x)}}
}
\;>
$$

$$
\cfrac{}{S}
\qquad
\lambda c.\,\textbf{arrive}\left(\pi_1\left(@_1 c :: \left[\begin{array}{l} x : \textbf{entity} \\ \textbf{book}(x) \end{array}\right]\right)\right)
$$

The underspecified term is indexed by a natural number i and each number assigned to an underspecified term is mutually distinct. In the above derivation, an underspecified term introduced by *the* has index 1. Here we assume that the predicate **book** is not context-sensitive so that vacuous abstraction is involved as in $\lambda x \lambda c.\textbf{book}(x)$; in such a case, the input local context c is simply discarded in the body of the semantic representation. As shown here, the term $@_1 c$ in the final representation is annotated with a Σ-type corresponding to the proposition that there is a book. In this way, the annotated type represents the existence presupposition triggered by the definite description *the book*.

---

[10] In CCG derivation trees, we use two standard combinatory rules: forward (>) and backward (<) function application rules.

$$
\cfrac{X/Y : m \quad Y : n}{X : mn} > \qquad \cfrac{Y : n \quad X\backslash Y : m}{X : mn} <
$$

For instance, the combinatory rule (>) means that an expression having a syntactic category X/Y and a meaning m, combined with an expression having a syntactic category Y and a meaning n, yields an expression having a category X and a meaning mn. Each meaning is represented as a lambda term. See Steedman (2000) for more details.

The resolution of an underspecified term in a semantic representation A amounts to checking that A is well-typed in a given context. More specifically, it is triggered by the following:

(14) $\Gamma, \delta : \mathbf{type} \vdash A : \delta \to \mathbf{type}$

Here, Γ is a set of assumptions, called a *global* context, which represents the background knowledge; δ is the type of a local context (representing the previous discourse); $A : \delta \to \mathbf{type}$ in the consequence shows that A is a dynamic proposition in DTS, that is, a function mapping a given local context of type δ to a static proposition; (14) reflects the requirement that the semantic representation of a (declarative) sentence, i.e., a static proposition, must be of type **type**. This requirement is called the *felicity condition* of a sentence in DTS.

In the case of (11), the resolution process is launched by the following judgement:

(15) $\Gamma, \delta : \mathbf{type} \vdash \lambda c.\,\mathbf{arrive}\left(\pi_1\left(@_1 c :: \begin{bmatrix} x : \mathbf{entity} \\ \mathbf{book}(x) \end{bmatrix} \right) \right) : \delta \to \mathbf{type}.$

Assuming that **arrive : entity** $\to$ **type** is in the global context Γ, the type of $@_1$ is determined by the following derivation.[11]

(16)

$$
\cfrac{
\cfrac{
\cfrac{
\cfrac{
\cfrac{@_1 : \delta \to \begin{bmatrix} x : \mathbf{entity} \\ \mathbf{book}(x) \end{bmatrix} \quad \overline{c : \delta}\,1}{@_1 c : \begin{bmatrix} x : \mathbf{entity} \\ \mathbf{book}(x) \end{bmatrix}}\ (\Pi E)
}{
\left(@_1 c :: \begin{bmatrix} x : \mathbf{entity} \\ \mathbf{book}(x) \end{bmatrix} \right) : \begin{bmatrix} x : \mathbf{entity} \\ \mathbf{book}(x) \end{bmatrix}
}\ (ann)
}{
\pi_1\left(@_1 c :: \begin{bmatrix} x : \mathbf{entity} \\ \mathbf{book}(x) \end{bmatrix} \right) : \mathbf{entity}
}\ (\Sigma E) \quad \cfrac{}{\mathbf{arrive} : \mathbf{entity} \to \mathbf{type}}\ (CON)
}{
\mathbf{arrive}\left(\pi_1\left(@_1 c :: \begin{bmatrix} x : \mathbf{entity} \\ \mathbf{book}(x) \end{bmatrix} \right) \right) : \mathbf{type}
}\ (\Pi E)
}{
\lambda c.\,\mathbf{arrive}\left(\pi_1\left(@_1 c :: \begin{bmatrix} x : \mathbf{entity} \\ \mathbf{book}(x) \end{bmatrix} \right) \right) : \delta \to \mathbf{type}
}\ (\Pi I), 1
$$

---

[11] Here we make use of the following rule, which ensures that one can obtain the annotated term $t :: A$ of type A from any term $t : A$.

$$\cfrac{t : A}{(t :: A) : A}\ (ann)$$

See also the Appendix for other derivation rules.

The open branch of the derivation, repeated in (17), requires that in order for the semantic representation in question to be well-typed, one has to construct a proof term for the proposition that there is a book. (This is due to the @-formation rule. See Definition 12 in the Appendix.)

(17)　$@_1 : \delta \rightarrow \begin{bmatrix} x : \textbf{entity} \\ \textbf{book}(x) \end{bmatrix}$

In other words, if one assumes that (11) is a felicitous utterance, the proposition that there is a book must be true. This requirement corresponds to the existence presupposition of (11).

At the final stage of presupposition resolution, a proof search is carried out to prove (17) and the underspecified term $@_1$ is replaced by the constructed term. More specifically, the process of anaphora/presupposition resolution is defined as follows (Bekki 2014).

(18)　Suppose that $\Gamma \vdash @_i : A$ and $\Gamma \vdash M : A$, where Γ is a global context and A is a type. Then a resolution of $@_i$ by M under the context Γ is an equation $@_i =_A M$.

In the example considered here, if a proof term for the presupposition that there is a book is constructed, it can replace the underspecified term $@_1$. Such a proof construction is possible when, for instance, *the book* appears in contexts as shown in (19a, b).

(19)　a.　If John ordered a book last week, the book will arrive today.

　　　b.　John ordered a book last week and the book arrived today.

In general, if S' entails the presuppositions of S, constructions such as S' and S and If S' then S do not inherit the presuppositions of S. In such a case, it is said that the presupposition is *filtered*.

In DTS, examples such as (19a, b) can be handled in the following way. First, the (somewhat simplified) semantic representation for (19a) is derived as shown in (20). The type checking derivation for the final representation of (20) is shown in (21). This derivation specifies the type of $@_1$. We can see that what is required for the representation to be well-typed is to find a term substituted for $@_1$ in (22).

(20)

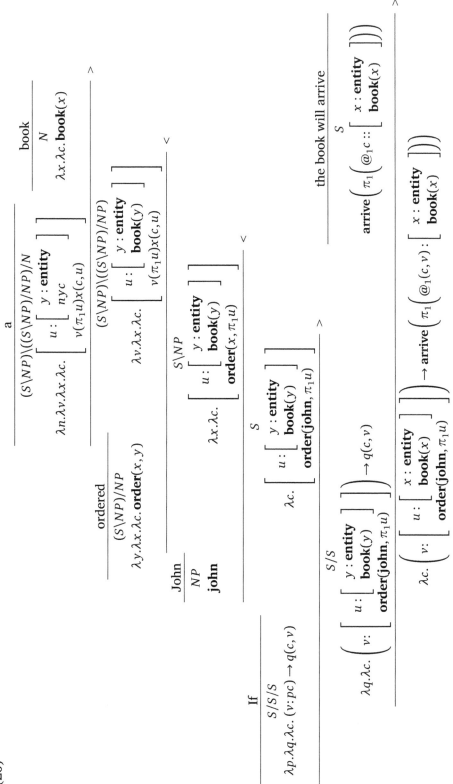

(21)

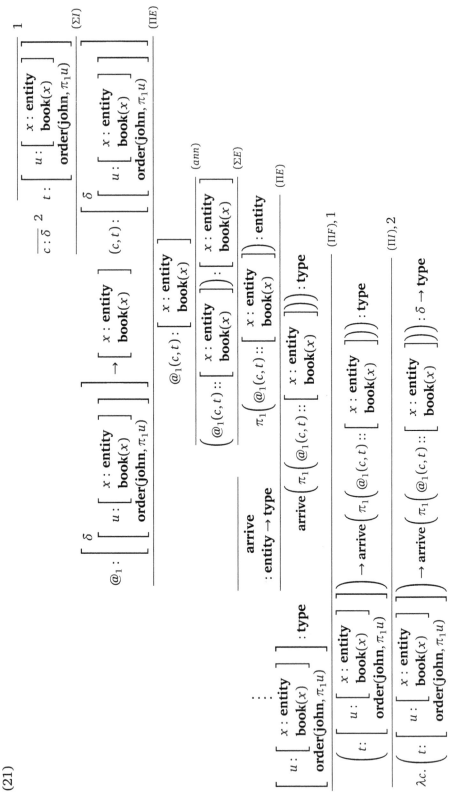

$$(22) \quad @_1 : \left[\begin{array}{c} \delta \\ \left[u : \left[\begin{array}{c} x : \textbf{entity} \\ \textbf{book}(x) \\ \textbf{order}(\text{john}, \pi_1 u) \end{array} \right] \right] \end{array} \right] \rightarrow \left[\begin{array}{c} x : \textbf{entity} \\ \textbf{book}(x) \end{array} \right]$$

In this case, without using the information provided in the previous discourse in δ, a proof of the proposition that there is a book can be obtained from the antecedent of the conditional; one can find a term that can replace $@_1$, namely, $\lambda c.\pi_1 \pi_2 c.$[12] By replacing $@_1$ with the constructed term $\lambda c.\pi_1 \pi_2 c$ in the representation given in (20), we can eventually obtain the following semantic representation for (19a), which captures the intended reading.

$$(23) \quad \left(t : \left[\begin{array}{c} u : \left[\begin{array}{c} x : \textbf{entity} \\ \textbf{book}(x) \\ \textbf{order}(\text{john}, \pi_1 u) \end{array} \right] \end{array} \right] \right) \rightarrow \textbf{arrive}\,(\pi_1 \pi_1 t)$$

Another well-known characteristic property of a presupposition is that it *projects* out of embedded contexts such as negation and the antecedent of a conditional. Thus, not only the positive sentence (11) but also the negated sentence (24a) and the antecedent of a conditional (24b) imply that there is a book.

(24)   a.   The book didn't arrive.   NEGATION

       b.   If the book arrives, Susan will be happy.   CONDITIONAL

In DTS, (24a, b) can be given the following semantic representations.

$$(25) \quad \text{a.} \quad \lambda c. \neg \textbf{arrive}\left(\pi_1 \left(@_1 c :: \left[\begin{array}{c} x : \textbf{entity} \\ \textbf{book}(x) \end{array} \right] \right) \right)$$

$$\text{b.} \quad \lambda c. \textbf{arrive}\left(\pi_1 \left(@_1 c :: \left[\begin{array}{c} x : \textbf{entity} \\ \textbf{book}(x) \end{array} \right] \right) \right) \rightarrow \textbf{happy}\,(\textbf{susan})$$

It can be shown that for the semantic representations (25a) and (25b) to be well-typed, it is required to find a proof term for the proposition that there is a book. Thus, in order to prove that (25b) has type $\delta \rightarrow \textbf{type}$, one has to prove that the antecedent is of type **type** under the given local context c. Since the antecedent in (25b) corresponds to the proposition that the book arrived, this yields the derivation that

---

[12] When such a filtration does not occur, the entire sentence can have a presupposition that is resolved by the information in δ (i.e., the information in the previous discourse) or by the information in the global context (background knowledge).

contains the type checking process in (16) as a sub-derivation. Accordingly, it is correctly predicted that (24b) has the same existence presupposition as the simple sentence in (11). Note that, in dependent type theory, the negation $\neg A$ is defined using the implication $A \rightarrow \bot$, which in turn is a degenerate form of a Π-type. Thus, the same explanation applies to the case of negation in (24a) as well. In this way, we can explain basic projection patterns of presuppositions within the framework of DTS.[13]

Before moving on to the case of factive presuppositions, let us mention one feature of underspecified terms in DTS; that is, an underspecified term can occur inside a type annotation of another underspecified term. This feature enables us to handle *nested* presuppositions. As a typical example, consider a definite noun phrase such as *the book that he wrote*. Omitting the details of compositional derivation, we can assign the following semantic representation to this complex NP.

$$(26) \quad \lambda v.\lambda c.v\left(\pi_1\left(@_1c :: \begin{bmatrix} x : \textbf{entity} \\ \begin{bmatrix} \textbf{book}(x) \\ \textbf{write}(@_2c :: \textbf{entity}, x) \end{bmatrix} \end{bmatrix}\right)\right)c$$

Here, the underspecified term $@_2$, introduced by the pronoun *he*, occurs inside the type annotation of the underspecified term $@_1$ introduced by *the*.[14] In this case, one can resolve the most embedded underspecified term $@_2$ first and then resolve the outer underspecified term $@_2$ subsequently. A more detailed discussion of nested presupposition is given in Bekki and Mineshima (2017).

3   ANALYZING FACTIVITY IN DTS

In this section, we provide an analysis of factive predicates in DTS. We take the verb *know* as a representative of a factive predicate and provide its semantic representation. We start by summarizing some semantic properties of *know*, in comparison with the non-factive verb *believe*.

---

[13] Bekki and Satoh (2015) provide a definition for decidable fragment of dependent type theory with an underspecified term and formulate its type-checking algorithm. They also provide an implementation of the algorithm.

[14] It is also possible to add gender information associated with personal pronouns as a presupposition. See Bekki and Mineshima (2017).

3.1   *Inferences with factive and non-factive verbs*

The factive verb *know* and the non-factive verb *believe* show different inference patterns with respect to the form of complements they take. In what follows, we will focus on two types of complements, declarative complements and NP-complements.

Consider the examples in (27), where the verbs *know* and *believe* take a declarative complement.

(27)   a. John knows that Mary is successful.

   b. John believes that Mary is successful.

(28)   Mary is successful.

(27a) implies (28), while (27b) does not. In the context of epistemic logic (Hintikka 1962; Meyer and van der Hoek 2004), the inference from (27a) to (28) has usually been treated as an instance of entailment (hereafter, we use the notion "entailment" in the sense of logical entailment). In the linguistics literature, by contrast, it has been widely agreed that the inference from (27a) to (28) is not an entailment but a presupposition (Kiparsky and Kiparsky 1970; Beaver 2001), as witness examples in (29) and (30).

(29)   a. John does not know that Mary is successful.   NEGATION

   b. If John knows that Mary is successful, ...   CONDITIONAL

(30)   a. If Mary is successful, John knows that she is.

   b. Mary is successful, and John knows that she is.

The examples in (29a, b) show that the proposition in (28) projects out of the embedded contexts; the examples in (30a, b) shows the filtering of presupposition. Because the antecedent of (30a) or the first conjunct of (30b) entails (28), the sentences do not inherit the presupposition of *know*, in a similar way to (19a, b).

Another interesting difference between *know* and *believe* is shown in (31), where they take an NP-complement of the form *the N that P*.

(31)   a. John believes the rumor that Mary came.
         ⇒ John believes that Mary came.

   b. John knows the rumor that Mary came.
         ⇏ John knows that Mary came.

K1	x knows that P	$\triangleright$	P
K2	x knows the N that P	$\not\Rightarrow$	x knows that P
K3	x knows the N that P	$\triangleright$	There is a N that P
B1	x believes that P	$\not\Rightarrow$	P
B2	x believes the N that P	$\Rightarrow$	x believes that P
B3	x believes the N that P	$\triangleright$	There is a N that P

Figure 3: Entailments ($\Rightarrow$) and presuppositions ($\triangleright$) associated with factive and non-factive verbs (N refers to a non-veridical content noun)

The non-factive verb *believe* licenses the inference from *x Vs the N that P* to *x Vs that P*, where N is a (non-veridical) content noun, such as *rumor, story,* and *hypothesis,* that takes a propositional complement; by contrast, the factive verb *know* does not license this pattern of inference (Vendler 1972; Ginzburg 1995a,b; Uegaki 2016).

Figure 3 shows a summary of the inference patterns for *know* and *believe* that we are concerned with in this paper. A remark is in order regarding the non-entailment in K2. There is a class of content nouns that does not follow the pattern in K2. A typical example is the content noun *fact*; "x knows the fact that P" entails "x knows that P", and vice versa. We call this class of nouns *veridical* content nouns and distinguish them from *non-veridical* content nouns such as *rumor* and *story*. The inference pattern in K2 only applies to non-veridical content nouns. We discuss the case of veridical content nouns at the end of Section 3.3.

To predict these inference patterns in a compositional setting, one needs to provide an adequate account of the lexical semantic differ- ence between factive and non-factive verbs. One possible approach is to consider the two types of verbs select for different semantic objects. More specifically, it has been proposed by a number of authors that the non-factive verb *believe* selects for a *proposition*, whereas the fac- tive verb *know* selects for a *fact* (Vendler 1972; Parsons 1993; Ginzburg 1995a,b; King 2002). In the next section, we will explore such a se- mantic analysis of factive and non-factive verbs within the framework of DTS.

3.2   *Declarative complements*

We treat factive and non-factive verbs as predicates having different semantic types. We analyze the non-factive verb *believe* as taking two arguments, a term of type **entity** and a proposition. In our notation, the predicate **believe** has the following type: [15]

(32) believe : **entity** → **type** → **type**

By contrast, we analyze the factive verb *know* as taking three arguments: (i) an entity representing the agent, (ii) a proposition that serves as the content of knowledge, and (iii) a proof term of that proposition. The predicate **know** has the following semantic type:

(33) know : **entity** → (P: **type**) → P → **type**.

As mentioned in Section 2.1, the existence of a proof term a of type P corresponds to the truth of proposition P. One may read **know**(x)(P)(a) as *the agent x obtains evidence a of the proposition* P.

The standard analysis of *know* in formal semantics follows Hintikka's (1969) possible world semantics, which fails to capture the notion of evidence or justification that has been traditionally associated with the concept of knowledge. An advantage of dependent type theory is that it is equipped with proofs as first-class objects and thus enables us to analyze the factive verb *know* as a predicate over a proof (evidence) of a proposition. Our analysis is also compatible with Vendler's view that *know* and *believe* select for different semantic objects. Note that, in our approach, the notion of facts is not taken as primitive but analyzed in terms of the notion of evidence of a proposition.

The idea that a proof term of a proposition serves as an antecedent of anaphor can be traced back to Ranta (1994), where under the assumption that proofs are identified with *events* it is claimed that aspectual verbs like *stop* presuppose the existence of a proof. Also, Krahmer and Piwek (1999) briefly mentioned that the presuppositions triggered by noun phrases like *the fact that P* can be treated in a similar way (see also Section 3.3 for some discussion). Our claim is that the idea that proof terms act as antecedents of anaphora can be applied to the presuppositions of factive verbs in general.

---

[15] We leave open the possibility of decomposing the semantic representation of belief sentences in terms of possible worlds. See Tanaka *et al.* (2015) for discussion in the context of DTS. The problem of opacity and hyperintensionality (Fox and Lappin 2005) is beyond the scope of the present paper.

To account for the presuppositional inferences summarized in Section 3.1, we use the following lexical entry for *know*. [16]

(34)   know; $(S\backslash NP)/\overline{S}$; $\lambda p.\lambda x.\lambda c.\textbf{know}(x)(pc)(@_i c)$

Here the argument p is a dynamic proposition expressed by the declarative complement of *know*. The underspecified term $@_i$ takes a local context c as an argument and requires one to construct a proof term of type pc, i.e., to find *evidence* of the (static) proposition pc being true. If such a proof term is constructed, it fills the third argument position of the predicate **know**. In sum, the sentence x *knows that P* presupposes that there is a proof (evidence) of P and asserts that the agent x obtains it, i.e., x has a proof (evidence) of the proposition P.

Let us illustrate with (27a) how to give a compositional analysis of a construction containing *know*. The semantic representation for (27a) is given by the following CCG derivation tree.

(35)

$$
\begin{array}{c}
\cfrac{
  \cfrac{
    \text{John}
  }{
    \cfrac{NP}{\textbf{john}}
  }
  \quad
  \cfrac{
    \cfrac{\text{knows}}{(S\backslash NP)/\overline{S} \quad \lambda p.\lambda x.\lambda c.\textbf{know}(x)(pc)(@_1 c)}
    \quad
    \cfrac{
      \cfrac{\text{that}}{\overline{S}/S \quad \lambda P.P}
      \quad
      \cfrac{\text{Mary is successful}}{S \quad \lambda c.\textbf{successful}(\textbf{mary})}
    }{\overline{S} \quad \lambda c.\textbf{successful}(\textbf{mary})} >
  }{S\backslash NP \quad \lambda x.\lambda c.\textbf{know}(x)(\textbf{successful}(\textbf{mary}))(@_1 c)} >
}{S} <
$$
$$\lambda c.\textbf{know}(\textbf{john})(\textbf{successful}(\textbf{mary}))(@_1 c)$$

Then, the derivation (36) checks whether the semantic representation is well-typed. The open branch ending up with $\delta \rightarrow \textbf{successful}(\textbf{mary})$ shows the presupposition of this representation, which is the factive presupposition of (27a). In this way, we can correctly predict that the presuppositional inference from (27a) to (28) holds. The inference mechanism we described in Section 2.3 for the existence presupposition of definite descriptions can be extended for the case of *know*. In particular, it is easy to see that the projection inference in (29) and the filtering inference in (30) can be accounted for in the same way as those in (24) and (19), respectively.

---

[16] In (34), the underspecified term $@_i c$ is not annotated with its type pc, since it is inferable from the type of the predicate **know**.

(36)

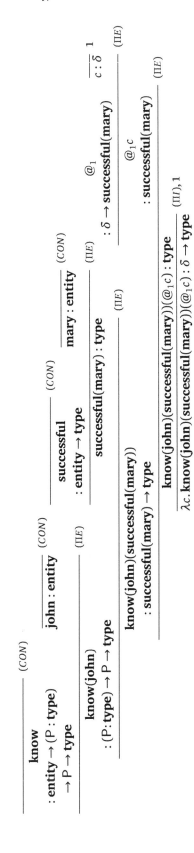

It is known that a sentence such as (37) poses the so-called *binding problem* (Karttunen 1971; Karttunen and Peters 1979; Cooper 1983).

(37) A student regrets that she talked.

Here, the existential quantification introduced by *a student* binds the pronoun *she* that appears in the presupposed content. This is an instance of the nested presuppositions that we mentioned in Section 2.3. In DTS, (37) can be given the semantic representation as shown in (38) (where the semantic representation of *regrets* is analogous to that of *knows* above). In this resulting representation, the Σ-type corresponding to the subject *a student* binds the variable u in the second argument of **regret**, which correponds to the type of $@_2(c, u)$ introduced by the factive presupposition of *regret*. With the help of the type checking procedure, this enables us to capture the dependency between assertion and presupposition.[17]

3.3   *NP-complements*

The analysis presented so far can be extended to the analysis of NP-complements. Let us first take the case of *believe*. Consider the example in (31a). The semantic representation of the definite NP *the rumor that Mary came* appearing in the object position can be derived as in (39). Since *rumor* is a content noun, we treat it as having the syntactic category N_{+c} with the syntactic feature +c. Correspondingly, the predicate **rumor** is analyzed as a predicate over propositions; its type is **type** $\rightarrow$ **type**. The semantic representation of definite article *the* is given in the same way as the one in Section 2.3 except that it combines with a predicate over propositions (i.e., objects of type **type**), rather than with a predicate over entities.[18]

The semantic representation for the premise sentence in (31a) can be derived as shown in (40). The resulting representation presupposes that there is a rumor whose content is identified with **come(mary)**. This is the existence presupposition triggered by the NP-complement

---

[17] See Bekki and Mineshima (2017) for more details.

[18] Strictly speaking, to combine Σ-types with predicates over propositions requires the notion of type hierarchy (Martin-Löf 1984). For ease of exposition, we refer to the base type (**type**$_0$) simply as **type**.

(38)

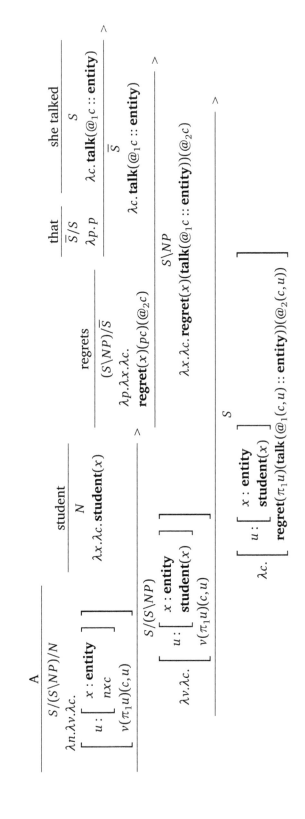

(39)

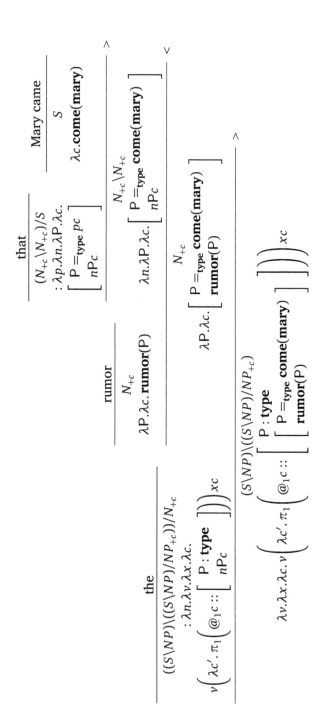

(40)

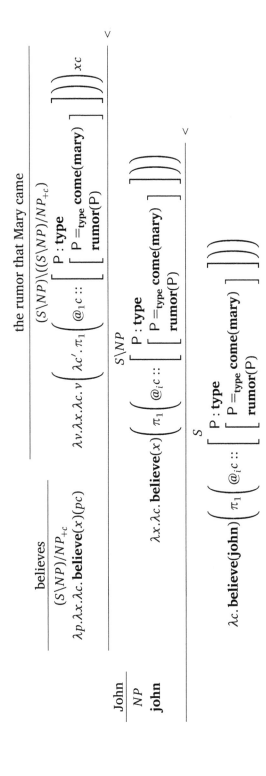

(cf. B3 in Figure 3). When this presupposition is satisfied, the resulting semantic representation can be reduced to **believe(john, P)**, where we have P : **type**, P $=_{type}$ **come(mary)**, and **rumor**(P). Thus, we can derive the representation **believe(john, come(mary))**, which is the representation for the conclusion in (31a). Hence, we can correctly derive the entailment pattern B2 in Figure 3.

It should be noted that, in the case of (31a), the predicate **rumor** does not contribute to the content of belief. By contrast, (31b) shows that, in the case of the factive verb *know* taking an NP-complement, the predicate **rumor** is part of the content of knowledge ascribed to the agent. The premise sentence in (31b) can be paraphrased as *John knows that there is a rumor that Mary came*. To handle (31b), then, we use the following lexical entries for the non-presuppositional use of *the*, which we refer to by *the$_{pred}$*.

(41) *the$_{pred}$* (subject position);

$$(S/(S\backslash NP_{+c}))/N_{+c} \, ; \, \lambda n.\lambda v.\lambda c. \, v\left(\lambda c'. \begin{bmatrix} P : \textbf{type} \\ nPc \end{bmatrix}\right) c$$

(42) *the$_{pred}$* (object position);

$$((S\backslash NP)\backslash((S\backslash NP)/NP_{+c}))/N_{+c} \, ; \, \lambda n.\lambda v.\lambda x.\lambda c. \, v\left(\lambda c'. \begin{bmatrix} P : \textbf{type} \\ nPc \end{bmatrix}\right) xc$$

In contrast to the entry given in (12), *the$_{pred}$* does not have existence presupposition and passes the whole existential proposition (Σ-type) to the main predicate.[19]

We take it that the existence presupposition associated with the premise sentence in (31b) comes from the factive verb *know*. Using the entry in (42), the semantic representation for the premise sentence in (31b) can be derived as in (43). The semantic representation derived in (43) presupposes that there is a rumor that Mary came and asserts that John has evidence for it. This is clearly distinguished from the reading

---

[19] Such a non-presuppositional use of definite description is also needed to handle examples such as *The king of France does not exist*, where the use of *the* does not presuppose the existence of the king of France.

(43)

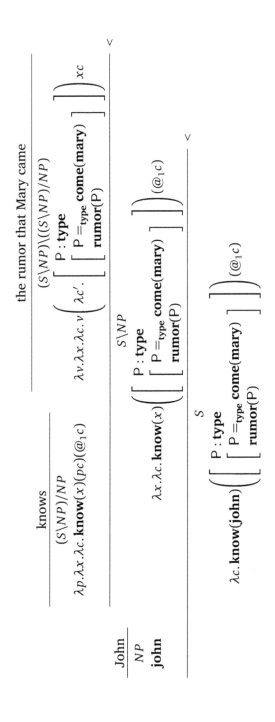

K4	x knows the fact that P	$\Longleftrightarrow$	x knows that P
K5	x knows the fact that P	$\triangleright$	There is a fact that P
K6	x knows the fact that P	$\triangleright$	P

Figure 4: Inferences associated with veridical content nouns

that John has evidence that Mary came, hence, we can account for the non-entailment in (31b), schematically given as K2 in Figure 3.[20]

As noted in Section 3.1, veridical content nouns such as *fact* and *truth* show a different entailment pattern from non-veridical content nouns such as *rumor* and *story*. The relevant inference patterns are summarized in Figure 4. The present analysis can naturally handle these inference patterns as well. Consider (44):

(44) John knows the fact that Mary came.

In the same way as the derivation in (43), we can obtain the semantic representation for (44):

$$(45) \quad \lambda c.\,\textbf{know(john)}\left(\left[\begin{array}{l} P : \textbf{type} \\ \left[\begin{array}{l} P =_{\text{type}} \textbf{come(mary)} \\ \textbf{fact}(P) \end{array}\right] \end{array}\right]\right)(@_1 c)$$

The underspecified term $@_1$ in (45) triggers the presupposition that there is the fact that Mary came, which accounts for K5 in Figure 4. To account for the other inference patterns, we may posit two axioms. The first axiom is the one concerning the lexical meaning of the veridical content noun *fact*:

(46) Axiom 1 : $(P:\textbf{type}) \rightarrow (\textbf{fact}(P) \longleftrightarrow P)$

Using this axiom, one can construct a proof term of **come(mary)** from the presupposition in (45), hence K6 in Figure 4 follows.

The second axiom we need is about the closure property of *know*:

(47) Axiom 2 : $(x:\textbf{entity}) \rightarrow (P:\textbf{type}) \rightarrow (Q:\textbf{type}) \rightarrow (a:P) \rightarrow$
      $\textbf{know}(x)(P)(a) \rightarrow (f:P \rightarrow Q) \rightarrow \textbf{know}(x)(Q)(f a)$

The sentence *John knows that Mary came* can be compositionally assigned the semantic representation in (48), in the same way as the derivation shown in (35).

---

[20] As pointed out by an anonymous reviewer, the current analysis allows the combination of the verb *know* and the presuppositional *the*. This yields an unintended reading for (31b) where it is presupposed that Mary came. Though this undesirable reading could be blocked by involving a complicated syntactic analysis, we consider details of such an analysis as beyond the scope of this paper.

(48) $\lambda c . \mathbf{know}(\mathbf{john})(\mathbf{come}(\mathbf{mary}))(@_2 c)$

It is easy to derive (48) from (45) given an initial context c. First, assume that the presupposition in (45) is satisfied, that is, there is a proof term substituted for $@_1$ in (45). Using Axiom 1, we can construct a proof term substituted for $@_2$ in (48), that is, a proof term of **come**(**mary**), as well as a proof term for the proposition in (49).

(49) $$\left[\begin{array}{l} \mathsf{P : type} \\ \left[\begin{array}{l} \mathsf{P} =_{\mathrm{type}} \mathbf{come}(\mathbf{mary}) \\ \mathbf{fact}(\mathsf{P}) \end{array} \right] \end{array} \right] \rightarrow \mathbf{come}(\mathbf{mary})$$

Hence, applying Axiom 2, we can obtain a proof term of (48). The other direction, i.e., the inference from (48) to (45), is derived in the same manner. Thus we can account for the pattern in K4.

Note that the present analysis of the inference pattern in K6 is different from what is suggested by Krahmer and Piwek (1999). These authors briefly discuss the presupposition triggered by the factive construction *(be) annoyed by the fact that P*. They treat this construction as one complex predicate, assuming that its presupposition is *P*. In our approach, *know the fact that P* is analyzed not as directly presupposing that *P*, but as presupposing the existence of the fact whose content is *P*. Under the present analysis, the inference in K6 is explained in terms of the lexical knowledge concerning the content noun *fact*.

4   CONCLUSION

This paper has attempted to provide an analysis of presuppositions and factivity within the framework of DTS. Under our analysis, factive and non-factive verbs are assigned different semantic types: while the non-factive predicate *believe* selects for a proposition as an object argument, the factive predicate *know* takes a proof-object as an extra argument. Using the machinery of underspecified semantics in DTS, we have illustrated how to account for a variety of inferences concerning factive and non-factive verbs.

Several open issues remain, most notably that of the interpretation of interrogative complements. It is acknowledged in the literature that the factive verb *know* takes interrogative complements, whereas the non-factive verb *believe* does not (Ginzburg 1995a,b; Egré 2008):

(50)   a. John {knows, *believes} whether Ann or Bob came.
       b. John {knows, *believes} who came.

Providing a detailed analysis of interrogative complements within our proof-theoretic framework is left for another occasion.

ACKNOWLEDGMENT

This paper is a revised and expanded version of a paper presented at the TYpe Theory and LExical Semantics (TYTLES) workshop during the 27th European Summer School in Logic, Language and Information (ESSLLI 2015). We are grateful to Robin Cooper, Christian Retoré, and the audience of TYTLES workshop for helpful discussions. We would also like to thank the three anonymous reviewers of this paper for their valuable comments and suggestions. This work was supported by JST CREST Grant Number JPMJCR1301, Japan. The first author acknowledges the financial support of the JSPS Grant-in-Aid for JSPS Fellows Grant Number 15J11772.

APPENDIX

Definition 1 (Alphabet for $\lambda_{\Pi\Sigma}$) *An alphabet for $\lambda_{\Pi\Sigma}$ is a $\langle Var, Con \rangle$, where Var is a set of variables, and Con is a set of constants. Dependent type semantics employs an alphabet as follows:*

$$Var \stackrel{def}{\equiv} \{x, y, z, u, v, ...\}$$

$$Con \stackrel{def}{\equiv} \{\textbf{entity}, \textbf{book}, \textbf{arrive}, ...\}$$

Definition 2 (Preterms) *The collection of preterms is recursively defined as follows (where $x \in Var$ and $c \in Con$, $j = 1, 2$, $i = 0, 1, 2, ...$).*

$$\Lambda := x \mid c \mid @_i \mid \textbf{type}_i \mid \Lambda :: \Lambda \mid (x : \Lambda) \to \Lambda \mid \lambda x.\Lambda \mid \Lambda\Lambda$$

$$\mid \left[\begin{array}{c} x : \Lambda \\ \Lambda \end{array} \right] \mid (\Lambda, \Lambda) \mid \pi_j(\Lambda) \mid \Lambda =_\Lambda \Lambda \mid \text{refl}_\Lambda(\Lambda) \mid \text{idpeel}(\Lambda, \Lambda)$$

$$\mid \bot \mid \top \mid \text{case}_\Lambda(\Lambda_1, ..., \Lambda_n)$$

Definition 3 (Signature) *A signature σ is defined recursively as follows.*

$$\sigma := () \mid \sigma, c : A$$

where () is an empty signature, $c \in Con$, $A \in \Lambda$ s.t. $\vdash_\sigma A : \textbf{type}_i$ for some $i \in \mathbb{N}$.

Definition 4 (Context) *A context is defined recursively as follows.*

$$\Gamma := () \mid \Gamma, x : A$$

where () is an empty context, $x \in Var$, $A \in \Lambda$ s.t. $\Gamma \vdash_\sigma A : \mathbf{type}_i$ for some $i \in \mathbb{N}$.

Definition 5 (Constant symbol rule) *For any $(c : A) \in \sigma$,*

$$\frac{}{c : A} \ (CON)$$

Definition 6 (Type rules) *For any $i \in \mathbb{N}$,*

$$\frac{A : \mathbf{type}_i}{A : \mathbf{type}_{i+1}} \ (\text{type}I) \qquad \frac{}{\mathbf{type}_i : \mathbf{type}_{i+1}} \ (\text{type}F)$$

Definition 7 (Π-type) *For any $i, j \in \mathbb{N}$,*

$$\frac{A : \mathbf{type}_i \quad \overset{\displaystyle \overline{x : A}^{\,j}}{\underset{\vdots}{} \ B : \mathbf{type}_i}}{(x{:}A) \to B : \mathbf{type}_i} \ (\Pi F),j \qquad \frac{A : \mathbf{type}_i \quad \overset{\displaystyle \overline{x : A}^{\,j}}{\underset{\vdots}{} \ M : B}}{\lambda x.M : (x{:}A) \to B} \ (\Pi I),j$$

$$\frac{M : (x{:}A) \to B \quad N : A}{MN : B[M/x]} \ (\Pi E)$$

Definition 8 (Σ-type) *For any $i, j \in \mathbb{N}$,*

$$\frac{A : \mathbf{type}_i \quad \overset{\displaystyle \overline{x : A}^{\,j}}{\underset{\vdots}{} \ B : \mathbf{type}_i}}{\begin{bmatrix} x : A \\ B \end{bmatrix} : \mathbf{type}_i} \ (\Sigma F),j \qquad \frac{M : A \quad N : B[M/x]}{(M, N) : \begin{bmatrix} x : A \\ B \end{bmatrix}} \ (\Sigma I)$$

$$\frac{M : \begin{bmatrix} x : A \\ B \end{bmatrix}}{\pi_1(M) : A} \ (\Sigma E) \qquad \frac{M : \begin{bmatrix} x : A \\ B \end{bmatrix}}{\pi_2(M) : B[\pi_1(M)/x]} \ (\Sigma E)$$

Definition 9 (Bottom type) *For any $i \in \mathbb{N}$,*

$$\frac{}{\bot : \mathbf{type}_0} \ (\bot F) \qquad \frac{M : \bot \quad C : \bot \to \mathbf{type}_i}{\mathrm{case}_M() : C(M)} \ (\bot E)$$

Definition 10 (Top type) *For any $i \in \mathbb{N}$,*

$$\frac{}{\top : \mathbf{type}_0} \; (\top F) \qquad \frac{}{() : \top} \; (\top I)$$

$$\frac{M : \top \quad C : \top \to \mathbf{type}_i \quad N : C()}{\mathrm{case}_M(N) : C(M)} \; (\top E)$$

Definition 11 (Id-type) *For any $i \in \mathbb{N}$,*

$$\frac{A : \mathbf{type}_i \quad M : A \quad N : A}{M =_A N : \mathbf{type}_i} \; (\mathrm{Id}F) \qquad \frac{A : \mathbf{type} \quad M : A}{\mathrm{refl}_A(M) : M =_A M} \; (\mathrm{Id}I)$$

$$\frac{E : M_1 =_A M_2 \quad C : (x{:}A) \to (y{:}A) \to (x =_A y \to \mathbf{type}_i) \quad N : (x{:}A) \to Cxx(\mathrm{refl}_A(x))}{\mathrm{idpeel}(e, N) : CM_1 M_2 E} \; (\mathrm{Id}E)$$

Definition 12 (@-formation rule) *For any $i, j \in \mathbb{N}$,*

$$\frac{A : \mathbf{type}_i \quad A \; true}{@_j : A} \; (@F)$$

Definition 13 (Type annotation rule)

$$\frac{t : A}{(t :: A) : A} \; (ann)$$

REFERENCES

Nicholas ASHER (2011), *Lexical Meaning in Context: A Web of Words*, Cambridge University Press, Cambridge.

Nicholas ASHER and Zhaohui LUO (2012), Formalisation of coercions in lexical semantics, in E. CHEMLA, V. HOMER, and G. WINTERSTEIN, editors, *Proceedings of Sinn und Bedeutung 17*, pp. 63–80, Paris, http://semanticsarchive.net/sub2012/.

David I. BEAVER (2001), *Presupposition and Assertion in Dynamic Semantics*, CSLI Publications, Stanford.

Daisuke BEKKI (2014), Representing anaphora with dependent types, in N. ASHER and S. SOLOVIEV, editors, *Logical Aspects of Computational Linguistics: 8th International Conference, LACL 2014, Proceedings*, volume 8535 of *Lecture Notes in Computer Science*, pp. 14–29, Springer, Heidelberg.

Daisuke BEKKI and Nicholas ASHER (2013), Logical polysemy and subtyping, in Y. MOTOMURA, A. BUTLER, and D. BEKKI, editors, *New Frontiers in Artificial Intelligence: JSAI-isAI 2012 Workshops, Revised Selected Papers*, volume 7856 of *Lecture Notes in Computer Science*, pp. 17–24, Springer, Heidelberg.

Daisuke BEKKI and Koji MINESHIMA (2017), Context-passing and underspecification in Dependent Type Semantics, in S. CHATZIKYRIAKIDIS and Z. LUO, editors, *Modern Perspectives in Type-Theoretical Semantics*, volume 98 of *Studies in Linguistics and Philosophy*, pp. 11–41, Springer, Heidelberg.

Daisuke BEKKI and Miho SATOH (2015), Calculating projections via type checking, in R. COOPER and C. RETORÉ, editors, *ESSLLI proceedings of the TYTLES workshop on Type Theory and Lexical Semantics ESSLLI2015*, Barcelona.

Stergios CHATZIKYRIAKIDIS and Zhaohui LUO (2014), Natural language inference in Coq, *Journal of Logic, Language and Information*, 23(4):441–480.

Robin COOPER (1983), *Quantification and Syntactic Theory*, Reidel, Dordrecht.

Rogelio DÁVILA-PÉREZ (1995), *Semantics and Parsing in Intuitionistic Categorial Grammar*, Ph.D. thesis, University of Essex.

Paul EGRÉ (2008), Question-embedding and factivity, *Grazer Philosophische Studien*, 77(1):85–125.

Delia Graff FARA (2001), Descriptions as predicates, *Philosophical Studies*, 102:1–42, originally published under the name "Delia Graff".

Chris FOX and Shalom LAPPIN (2005), *Foundations of Intensional Semantics*, Blackwell, Oxford.

Jonathan GINZBURG (1995a), Resolving questions, I, *Linguistics and Philosophy*, 18(5):459–527.

Jonathan GINZBURG (1995b), Resolving questions, II, *Linguistics and Philosophy*, 18(6):567–609.

Jeroen GROENENDIJK and Martin STOKHOF (1991), Dynamic predicate logic, *Linguistics and Philosophy*, 14(1):39–100.

Irene HEIM (1982), *The Semantics of Definite and Indefinite Noun Phrases*, Ph.D. thesis, University of Massachusetts, Amherst.

Irene HEIM (1983), On the projection problem for presuppositions, in M. BARLOW, D. FLICKINGER, and M. WESCOAT, editors, *Proceedings of the Second West Coast Conference on Formal Linguistics*, pp. 114–125, Stanford University Press, Stanford, CA.

Jaakko HINTIKKA (1962), *Knowledge and Belief: An Introduction to the Logic of the Two Notions*, Cornell University Press, Ithaca, NY.

Jaakko HINTIKKA (1969), Semantics for propositional attitudes, in J. W. DAVIS, D. J. HOCKNEY, and W. K. WILSON, editors, *Philosophical Logic*, volume 20 of *Synthese Library*, pp. 21–45, Reidel, Dordrecht.

William Alvin HOWARD (1980), The formulae-as-types notion of construction, in J. P. SELDIN and J. R. HINDLEY, editors, *To H. B. Curry: Essays on Combinatory Logic, Lambda Calculus and Formalism*, pp. 480–490, Academic Press, London.

Hans KAMP, Josef VAN GENABITH, and Uwe REYLE (2011), Discourse Representation Theory, in D. M. GABBAY and F. GUENTHNER, editors, *Handbook of Philosophical Logic*, volume 15, pp. 125–394, Springer, Heidelberg.

Lauri KARTTUNEN (1971), Implicative verbs, *Language*, 47(2):340–358.

Lauri KARTTUNEN and Stanley PETERS (1979), Conventional implicatures, in C. K. OH and D. A. DINNEEN, editors, *Syntax and Semantics 11: Presupposition*, pp. 1–56, Academic Press, New York, NY.

Jeffrey C. KING (2002), Designating propositions, *The Philosophical Review*, 111(3):341–371.

Eriko KINOSHITA, Koji MINESHIMA, and Daisuke BEKKI (2016), An analysis of selectional restrictions with Dependent Type Semantics, in *Proceedings of the 13th International Workshop on Logic and Engineering of Natural Language Semantics (LENLS13)*, pp. 100–113, Kanagawa.

Paul KIPARSKY and Carol KIPARSKY (1970), Fact, in M. BIERWISCH and K. E. HEIDOLPH, editors, *Progress in Linguistics*, pp. 143–173, de Gruyter Mouton, Berlin.

Emiel KRAHMER and Paul PIWEK (1999), Presupposition projection as proof construction, in H. BUNT and R. MUSKENS, editors, *Computing Meaning: Volume 1*, volume 73 of *Studies in Linguistics and Philosophy*, pp. 281–300, Kluwer Academic Publishers, Dordrecht.

Yusuke KUBOTA and Robert LEVINE (2017), Scope parallelism in coordination in Dependent Type Semantics, in M. OTAKE, S. KURAHASHI, Y. OTA, K. SATOH, and D. BEKKI, editors, *New Frontiers in Artificial Intelligence: JSAI-isAI 2015 Workshops, Revised Selected Papers*, volume 10091 of *Lecture Notes in Artificial Intelligence*, pp. 149–162, Springer, Heidelberg.

Susumu KUNO (1970), Some properties of non-referential noun phrases, in R. JAKOBSON and S. KAWAMOTO, editors, *Studies in General and Oriental Linguistics. Presented to S. Hattori on Occasion of his Sixtieth Birthday*, pp. 348–373, TEC, Tokyo.

Zhaohui LUO (2012a), Common nouns as types, in D. BÉCHET and A. DIKOVSKY, editors, *Logical Aspects of Computational Linguistics: 7th International Conference, LACL 2012, Proceedings*, volume 7351 of *Theoretical Computer Science and General Issues*, pp. 173–185, Springer, Heidelberg.

Zhaohui LUO (2012b), Formal semantics in modern type theories with coercive subtyping, *Linguistics and Philosophy*, 35(6):491–513.

Per MARTIN-LÖF (1984), *Intuitionistic Type Theory. Notes by G. Sambin*, Bibliopolis, Naples.

John-Jules Ch MEYER and Wiebe VAN DER HOEK (2004), *Epistemic Logic for AI and Computer Science*, Cambridge University Press, Cambridge.

Line MIKKELSEN (2005), *Copular Clauses: Specification, Predication and Equation*, John Benjamins, Amsterdam.

Line MIKKELSEN (2011), Copular clauses, in C. MAIENBORN, K. VON HEUSINGER, and P. PORTNER, editors, *Semantics: An International Handbook of Natural Language Meaning*, volume 2, pp. 1805–1829, de Gruyter Mouton, Berlin.

Richard MONTAGUE (1973), The proper treatment of quantification in ordinary English, in P. SUPPES, J. MORAVCSIK, and J. HINTIKKA, editors, *Approaches to Natural Language*, pp. 221–242, Kluwer Academic Publishers, Dordrecht.

Bengt NORDSTRÖM, Kent PETERSSON, and Jan M. SMITH (1990), *Programming in Martin-Löf's Type Theory: An Introduction*, Oxford University Press, Oxford.

Terence PARSONS (1993), On denoting propositions and facts, *Philosophical Perspectives*, 7:441–460.

Paul PIWEK and Emiel KRAHMER (2000), Presuppositions in context: constructing bridges, in P. BONZON, M. CAVALCANTI, and R. NOSSUM, editors, *Formal Aspects of Context*, volume 20 of *Applied Logic Series*, pp. 85–106, Kluwer Academic Publishers, Dordrecht.

Aarne RANTA (1994), *Type-Theoretical Grammar*, Oxford University Press, Oxford.

Christian RETORÉ (2014), The Montagovian generative lexicon ΛTy_n: a type theoretical framework for natural language semantics, in R. MATTHES and A. SCHUBERT, editors, *19th International Conference on Types for Proofs and Programs (TYPES 2013)*, volume 26 of *Leibniz International Proceedings in Informatics*, pp. 202–229, Schloss Dagstuhl–Leibniz-Zentrum fuer Informatik, Dagstuhl, `http://drops.dagstuhl.de/opus/volltexte/2014/4633/`.

Bertrand RUSSELL (1919), *Introduction to Mathematical Philosophy*, George Allen & Unwin, London.

Mark STEEDMAN (2000), *The Syntactic Process*, MIT Press, Cambridge, MA.

Göran SUNDHOLM (1986), Proof Theory and Meaning, in D. M. GABBAY and F. GUENTHNER, editors, *Handbook of Philosophical Logic*, volume 3, pp. 471–506, Reidel, Dordrecht.

Göran SUNDHOLM (1989), Constructive generalized quantifiers, *Synthese*, 79(1):1–12.

Ribeka TANAKA (2014), A proof-theoretic approach to generalized quantifiers in dependent type semantics, in R. DE HAAN, editor, *Proceedings of the ESSLLI2014 Student Session*, pp. 140–151, Tübingen, `http://www.kr.tuwien.ac.at/drm/dehaan/stus2014/proceedings.pdf`.

Ribeka TANAKA, Koji MINESHIMA, and Daisuke BEKKI (2015), Resolving modal anaphora in Dependent Type Semantics, in T. MURATA, K. MINESHIMA, and D. BEKKI, editors, *New Frontiers in Artificial Intelligence: JSAI-isAI 2014 Workshops, Revised Selected Papers*, pp. 83–98, Springer, Heidelberg.

Ribeka TANAKA, Yuki NAKANO, and Daisuke BEKKI (2014), Constructive generalized quantifiers revisited, in Y. NAKANO, K. SATOH, and D. BEKKI, editors, *New Frontiers in Artificial Intelligence: JSAI-isAI 2013 Workshops, Revised Selected Papers*, volume 8417 of *Lecture Notes in Computer Science*, pp. 115–124, Springer, Heidelberg.

Wataru UEGAKI (2016), Content nouns and the semantics of question-embedding, *Journal of Semantics*, 33(4):623–660.

Rob A. VAN DER SANDT (1992), Presupposition projection as anaphora resolution, *Journal of Semantics*, 9:333–377.

Zeno VENDLER (1972), *Res Cogitans: An Essay in Rational Psychology*, Cornell University Press, Ithaca, NY.

5

Representing syntax by means of properties: a formal framework for descriptive approaches

Philippe Blache
CNRS & Aix-Marseille Université
Laboratoire Parole et Langage

Keywords: *syntax, constraints, linguistic theory, usage-based theories, constructions, Property Grammars*

ABSTRACT

Linguistic description and language modelling need to be formally sound and complete while still being supported by data. We present a linguistic framework that bridges such formal and descriptive requirements, based on the representation of syntactic information by means of *local properties*. This approach, called *Property Grammars*, provides a formal basis for the description of specific characteristics as well as entire constructions. In contrast with other formalisms, all information is represented at the same level (no property playing a more important role than another) and independently (any property being evaluable separately). As a consequence, a syntactic description, instead of a complete hierarchical structure (typically a tree), is a set of multiple relations between words. This characteristic is crucial when describing unrestricted data, including spoken language. We show in this paper how local properties can implement any kind of syntactic information and constitute a formal framework for the representation of *constructions* (seen as a set of interacting properties). The *Property Grammars* approach thus offers the possibility to integrate the description of local phenomena into a general formal framework.

1   INTRODUCTION

The description and modelling of local language phenomena contributes to a better understanding of language processing. However, this data-driven perspective needs to provide a method of unifying models into a unique and homogeneous framework that would form an effective theory of language. Reciprocally, from the formal perspective, linguistic theories provide general architectures for language processing, but still have difficulty in integrating the variability of language productions. The challenge at hand is to test formal frameworks using a large range of unrestricted and heterogeneous data (including spoken language). The feasibility of this task mainly depends on the ability to describe all possible forms, regardless of whether they are well-formed (i.e. grammatical) or not. Such is the goal of the linguistic trend known as *usage-based* (Langacker 1987; Bybee 2010), which aims to describe how language works based on its concrete use. Our goal is to propose a new formal framework built upon this approach.

Moving away from the generative framework. Addressing the question of the syntactic description independently of grammaticality represents an epistemological departure from the generative approach in many respects. In particular, it consists in moving away from the representation of competence towards that of performance. Several recent approaches in line with this project consider grammar not as a device for generating language, but rather as a set of statements, making it possible to describe any kind of input, addressing at the same time the question of gradience in grammars (Aarts 2004; Blache and Prost 2005; Fanselow *et al.* 2005). To use a computational metaphor, this comes to replace a *procedural approach* where grammar is a set of operations (rules), with a *declarative approach* where grammar is a set of descriptions. This evolution is fundamental: it relies on a clear distinction between linguistic knowledge (the grammar) and parsing mechanisms that are used for building a syntactic structure. In most current formalisms, this is not the case. For example, the representation of syntactic information with trees relies on the use of phrase-structure rules which encode both a syntactic relation (government) and operational information (the local tree to be used in the final structure). Such merging of operational information within the grammar can also be found in other formalisms such as *Tree-Adjoining Grammars* (Joshi *et al.* 1975) in which the grammar is made of sub-parts of the final syntactic tree. It is also the case in *Dependency Grammars* (Tesnière 1959) with the projectivity principle (intended to control tree well-formedness) as well as in HPSG (Pollard and Sag 1994; Sag and Wasow 1999) and its feature percolation principles.

We propose disentangling these different aspects by excluding information solely motivated by the kind of structure to be built. In other words, linguistic information should be encoded independently of the form of the final representation. Grammar is limited then to a set of descriptions that are linguistic facts. As explained by Pullum and Scholz (2001), doing this enables a move away from *Generative-Enumerative Syntax* (GES) towards a *Model-Theoretic Syntax* (MTS) (Cornell and Rogers 2000; Blackburn and Meyer-Viol 1997; Blache 2007).

Several works are considered by Pullum and Scholz (2001) to exhibit the seeds of MTS, in particular *HPSG* and *Construction Grammars* (Fillmore 1988; Kay and Fillmore 1999). These two approaches have recently converged, leading to a new framework called *Sign-Based Construction Grammars* (Sag 2012; Sag *et al.* 2012). SGBG is motivated by providing a formal basis for *Construction Grammars*, paving the way towards modelling language usage. It starts to fulfill the MTS requirements in that it proposes a monotonic system of declarative constraints, representing different sources of linguistic information and their interaction. However, there still remains a limitation that is inherent to HPSG: the central role played by *heads*. Much information is controlled by this element, as the theory is *head-driven*. All principles are stipulated on the basis of the existence of a context-free skeleton, implemented by dominance schemas. As a consequence, the organization of the information is *syntacto-centric*: the interaction of the linguistic domains is organized around a head/dependent hierarchical structure, corresponding to a tree.

In these approaches, representing the information of a domain, and more to the point the interaction among the domains, requires one to first build the schema of mother/daughters. Constraints are then applied as filters, so as to identify well-formed structures. As a side effect, no description can be given when no such structures can be built. This is a severe restriction both for theoretical and cognitive reasons: one of the requirements of MTS is to represent all linguistic domains independently of each other (in what Pullum and Scholz 2001 call a *non-holistic* manner). Their interaction is to be implemented directly, without giving any priority to any of them with respect to the others. Ignoring this requirement necessarily entails a modular and serial conception of language processing, which is challenged now both in linguistics and in psycholinguistics (Jackendoff 2007; Ferreira and Patson 2007; Swets *et al.* 2008). Evidence supporting this challenge includes: language processing is very often underspecified; linguistic information comes from different and heterogeneous sources that may vary depending on usage; the understanding mechanisms are often non-compositional; etc.

One goal of this paper is to propose an approach that accommodates such different uses of language so as to be able to process canonical or non-canonical, mono- or multimodal inputs.

Describing any kind of input. Linguistic information needs to be represented separately when trying to account for unrestricted material, including non-canonical productions (e.g. in spoken language). The main motivation is that, whatever the sentence or the utterance to be parsed, it becomes then possible to identify its syntactic characteristics independently of the structure to be built. If we adopt this approach, we still can provide syntactic information partly describing the input even when no structure can be built (e.g. ill-formed realizations). In other words, it becomes possible to provide a description (in some cases a partial description) of an input regardless of its form.

This type of approach allows one to describe any type of sentence or utterance: it is no longer a question of establishing whether the sentence under question is grammatical or not, but rather of describing the sentence itself. This task amounts to deciding which descriptions present in the grammar are relevant to the object to be described and then to assessing them.

Grammar as set of constructions. One important advance for linguistic theories has been the introduction of the notion of *construction* (Fillmore 1988; Kay and Fillmore 1999). A construction is the description of a specific linguistic phenomenon, leading to a specific form-function pairing that is conventionalized or even not strictly predictable from its component parts (Goldberg 2003, 2009). These pairings result from the convergence of several properties or characteristics, as illustrated in the following examples:

1. Covariational conditional construction
   The Xer the Yer: *"The more you watch the less you know"*

2. Ditransitive construction
   Subj V Obj1 Obj2: *"She gave him a kiss"*

3. Idiomatic construction: *"kick the bucket"*

Several studies and new methodologies have been applied to syntactic description in the perspective of modelling such phenomena (Bresnan 2007). The new challenge is to integrate these constructions, which are the basic elements of usage-based descriptions, into a homogeneous framework of a grammar. The problem is twofold: first, how to represent the different properties characterizing a construction; and second, how to represent the interaction between these properties in order to form a construction.

Our proposal. We seek an approach where grammars comprise usage-based descriptions. A direct consequence is to move the question away from building a syntactic structure to describing the characteristics of an input. Specifically, grammatical information should be designed in terms of statements that are not conceived of with the aim of building a structure.

We propose a presentation of a theoretical framework that integrates the main requirements of a *usage-based* perspective. Namely, it first integrates constructions into a grammar and secondly describes non-grammatical exemplars. This approach relies on a clear distinction of operational and declarative aspects of syntactic information. A first step in this direction has been achieved with *Property Grammars* (Blache 2000; Blache and Prost 2014), in which a grammar is only made of properties, all represented independently of each other. *Property Grammars* offer an adequate framework for the description of linguistic phenomena in terms of interacting properties instead of structures. We propose going one step further by integrating the notion of construction into this framework. One of the contributions of this paper, in comparison to previous works, is a formal specification of the notion of construction based on constraints only, instead of structures as in SBCG. It proposes moreover a computational method for recognizing them.

In the first section, we present a formal definition of the syntactic properties; these are used for describing any type of input. We then discuss more theoretical issues that constitute obstacles when trying to represent basic syntactic information independently of the rest of the grammar.[1] We explore in particular the consequences of representing relations between words directly, without the mediating influence of any higher-level structures or elements (i.e. without involving the notion of phrases or heads). Last, we describe how this framework can incorporate the notion of construction and detail its role in the parsing process.

2   NEW PROPERTIES FOR GRAMMARS

We seek to abstract the different types of properties that encode syntactic information. As explained above, we clearly separate the representation of such information from any pre-defined syntactic structure. In other words, we encode this information by itself, and not in respect to any structure: a basic syntactic property should not be involved in the building of a syntactic structure. It is thus necessary to provide a framework that excludes any notion of hierarchical information, such as heads or phrases: a property is a relation between two words, nothing more. Disconnecting structures and relations is the key towards the description of any kind of input as well as any type of construction.

Unlike most syntactic formalisms, we limit grammar to those aspects that are purely descriptive, excluding *operational* information. Here, the grammatical information as well as the structures proposed for representing syntactic knowledge are not determined by how they may be used during analysis. We want to avoid defining (e.g. as in constituency-based grammars) a phrase-structure rule as a step in the derivational process (corresponding to a sub-tree). In this case, the notions of projection and sisterhood eclipse all other information (linear order, co-occurrence, etc.), which becomes implicit. Likewise, in *dependency grammars*, a dependency relation corresponds to a branch on the dependency tree. In this context, subcategorization or modification information becomes dominant and supersedes other information which, in this case too, generally becomes implicit. This issue also affects modern formalisms, such as HPSG (Pollard and Sag 1994; Sag and Wasow 1999; Sag 2012) which, strictly speaking does not use

---

[1] Pullum and Scholz (2001) emphasize this characteristic as a requirement for moving away from the holistic nature of generative grammars.

phrase-structure rules but organizes syntactic information by means of principles in such a way that it has to percolate through the heads, building as a side-effect a tree-like structure.

Our approach, in the context of *Property Grammars* (hereafter *PG*) consists in identifying the different types of syntactic information in order to represent them separately. At this stage, we will organize grammatical statements around the following types of syntactic information:

- the *linear order* that exists among several categories in a construction
- the *mandatory co-occurrence* between two categories
- the *exclusion of co-occurrence* between two categories
- the impossibility of *repeating* a given category
- syntactic-semantic *dependency* between two categories (generally a category and the one that governs it)

This list of information is neither fixed nor exhaustive and could be completed according to the needs of the description of specific languages, for example with adjacency properties, completing linearity, or morphological dependencies.

Following previous formal presentations of *Property Grammars* (Duchier *et al.* 2010; Blache and Prost 2014) we propose the following notations: x, y (lower case) represent individual variables; X, Y (upper case) are set variables. We note $C(x)$ the set of individual variables in the domain assigned to the category C (cf. Backofen *et al.* (1995) for more precise definitions). We use the binary predicates $\prec$ and $\approx$ respectively for linear precedence and equality.

2.1   *Linearity*

In PG, word order is governed by a set of linearity constraints, which are based on the clause established in the ID/LP formalism (Gazdar *et al.* 1985). Unlike phrase-structure or dependency grammars, this information is, therefore, explicit. The linearity relationship between two categories is expressed as follows ($pos(x)$ being the function returning the position of x in the sentence):

$$Prec(A, B) : (\forall x, y)[(A(x) \wedge B(y) \rightarrow pos(x) < pos(y))] \qquad (1)$$

This is the same kind of linear precedence relation as proposed in GPSG (Gazdar *et al.* 1985). If the nodes x and y, respectively of category A and B, are realized,[2] then y cannot precede x.

For example, in a nominal construction in English, we can specify the following linearity properties:

$$Det \prec Adj; \quad Det \prec N; \quad Adj \prec N; \quad N \prec WhP; \quad N \prec Prep \quad (2)$$

Note that, in this set of properties, relations are expressed directly between the lexical categories (the notion of phrase-structure category is no longer used). As such, the $N \prec Prep$ property indicates precedence between these two categories regardless of their dependencies. This aspect is very important and constitutes one of the major characteristics of PG: all properties can be applied to any two items, including when no dependency or subcategorization link them.

The following example illustrates all the linearity relationships in the nominal construction *"The very old reporter who the senator attacked"* (the relative clause is not described here):

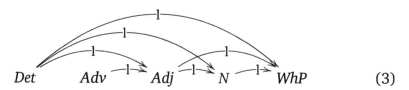

$$(3)$$

In this example, the linearity properties between two categories are independent of the *rection* (government) relations that these categories are likely to have. The linearity between *Det* and *Adj* holds even if these two categories have other dependencies (for example between the *Adj* and a modifier such as *Adv*). In theory, it could even be possible that a word dependent from the second category of the relation is realized before the first one: as such, there is no projectivity in these relations.[3] The same situation can be found for non-arguments: a linearity can be directly stipulated for example between a negative adverb and a verb. This is an argument in favour of stipulating properties directly between lexical categories rather than using phrase-structures.

---

[2] A word or a category is said to be *realized* when it occurs in the sentence to be parsed.

[3] Such a phenomenon does not exist in languages with fixed word order such as English or French.

In addition to the representation of syntactic relations, properties may be used to instantiate attribute values. For example, we can
distinguish the linearity properties between the noun and the verb,
depending on whether N is *subject* or *object* by specifying this value in
the property itself:

$$N_{[subj]} \prec V; \quad V \prec N_{[obj]} \tag{4}$$

As we shall see, all properties can be used to instantiate certain
attribute values. As is the case in *unification grammars*, attributes can
be used to reduce the scope of a property by limiting the categories
to which it can be applied. Generally speaking, a property (playing
the role of a constraint) has a dual function: control (limiting a definition domain) and instantiation (assigning values to variables, by
unification).

2.2   *Co-occurrence*

In many cases, some words or categories must co-occur in a domain,
which is typically represented by subcategorization properties. For example, the transitive schema for verbs implies that a nominal object
(complement) must be included in the structure. Such co-occurrence
constraint between two categories x and y specifies that if x is realized in a certain domain, then y must also be included. This is formally
represented as follows:

$$Req(A,B) : (\forall x)[A(x) \rightarrow \exists y B(y)] \tag{5}$$

If a node x of category A is realized, so too is a node y of category B. The co-occurrence relation is not symmetric.

As for verbal constructions, a classical example of co-occurrence
concerns nominal and prepositional complements of ditransitive
verbs, which are represented through the following properties:

$$V \Rightarrow N; \quad V_{[dit]} \Rightarrow Prep \tag{6}$$

As described in the previous section, a property is stipulated over
lexical categories, independently of their dependents and their order.

Co-occurrence represents not only complement-type relations; it
can also include co-occurrence properties directly between two categories independently from the head (thus regardless of rection rela-

tions). For example, the indefinite determiner is not generally used with a comparative superlative:[4]

(1) a. *The most interesting book of the library*
     b. **A most interesting book of the library*

In this case, there is a co-occurrence relation between the determiner and the superlative, which is represented by the property:

$$Sup \Rightarrow Det_{[def]} \tag{7}$$

Furthermore, this example shows that we can also specify variable granularity properties by applying general or more specific categories by means of attribute values.

A key point must be emphasized when using co-occurrence properties: the notion of head does not play a preponderant role in our approach. Moreover, we do not use sets of constituents within which, in constituency-based grammar, the head is distinct and indicates the type of projection. Classically in syntax, the head is considered to be the governing category, which is also the minimum mandatory component required to create a phrase. This means that the governed components must be realized together with the head. As such, this information is represented by properties establishing co-occurrence between the head and its complements. Defining a specific property that identifies the head is, therefore, not necessary.

In the case of nominal construction, the fact that N is a mandatory category is stipulated by a set of co-occurrence properties between the complements and the adjuncts to the nominal head:

$$Det \Rightarrow N_{[common]}; \quad Adj \Rightarrow N; \quad WhP \Rightarrow N; \quad Prep \Rightarrow N \tag{8}$$

The set of co-occurrence properties for the nominal construction described so far can be represented by the following graph:

$$\text{The} \quad \text{most} \quad \text{interesting} \quad \text{book} \quad \text{of} \quad \text{the} \quad \text{library} \tag{9}$$

---

[4] This constraint is limited to comparative superlatives. In some cases the use of an indefinite determiner entails a loss of this characteristic. In the sentence *"In the crowd, you had a former fastest man in the world."* the superlative becomes absolute, identifying a set of elements instead of a unique one.

We shall see later how the conjunction between co-occurrence and dependency properties is used to describe the syntactic characteristics of a head, without the need for other types of information. As such (unlike previous versions of PG), using specific properties for describing the head is not required.

At this stage, we can note that different solutions exist for representing non-headed constructions, for example when no noun is realized in a nominal construction. As we will see later, all constraints are violable. This means that a nominal construction without a noun such as in *"The very rich are different from you and me"* can be described with a violation of the co-occurrence properties stipulated above. This comes to identify a kind of implicit relation, not to say an empty category. Another solution consists in considering the adjective as a possible head of the nominal construction. In such a case, the grammar should contain another set of co-occurrence and dependency properties that are directly stipulated towards the adjective instead of the noun.

2.3   *Exclusion (co-occurrence restriction)*

In some cases, restrictions on the possibilities of co-occurrence between categories must be expressed. These include, for example, cases of lexical selection, concordance, etc. An exclusion property is defined as follows:

$$Excl(A, B) : (\forall x)(\nexists y)[A(x) \wedge B(y)] \qquad (10)$$

When a node x of category A exists, a sibling y of category B cannot exist. This is the *exclusion* relation between two constituents, that corresponds to the co-occurrence restriction in GPSG. The following properties show a few co-occurrence restrictions between categories that are likely to be included in nominal constructions:

$$Pro \otimes N; \quad N_{[prop]} \otimes N_{[com]}; \quad N_{[prop]} \otimes Prep_{[inf]} \qquad (11)$$

These properties stipulate that, in a nominal construction, the following co-occurrences cannot exist: a pronoun and a noun; a proper noun and a common noun; a proper noun and an infinitive construction introduced by a preposition.

Likewise, relative constructions can be managed based on the syntactic role of the pronoun. A relative construction introduced by a subject relative pronoun, as indicated in the following property, cannot contain a noun with this same function. This restriction is compulsory in French, where relative pronouns are case marked:

$$WhP_{[subj]} \otimes N_{[subj]} \tag{12}$$

It is worth noting that a particularity of this type of property is that it can only be verified when the entire government domain (i.e. a head and its complements/adjuncts) is known. We will discuss later the different cases of constraint satisfiability, which depend on their scope.

2.4   *Uniqueness*

Certain categories cannot be repeated inside a rection domain. More specifically, categories of this kind cannot be instantiated more than once in a given domain. This property is defined as follows:

$$Uniq(A) : (\forall x, y)[A(x) \wedge A(y) \rightarrow x \approx y] \tag{13}$$

If one node x of category A is realized, other nodes y of the same category A cannot exist. Uniqueness stipulates that constituents cannot be replicated in a given construction. Uniqueness properties are common in domain descriptions, although their importance depends upon the constructions to which they belong. The following example describes the uniqueness properties for nominal constructions:

$$Uniq = \{Det, Rel, Prep_{[inf]}, Adv\} \tag{14}$$

These properties are well established for the determiner and the relative pronoun. They also specify here that it is impossible to replicate a prepositional construction that introduces an infinitive ("*the will to stop*") or a determinative adverbial phrase ("*always more evaluation*").

Uniqueness properties are represented by a loop:

$$\overset{\curvearrowright^u}{The} \qquad book \qquad \overset{\curvearrowright^u}{that} \qquad I\ read \tag{15}$$

2.5   *Dependency*

The dependency relation in *PG* is in line with the notion of syntactic-semantic dependency defined in *Dependency Grammars*. It describes

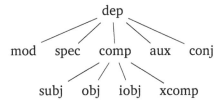

Figure 1: The hierarchy of the *dependency* relation

Table 1: The sub-types of the *dependency* relation

dep	generic relation, indicating dependency between a constructed component and its governing component
mod	modification relation (typically an adjunct)
spec	specification relation (typically *Det-N*)
comp	the most general relation between a head and an object (including the subject)
subj	dependency relation describing the subject
obj	dependency relation describing the direct object
iobj	dependency relation describing the indirect object
xcomp	other types of complementation (for example between *N* and *Prep*)
aux	relation between the auxiliary and the verb
conj	conjunction relation

different types of relations between two categories (complement, modifier, specifier, etc.). In terms of representation, this relation is arbitrarily oriented from the dependent to the head. It indicates the fact that a given object complements the syntactic organization of the target (usually the governor) and contributes to its semantic structure. In this section, we we leave aside semantics and focus on the syntactic aspect of the dependency relation.

Dependency relations are type-based and follow a type hierarchy (Figure 1); note that this hierarchy can be completed according to requirements of specific constructions or languages.

Since the dependency relation is a hierarchy, it is possible to use in a description one of these types, from the most general to the most specific, depending on the required level of precision. Each of these types and/or sub-types corresponds to a classic syntactic relation (Table 1).

Dependency relations (noted ⤳) possibly bear the dependency sub-type as an index. The following properties indicate the dependency properties applied to nominal constructions:

$$Det \leadsto_{spec} N_{[com]}; \quad Adj \leadsto_{mod} N; \quad WhP \leadsto_{mod} N \qquad (16)$$

The following example illustrates some dependencies into a nominal construction:

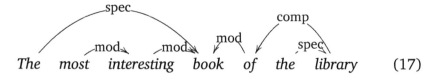

$$\text{The \quad most \quad interesting \quad book \quad of \quad the \quad library} \qquad (17)$$

In this schema, we can see the specification relations between the determiners and the corresponding nouns, and the modification relations between the adjectival and prepositional constructions as well as between the adverb and the adjective inside the adjectival construction.

Feature control: The types used in the dependency relations, while specifying the relation itself, also provide information for the dependent element. In PG, the dependency relation also assigns a value to the FUNCTION attribute of the dependent. For example, a *subject* dependency between a noun and a verb is expressed by the following property:

$$N_{[subj]} \leadsto_{subj} V \qquad (18)$$

This property instantiates the function value in the lexical structure [FUNCTION *subject*]. Similarly, dependency relations (as it is also the case for properties) make it possible to control attribute values thanks to unification. This is useful, for example, for agreement attributes that are often linked to a dependency. For instance, in French, a gender and number agreement relation exists between the determiner, the adjective and the noun. This is expressed in the following dependencies:

$$Det_{[agr_i]} \leadsto_{spec} N_{[agr_i]}; \quad Adj_{[agr_i]} \leadsto_{mod} N_{[agr_i]} \qquad (19)$$

Formal aspects: Unlike dependency grammars, this dependency relation is not strict. First of all, as the dependencies are only a part of the syntactic information, a complete dependency graph connecting all the categories/words in the sentence is not required. Moreover, dependency graphs may contain cycles: certain categories may have dependency relations with more than one component. This is the case, for example, in relative constructions: the relative pronoun depends on the main verb of the construction (a complementation relation with the verb of the relative, regardless whether it is the subject, direct object, or indirect object). But it is also a dependent of the noun that it modifies.

In PG, a cycle may also exist between two categories. Again, this is the case in the relative construction, between the verb and the relative pronoun. The relative pronoun is a complement of the main verb of the relative. It is also the target of the dependency relation originating from the verb. This relation indicates that the verb (and its dependencies) will play a role in establishing the sense of the relative construction. In this case, the dependency relation remains generic (at the higher level of the type hierarchy). The dependency properties of the relative construction stipulate:

$$WhP_{[comp]} \leadsto_{comp} V; \quad WhP \leadsto_{mod} N; \quad V \leadsto_{dep} WhP \quad (20)$$

It should be noted that the dependency relation between WhP and V bears the $comp$ type. This generic type will be specified in the grammar by one of its sub-types $subj$, obj or $iobj$, each generating different properties (in particular exclusion) for the relative. The following schema illustrates an example of a relative construction, with two particularities (the double dependency for the WhP, and the cycle between WhP and V):

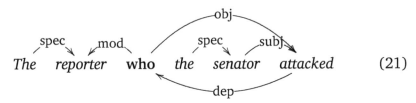

$$(21)$$

As we can see, the dependency graph in PG (as with the other properties) is not necessarily connected or cycle-free. Table 2 summarizes the main characteristics of the dependency relation.

It should be noted that these relations are stipulated taking into account the precise type of the dependency relations: they are true

Table 2: Characteristics of the *dependency* relation

Antisymmetric:	if $A \leadsto_x B$, then $B \not\leadsto_x A$
Antireflexive:	if $A \leadsto B$, then $A \neq B$
Antitransitive:	if $A \leadsto_x B$ and if $B \leadsto_x C$ then $A \not\leadsto_x C$

only for a given type, but not as a general rule. For example, a symmetric complementation relation cannot exist (if A is a complement of B, then B cannot be a complement of A). However, a cycle can appear when the dependency types are different (as seen above for $V - WhP$ dependencies).

Apart from the type-based restrictions, properties are identical to those found in dependency grammars. The main difference in PG is that the dependency graph is not necessarily connected and does not necessarily have a unique root.

Furthermore, we can see that when two realized categories (i.e. each corresponding to a word in the sentence) are linked by a property, they are usually in a dependency relation, directly or otherwise. Formally speaking, this characteristic can be expressed as follows:

Let $\mathscr{P}$ be a relation expressing a PG property, let x, y and z be categories:

$$\text{If } x \mathscr{P} y, \text{ then } x \rightsquigarrow y \vee y \rightsquigarrow x \vee [\exists z \text{ such that } x \rightsquigarrow z \wedge y \rightsquigarrow z] \quad (22)$$

Finally, dependency relations comprise two key constraints, ruling out some types of dual dependencies:

- A given category cannot have the same type of dependency with several categories[5]:

$$\text{If } x \rightsquigarrow_{dep_i} y, \text{ then } \nexists z \text{ such that } y \not\approx z \wedge x \rightsquigarrow_{dep_i} z \quad (23)$$

Example : $Pro_i \rightsquigarrow_{subj} V_j$; $Pro_i \rightsquigarrow_{subj} V_k$
The same pronoun cannot be subject of two different verbs.

- A given category cannot have two different types of dependencies with the same category:

$$\text{If } x \rightsquigarrow_{dep_i} y, \text{ then } \nexists dep_j \neq dep_i \text{ such that } x \rightsquigarrow_{type\_dep_j} y \quad (24)$$

Example : $Pro_i \rightsquigarrow_{obj} V_j$; $Pro_i \rightsquigarrow_{subj} V_j$
A given pronoun cannot simultaneously be the subject and object of a given verb.

Note that such restrictions apply for dependencies at the same level in the dependency type hierarchy. In the above example, this is

---

[5] This constraint is to be relaxed for some phenomena such as coordination, depending on the conjuncts are considered at the same level or not.

Table 3: Properties of the nominal construction

$Det \prec \{Det, Adj, WhP, Prep, N\}$	$Det \leadsto_{spec} N$
$N \prec \{Prep, WhP\}$	$Adj \leadsto_{mod} N$
$Det \Rightarrow N_{[com]}$	$WhP \leadsto_{mod} N$
$\{Adj, WhP, Prep\} \Rightarrow N$	$Prep \leadsto_{mod} N$
$Uniq = \{Pro, Det, N, WhP, Prep\}$	$Pro \otimes \{Det, Adj, WhP, Prep, N\}$
	$N_{[prop]} \otimes Det$

the case for *subj* and *obj*: such dual dependency cannot exist. Also note that these constraints do not rule out licit double dependencies such as that encountered in control phenomena (the same subject is shared by two verbs) or in the case of the relative pronoun which is both the modifier of a noun and the complement of the verb of the relative:

$$WhP \leadsto_{comp} V; \qquad WhP \leadsto_{mod} N \qquad (25)$$

In this case, the relation types represent dependencies from both inside and outside the relative clause.

2.6 *A comprehensive example*

Each property as defined above corresponds to a certain type of syntactic information. In *PG*, describing the syntactic units or linguistic phenomena (chunks, constructions) in the grammar consists in gathering all the relevant properties into a set. Table 3 summarizes the properties describing the nominal construction.

In this approach, a syntactic description, instead of being organized around a specific structure (for example a tree), consists in a set of independent (but interacting) properties together with their status (satisfied or violated). The graph in the figure below illustrates the *PG* description of the nominal construction: *"The most interesting book of the library"*.

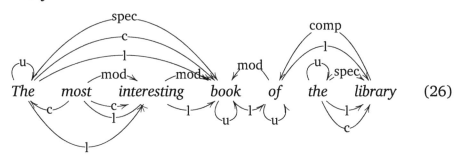

$$(26)$$

In *PG*, a syntactic description is therefore the graph containing all the properties of the grammar that can be evaluated for the sentence to be parsed. As illustrated in the example, this property graph represents explicitly all the syntactic characteristics associated to the input; each is represented independently of the others.

3   BRINGING CONSTRUCTIONS INTO PROPERTY GRAMMARS

A *construction* is defined as the convergence of several properties. For example, the ditransitive construction is, among other features, characterized by the fact that the argument roles are filled by two nominal objects in a specific order. The first step towards the recognition of a construction consists in identifying such basic properties. At this stage, no other process but the spotting of the properties needs to be used. This means that all properties should be identified directly and independently of the rest of the grammar. For example, in the case of the ditransitive construction, this consists in identifying the linear order between the nominal objects.

The issue, then, is to describe such local and basic properties, without relating them to any higher level information. As a consequence, we propose a representation in which all properties are self-contained (as presented in the previous section) in the sense that their evaluation should not depend on the recognition of other elements or structure. However, the two classical means of representing syntactic information (*constituency* or *dependency*) consist either in structuring higher-level groups (phrases in the case of constituency-based grammars) or assigning a specific role to the head in the definition of a branching structure (in the case of dependency grammars). In this section, we explore in greater detail these aspects and their consequences when trying to represent basic properties directly. Our analysis is built around three issues: the notion of syntactic group, the status of the head, and the kind of information to be encoded in the lexicon for the representation of basic properties.

3.1   *Constructions as sets of properties*

Constituency-based approaches rely on the definition of syntactic properties in terms of membership: a syntactic object is characterized by its set of constituents. This approach offers several advantages in describing the distributional properties of syntactic groups, for example. Moreover, it constitutes a direct framework for controlling the scope of local properties (such as linearity or co-occurrence restriction): they are valid within a *domain* (a phrase).

Using this notion of domain proves interesting for constraint-based frameworks in which a phrase is described by a set of categories to which several constraints apply (offering a direct control of the scope of constraints). However, such an approach requires the organization of syntactic information into two separate types, forming two different levels: on the one hand, the definition of the domain (the set of categories, the phrase) and, on the other hand, their linguistic properties. In terms of representation (in the grammar), this means giving priority to the definition of the domain (the identification of the set of constituents, for example by means of rules or schemas). The constraints come on top of this first level, adding more information. In terms of parsing, the strategy also follows this dual level organization: first recognizing the set of categories (for example *Det, N, Rel, ...* for the *NP*), then evaluating constraint satisfaction.

The problem with this organization is that it gives priority to a certain type of information, namely constituency, that is motivated by operational matters (representation and construction of the syntactic structure) more than by linguistic considerations: sisterhood in itself does not provide much syntactic knowledge or, more precisely, is too vague in comparison with the syntactic properties binding two categories (e.g. co-occurrence, restriction, dependency). Moreover, this organization has a severe drawback: a linguistic description is only possible when the first level (identification of the set of categories) is completed. In other words, it is necessary to build a phrase before being able to evaluate its properties. This approach does not fit with the notion of construction for several reasons. First, a construction is not necessarily composed of adjacent constituents. A constituency-based grammar cannot handle such objects directly. Moreover, constructions can be formed with a variable structure (elements of varying types, non-mandatory elements, etc.), due to the fact that they encode a convergence of different sources of information (phonology, morphology, semantics, syntax, etc.). An organization in terms of constituents relies on a representation driven by syntax, which renders impossible a description in terms of interaction of properties and domains as is the case with construction-based approaches.

Our goal is to integrate a multi-domain perspective, based on a description in terms of constructions, that is capable of dealing with any kind of input (including ill-formed or non-canonical realizations). We propose a representation of the linguistic information in terms of properties that are all at the same level. In other words, all information needs to be represented in the same manner, without any priority given to one type of information over another. No domain, set of categories or phrase should be built before being able to describe the linguistic characteristics of an input: a linguistic property should be identified directly, independently of any other structure.

As a consequence, properties need to be represented as such in the grammar (i.e. independently of any notion of constituency) and used directly during parsing (i.e. without needing to build a set of categories first). This goal becomes possible provided that the scope of the property is controlled. One way to do this consists in specifying precisely the categories in relation. Two types of information can be used with this perspective: the specification of certain features (limiting the kinds of objects to which the property can be applied), and the use of an HPSG-like category indexing (making it possible to specify when two categories from two properties refer to the same object).

As such, integrating the notion of construction should not make use of the notion of constituency but rather favour a description based on direct relations between words (or lexical categories). Thus, we fall in line with a perspective that is akin to dependency grammars, except for the fact that we intend to use a larger variety of properties to describe the syntax and not focus exclusively on dependency. In the remainder of this section we will present a means of representing constructions only using such basic properties.

3.2   *The question of heads: to have or not to have?*

The notion of head plays a decisive role in most linguistic theories: syntax is usually described in terms of government or dependency between a head and its dependents. In *constituency-based grammars*, the head bears a special relation to its projection (the root of the local tree it belongs to). In *dependency grammars*, a head is the target of the relations from the depending categories. The role of the head can be even more important in lexicalized theories such as LFG (Bresnan 1982) or HPSG. In this case, the head is also an operational element in the construction of the syntactic structure: it represents the site through which all information (encoded by features) percolates. All exocentric syntactic relations (between a phrase constituent and another component outside this phrase) are expressed as feature values which, as a result of a number of principles, move from the source constituent to the target, passing through the head.

A direct consequence is that when heads play a central role, syntactic information needs to be represented in a strictly hierarchical manner: as the head serves as a gateway, it is also a *reduction* point from which all information relating to the head's dependents may be accessed. Such a strict hierarchical conception of syntax has a formal consequence: the syntactic structure must be represented as a hierarchical (or a tree-like) structure in which every component (word, category, phrase, etc.) is dependent on a higher-level element. Such a syntactic organization is not suited for the description of many phenomena that we come across in *natural* language. For example, many constructions have no overt head:

(2) a. *John sets the red cube down and takes the black.*
     b. *First trip, New York.*
     c. *Monday, washing, Tuesday, ironing, Wednesday, rest.*

Example (2a) presents a classical elision as part of a conjunction: the second NP has no head. This is also the case in the nominal sentences in examples (2b) and (2c), which correspond to binary structures where each nominal component holds an argumentative position (from the semantic point of view) without a head being realized. We already gave some arguments towards the non-headed construction analysis in the second section. In the case of the last two examples, little information can be given at the syntactic level; it mainly comes from the interaction of morphology, prosody and discourse. The solution in PG (not developed in this paper) consists in implementing interaction constraints for controlling the alignment of properties coming from the different domains (Blache and Prévot 2010).

This raises the issue of structures that can be adapted to the representation of linguistic relations outside the head/dependent relation. The example of collective nouns in French illustrates such a situation:

(3) a. *un ensemble de catégories* (a set of categories)
     b. **un ensemble des catégories* (a set of-plu categories)
     c. *l'ensemble de catégories* (the set of categories)
     d. *l'ensemble des catégories* (the set of-plu categories)

If a collective noun is specified by an indefinite determiner, then the complex category preposition-determiner *de* ("of") – which, in this case, is a partitive – can only be used in its singular form. This construction is controlled by the exclusion property:

$$Det_{[ind]} \otimes \{Prep + Det_{[plu]}\} \qquad (27)$$

Inside a nominal construction with a collective noun, we have a direct constraint between the type of determiner (definite or indefinite) and the preposition agreement feature without any mediation of the head. In order to be complete, this property has to be restricted to those determiners which specify a collective noun. This is implemented by a co-indexation mechanism between categories, that is described in section 3.4 below.

Generally speaking, the head plays a fundamental role in specifying the subcategorization or the argument structure. It is not, however, necessary to give it an operational role when constructing the syntactic structure. We shall see that the head, even with no specific role, can be identified only as being the category to which all dependency relations converge.

3.3   *The structure of lexical entries*

As in unification grammars, the lexical information is highly important. Nonetheless, the lexicalization of syntactic information (emphasized in theories such as LFG or HPSG) is more limited in PG. In particular, the lexicon does not play a direct role in the construction of the syntactic structure; rather, all information is borne by the properties. Lexical information, although rich, is only used on the one hand to control the scope of the properties (as described above) and on the other hand to instantiate the subcategorization or the specific dependencies that one category can have with others.

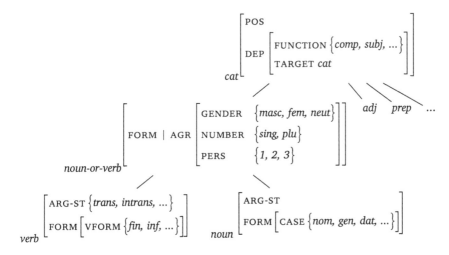

Figure 2: Inheritance in nominal and verbal categories

In general, a lexical entry is associated with an attribute-value matrix which basically contains the category, agreement, morpho-syntactic features, subcategorization list and grammatical function (when relevant). This structure can be enriched with other features, for example those describing semantics, phonology, etc. It can also be completed depending on the category, with more specific information such as mood, tense, person, or the valence feature that gives the list of arguments required.

Figure 2 summarizes the main features of nominal and verbal cat-egories. It represents a type hierarchy, while the subtypes inherit "ap-propriate" features from the higher-level types.

The most general type, *cat*, comprises features appropriate to the description of all categories: the category label as well as the descrip-tion of its dependency with other categories. This relation is described by the type of the dependency and the target value of the relation. In the above example, the lower level subtypes describe the features ap-propriate to *N* and *V*: both categories take agreement. Moreover, the verb has an argument structure which specifies its valence as well as its form attributes. As for the noun, it is associated with case features.

3.4   *The role of features*

Properties are relations between two lexical categories (that may po-tentially have other dependencies). For example, a linear property such as $V \prec N_{[obj]}$ indicates that the verb precedes the direct object.

This relation holds regardless of the other dependency relations of V and N. However, in this example, specifying the function value is mandatory: without it, the property would not be valid ($V \prec N$ is not licit as such in English).

The instantiation of feature values of a category involved in a property reduces its definition domain and, as a side effect, the scope of the property. Moreover, with all properties being independent of each other, it is necessary to provide as much information as possible to identify precisely the categories to be linked. Representing a property in this way renders them absolute, in the manner of *Optimality Theory* (Prince and Smolensky 1993), in which all constraints are universal. In this approach, a property can be evaluated directly, without needing any knowledge of the context or the rest of the syntactic structure. This condition is imperative when trying to consider a grammar as a set of properties.

We present two series of examples illustrating how feature instantiation helps in controlling the application of a property.

Control by feature values. The specification of feature values in properties can be used in order to describe certain phenomena directly. For example, the argument structure can be described by means of linearity and dependency properties, assigning subcategorization and case feature values:

$$
\begin{array}{ll}
V \Rightarrow N_{[subj]} & V_{[trans]} \Rightarrow N_{[obj]} \\
V_{[intrans]} \otimes N_{[obj]} & V_{[ditrans]} \Rightarrow N_{[iobj]}
\end{array}
\qquad (28)
$$

Likewise, the different possible constructions of the relative in French can be described by specifying the case of the relative pronoun:

$$
\begin{array}{ll}
WhP_{[nom]} \otimes N_{[subj]} & WhP_{[nom]} \rightsquigarrow_{subj} V \\
WhP_{[acc]} \otimes N_{[obj]} & WhP_{[nom]} \rightsquigarrow_{obj} V
\end{array}
\qquad (29)
$$

These properties stipulate that the nominative relative pronoun *qui* ("who") excludes the possibility to realize a subject within the relative construction and specifies a subject-type dependency relation between the relative pronoun and the verb. The same type of restriction is specified for the accusative pronoun *que* ("which") and could also be extended to the dative pronoun *dont* ("of which/of whom"). These properties implement the long-distance dependency between *WhP* and the "gap" in the argument structure of the main verb.

Table 4: Inverse dependencies between *Prep* and *N*

Construction	Properties	Example	Property graph
Prepositional	$Prep \prec N$ $N \leadsto_{xcomp} Prep$	*"on the table"*	
Nominal	$N \prec Prep$ $Prep \leadsto_{mod} N$	*"the book on ..."*	

Control by co-indexation. We illustrate here the possibility of controlling the application of properties thanks to the co-indexation of the categories involved in different properties. The following example describes the relative order between *Prep* and *N*, which is governed by the type of construction in which they are involved: the preposition precedes the noun in a prepositional construction whereas it follows it in a nominal one. Table 4 presents a first description of these different cases, illustrated with an example.

As such, it is necessary to specify the *linearity* and *dependency* properties between *Prep* and *N* according to the construction they belong to. In order to distinguish between these two cases, we specify the syntactic functions. The following feature structures specify the dependency features of *N*, illustrating here the cases of the subject of a *V* and a complement of a *Prep*:

$$
\text{(a) } N \begin{bmatrix} \text{DEP} \begin{bmatrix} \text{FUNCTION } mod \\ \text{TARGET } V \end{bmatrix} \end{bmatrix}
\qquad
\text{(b) } N \begin{bmatrix} \text{DEP} \begin{bmatrix} \text{FUNCTION } xcomp \\ \text{TARGET } Prep \end{bmatrix} \end{bmatrix}
$$

(30)

Using this representation, the distinction between the two cases of dependency between *N* and *Prep* relies on the specification of the function and target features of the categories (Table 5). Moreover, a co-indexation makes it possible to link the properties.

These properties stipulate an order and a dependency relation; these are determined by the syntactic roles. In a nominal construction, the noun precedes the prepositional construction that modifies it, whereas the preposition precedes the noun in the other construction. Two classical mechanisms, based on unification, are used in these

Table 5: Co-indexation between constraints

Construction type	Constraints
Nominal	$N_i \prec Prep \begin{bmatrix} \text{FCT } mod \\ \text{TGT } N_i \end{bmatrix}$ $Prep \begin{bmatrix} \text{FCT } mod \\ \text{TGT } N_i \end{bmatrix} \rightsquigarrow_{mod} N_i$
Prepositional	$Prep_i \prec N \begin{bmatrix} \text{FCT } xcomp \\ \text{TGT } Prep_i \end{bmatrix}$ $N \begin{bmatrix} \text{FCT } xcomp \\ \text{TGT } Prep_i \end{bmatrix} \rightsquigarrow_{xcomp} Prep_i$

properties: first, the specification of the dependency attribute controls the application of the properties (the N following $Prep$ is its complement, the $Prep$ that follows N modifies it). Moreover, index unification (marked by the use of the same index i in the previous examples) ensures that the category is identical across all relations: the co-indexation of the categories in the different properties imposes a reference to the same object.

4   REPRESENTING AND PROCESSING CONSTRUCTIONS

Syntactic information is usually defined with respect to a specific domain (a set of categories). For example, the precedence property between Det and N only makes sense within a nominal construction. The following example illustrates this situation, showing the possible relations corresponding to the linearity property $Det \prec N$. These relations are represented regardless of any specific domain (i.e. between all the determiners and nouns of the sentence). Same-category words are distinguished by different indices:

$$
\begin{array}{ccccc}
Det_1 & \longleftrightarrow N_1 & V & Det_2 & \longrightarrow N_2 \\
\text{The} & \text{man} & \text{reads} & \text{the} & \text{book}
\end{array} \tag{31}
$$

In this example, the relation $Det_1 \prec N_2$ connects two categories that clearly do not belong to the same domain. More generally, the subsets of categories $\{Det_1, N_1\}$ and $\{Det_2, N_2\}$ form possible units, unlike $\{Det_1, N_2\}$. The problem is that, as explained in the previous section, properties need to be assessed and evaluated independently of any a priori knowledge of a specific domain: a property in the grammar is not specifically attached to a set of categories (a phrase or a dependent). However, linguistic description relies mainly on the identification of local phenomena that corresponds to the notion of *construction* such as that specified in *Construction Grammars* (Fillmore 1988). It is, therefore, necessary to propose an approach fulfilling both requirements: the representation of properties independently and the description of local phenomena as sets of properties.

We propose in the next two sections to examine constructions through two different perspectives: one concerning their representation and the other describing their processing. In the first perspective, constructions are described as sets of interacting properties. In the latter, constructions are recognized on the basis of topological characteristics of the property graph (representing sets of evaluated properties).

4.1   *In grammar: construction = set of properties*

Grammars organize syntactic information on the basis of structures to which different relations can be applied. In phrase-structure grammars, the notion of *phrase* implicitly comprises the definition of a domain (the set of constituents) in which the relations are valid. This notion of domain also exists in theories like HPSG, using generic tree schemata that are completed with the subcategorization information borne by lexical entries (both pieces of information together effectively correspond to the notion of constituency). Dependency grammars, in contrast, integrate syntactic information in the dependency relation between a head and its dependents. In both cases, the question of the scope of syntactic relations relies on the topology of the structures: a relation is valid inside a local tree. Therefore, a domain typically corresponds to a set of categories that share common properties.

Our approach relies on a *decentralized* representation of syntactic information by means of relations that can be evaluated independently of the entire structure. In other words, any property can be assessed alone, without needing to evaluate any other. For example, the assessment of linearity between two categories is done without taking into account any other information such as subcategorization. In this case, we can evaluate the properties of a construction without having to create a syntactic tree: *PG* is based on a *dynamic* definition of the notion of construction. This means that all properties are assessed separately, a construction being the set of independently evaluated properties.[6]

In *Construction Grammars*, a construction is defined by the interaction of relations originating from different sources (lexical, syntactic, semantic, prosodic, etc.). This approach makes it possible to describe a wide variety of facts, from lexical selection to syntactico-semantic interactions (Goldberg 2003; Kay and Fillmore 1999; Lambrecht 1995). A construction is then intended as a linguistic *phenomenon* that is composed of syntactic units as well as other types of structures such as multi-word expressions, specific turns, etc. The notion of construction is, therefore, more general than that of syntactic unit and not necessarily based on a structured representation of information (e.g. a tree).

PG provides an adequate framework for the representation of constructions. First, a syntactic description is the interaction of several sources of information and properties. Moreover, *PG* is a constraint-based theory in which each piece of information corresponds to a constraint (or property). The description of a construction in a *PG* grammar is a set of properties connecting several categories. This definition gives priority to the relations instead of their arguments, which means that a prior definition of the set of constituents involved in the construction is not necessary.[7] As a consequence, the notion of constraint scope is not directly encoded: each property is specified independently and the grammar is a set of constructions, each described by a set of properties.

The following example illustrates the encoding of the ditransitive construction, focusing on the relation between the type of categories (*N* or *Prep*), their linear order and their function:

---

[6] A direct implementation of this mechanism consists in assessing all the possible properties, for all the combinations of words/categories, which is exponential. Different possibilities of controlling this complexity exists, such as delayed evaluation or probabilistic selection.

[7] In previous versions of *PG*, all categories belonging to a construction were indicated in a list of constituents.

$$V_{[ditrans]} \Rightarrow N_{[obj]} \qquad N_{[obj]} \rightsquigarrow_{obj} V_{[ditrans]}$$
$$V_{[ditrans]} \Rightarrow X_{[iobj]} \qquad N_{[iobj]} \rightsquigarrow_{iobj} V_{[ditrans]}$$
$$N_{[iobj]} \prec N_{[obj]} \qquad Prep_{[iobj]} \rightsquigarrow_{iobj} V_{[ditrans]}$$
$$N_{[obj]} \prec Prep_{[iobj]}$$

The two first co-occurrence properties stipulate that the ditransitive verb governs a nominal object plus an indirect object of unspecified category encoded by X (that could be, according to the rest of the properties, either a nominal or a prepositional construction). Linearity properties stipulate that in the case of a double nominal construction, the nominal indirect object should precede the direct object. Otherwise, the direct object precedes the indirect prepositional construction. Finally, the dependency relations instantiate, according to their function, the type of the dependency with the verb.

4.2   *In analysis: construction = government domain*

The theoretical and naïve parsing principle in PG consists in evaluating all properties that may exist between all categories corresponding to the words in a sentence. This set of properties contains considerable noise: most of the properties evaluated in this way link categories which do not belong to the same domain. The issue is to elicit the constructions existing in this set. Concretely, the set of properties forms a graph from which the connected categories may correspond to a construction. In the following, we put forward a formal characterisation of the notion of construction in terms of graph topology.

Generally speaking, two types of properties can be distinguished, based on the number of categories they involve:

- Binary properties, where two categories are connected: linearity, dependency, co-occurrence
- Unary properties: uniqueness, exclusion

Unary relations, because of their specificity, do not have any features that may be used to identify the construction. On the contrary, the three types of binary properties are the basis of the domain identification mechanism. The following graph illustrates the characterisation of the sentence "*A very old book is on the table.*":

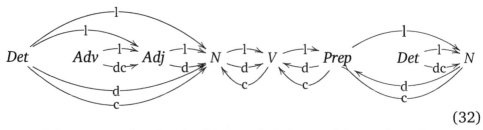

$$(32)$$

It is noteworthy that in this graph, it is possible to identify several subgraphs in which all the categories are interconnected. Formally, they are referred to as being *complete*: a complete graph is a graph where all nodes are connected[8]. In this example, the nodes labelled by *Adv* and *Adj* form a complete subgraph: both categories are connected. On the other hand, the set of categories {*Det, Adv, Adj*} does not form a complete subgraph, the *Det* and *Adv* categories being disconnected.

Furthermore, when eliciting a construction, it is necessary to take into account all the categories of the same constraint network. For example, the *Adj* and *N* nodes could form a complete subgraph, but it would be a subset of another more complete subgraph {*Det, Adj, N*} subset. As a consequence, we only take into consideration *maximal complete subgraphs*.

The maximal complete subgraphs in the previous example correspond to the subsets of the following nodes (Table 6) to which we have associated a construction type.

Table 6: Constructions as complete subgraphs

Adv − Adj	Adjectival construction
Det − Adj − N	Nominal construction
N − V	Subject/verb construction
V − Prep	Verb/indirect object construction
Prep − N	Prepositional construction
Det − N	Nominal construction

As such, based on a graph topology, we can identify constructions for which the following definition can be given:

---

[8] For clarity's sake, only such subgraphs have been represented here. A complete graph would bear all possible relations, including not relevant ones, such as linearity between the first *Det* and the lat *N*. This would not change the identification and the properties of the complete subgraphs such as described here.

Definition: *A construction is a maximal complete subgraph of the property graph.*

Concretely, these subsets correspond to syntactic units. Yet, where classical approaches rely on the definition of constructions a priori in the grammar, this definition proposes a dynamic and a posteriori description. This is fundamental: it makes it possible to describe any type of sentence, regardless of its grammaticality. Analyzing a sentence consists in interpreting the property graph. This structure may contain constructions that lead directly to a semantic interpretation. But it can also be the case that the property graph contains subparts that are not necessarily connected with the rest of the sentence. This situation occurs with ungrammatical sentences.

At this stage, exhibiting the set of relevant constructions for the description of a sentence consists in identifying, among the set of maximal complete subgraphs, those that cover the set of words: in the optimal case, the set of nodes of the exhibited constructions corresponds to the set of words in the sentence. Note that in theory, constructions can overlap, which means that the same node could belong to different constructions. This characteristic is useful when combining different domains of linguistic description, including prosody, discourse, etc. However, when studying a single domain, for example syntax, it is useful to reduce overlapping: a category belonging to a construction can contribute to another construction provided it is its head. The task is therefore to exhibit the optimal set of constructions, covering the entire input.

5   PARSING BY SATISFYING CONSTRAINTS

Parsing a sentence S consists in firstly determining and evaluating the set of properties relevant for the input and secondly in exhibiting the constructions. In the second stage, it is necessary to establish all the partitions of the suite of categories that correspond to S. The issue is to know which parts correspond to a construction and whether an *optimal* partition exists.

In the first stage, an operational semantics describing conditions of satisfiability must be assigned to the properties. In this perspective, we introduce some preliminary notions:

- **Set of property categories**: Let p be a property. We define a function **Cat(p)** building the set of categories contained in p. For example, $Cat(Det \prec N) = \{Det, N\}$.
- **Applicable properties**: Given a grammar G and a set of categories C, the set of *C-applicable properties* is the set of all the properties of G in which the categories of C appear. More specifically, a property p is *applicable* when its evaluation becomes possible. Two types of properties can be distinguished: those requiring the realization of all the categories they involve (uniqueness, linearity and dependency) and the properties needing at least one of their categories to be evaluated (co-occurrence and exclusion). As such, we have:

Definition: Let $p \in G$:

  - p is a *uniqueness, linearity* or *dependency* property: p is an *applicable property* for C iff $[Cat(p) \subset C]$
  - p is a *co-occurrence* or *exclusion* property: p is an *applicable property* for C iff $[Cat(p) \cap C \neq \emptyset]$

- **Position in the string** : We define a function **Pos(c, C)**, returning the rank of c in the category suite C

An operational semantic definition may be assigned to each property as in Table 7 (C being a set of categories).

Table 7: Properties' operational semantics

- Uniqueness: $Uniq_x$ holds in C iff $\forall y \in C - \{x\}$, then $x \not\approx y$
- Exclusion: $x \otimes y$ holds in C iff $\forall z \in C - \{x\}$, then $z \not\approx y$
- Co-occurrence: $x \Rightarrow y$ holds in C iff $\{x, y\} \subset C$
- Linearity: $x \prec y$ holds in C iff $pos(x, C) < pos(y, C)$

These definitions provide the conditions of satisfiability of the different properties. It now becomes possible to illustrate how the description of the syntactic structure can be built.

The construction of the syntactic description (called the *characterisation*) of a construction consists in evaluating the set of its applicable properties. In more general terms, parsing a sentence consists in evaluating all the relevant properties and then determining the corresponding constructions. Formally:

let S be the set of categories of a sentence to be parsed,
let $Part_S$ be a partition of S,

let p be one subpart of $Part_S$,

let $Prop_p$ be the set of applicable properties of p.

The categories belonging to p part are instantiated: their feature values, as determined by the corresponding lexical entries, are known insofar as they correspond to the words of the sentence to be parsed. The properties in $Prop_p$ stipulate constraints in which the categories are fully instantiated (by the unification of the categories of the properties in the grammar and those realized in the sentence). We define $Sat(Prop_p)$ as the constraint system formed by both applicable properties and the state of their satisfaction after evaluation (true or false).

Table 8 presents two examples of nominal constructions along with their characterisations; the second example contains a linear constraint violation between *Det* and *Adj*.

This example illustrates a key aspect of *Property Grammars*: their ability to describe an ill-formed sentence. Furthermore, we also note that in this description, in spite of the property violation, the nominal construction is characterized by a large number of satisfied constraints. This characteristic allows one to introduce a crucial element for usage-based grammars: *compensation* phenomena between positive and negative information. We know that constraint violation can be an element of difficulty for human or automatic processing. The idea is that the violation of constraints can be compensated by the satis-

Table 8: Characterisations of nominal constructions

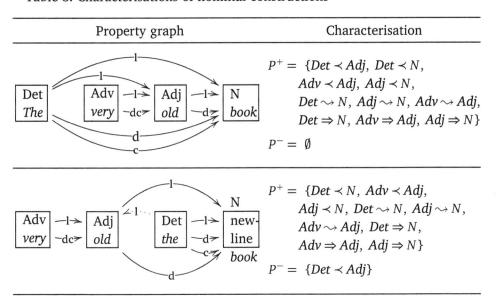

Property graph	Characterisation
	$P^+ = \{Det \prec Adj,\ Det \prec N,$ $Adv \prec Adj,\ Adj \prec N,$ $Det \rightsquigarrow N,\ Adj \rightsquigarrow N,\ Adv \rightsquigarrow Adj,$ $Det \Rightarrow N,\ Adv \Rightarrow Adj,\ Adj \Rightarrow N\}$ $P^- = \emptyset$
	$P^+ = \{Det \prec N,\ Adv \prec Adj,$ $Adj \prec N,\ Det \rightsquigarrow N,\ Adj \rightsquigarrow N,$ $Adv \rightsquigarrow Adj,\ Det \Rightarrow N,$ $Adv \Rightarrow Adj,\ Adj \Rightarrow N\}$ $P^- = \{Det \prec Adj\}$

faction of some others. For example, the violation of a precedence constraint can be compensated by the satisfaction of co-occurrence and dependency ones. PG offers the possibility to quantify these compensation effects, on the basis of complexity evaluation (Blache *et al.* 2006; Blache 2011).

One important issue when addressing the question of parsing is that of ambiguity. The problem is twofold: how to represent ambiguity and how to deal with it. With syntactic information being represented in terms of graphs, it is theoretically possible to represent different types of attachment at the same time. It is possible to have in the property graph two dependency relations of the same type, which are then mutually exclusive. The control of ambiguity resolution can be done classically, thanks to preference options implemented by property weights.

6   AN APPLICATION TO TREEBANKING

The use of treebanks offers a direct framework for the experimentation and the comparison of syntactic formalisms. Most of them have been developed using classical constituency or dependency-based representations. They have then to be adapted when studying more specific proposals. We present in this section an approach making it possible to extract properties from existing treebanks.

Most of the properties presented in this paper can be extracted automatically under some conditions, following a method presented in Blache *et al.* (2016). This is in particular the case with linearity, uniqueness, co-occurrence and exclusion, on which we focus in this section. The three first properties can be inferred fully automatically, the last one has to be filtered manually after its automatic extraction. The mechanism consists of two steps:

1. Extraction of the implicit context-free grammar
2. Generation of the properties from the CFG

In order to validate the approach, we have tested the method on several treebanks that offer different representations. We used first a set of four large constituency-based treebanks: the *Penn Treebank* (Marcus *et al.* 1994) itself, the *Chinese Treebank* (Xue *et al.* 2010), the *Arabic Treebank* (Maamouri *et al.* 2003), and the *French Treebank*

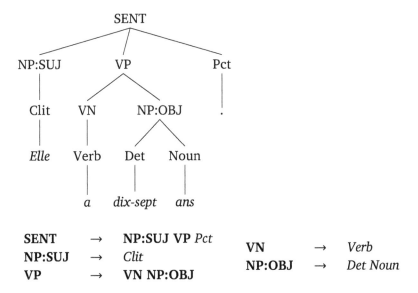

Figure 3: Constituent tree and inferred CFG rules

(Abeillé *et al.* 2003). In a second stage, we have applied property extraction to the *Universal Dependencies Treebank* (Nivre *et al.* 2015). We offer a brief overview of this ongoing work presently.

The extraction of a context-free grammar (CFG) from a constituency treebank is based on a simple method described in Charniak (1996). Each internal node of a tree is converted into a rule in which the left-hand side (LHS) is the root and the right-hand side (RHS) is the sequence of constituents. The implicit grammar is composed of the complete set of rules. Figure 3 shows the syntactic tree associated with the French sentence *Elle a dix-sept ans* ("She is seventeen"), together with the corresponding CFG rules.

We applied a similar approach to dependency treebanks. In this case, a root node (LHS of a rule) is a head, while the constituents (RHS) form its list of dependents, following the projection order by which the head is added (encoded with the symbol *).

Figure 4 illustrates the dependency tree of the same sentence as in Figure 3 with the extracted CFG rules.

Using these grammars, it is straightforward to extract the properties that we consider in this experiment, which we describe in Figure 5.

The treebanks and the generated resources are serialized as XML; this facilitates editing and visualization. We have developed software to view the different types of information: treebanks, tagset, extracted grammar, rules, and properties. Each type of information is associated

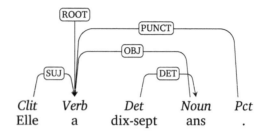

$$Verb:ROOT \quad \rightarrow \quad Clit:SUJ * Noun:OBJ\ Pct:PUNCT$$
$$Noun:OBJ \quad \rightarrow \quad Det:DET *$$

Figure 4: Dependency tree and inferred CFG rules

Linearity: the precedence table is built while verifying – for each category preceding another category into a construction (or a right-hand side) – whether this relation is valid throughout the set of constructions	$\forall\ rhs_m \in RHS(XP)$ $\quad$**if** $((\exists\ (c_i, c_j) \in rhs_m \mid c_i \prec c_j)$ $\quad$**and** $(\nexists\ rhs_n \in RHS(XP) \mid (c_i, c_j) \in rhs_n$ $\quad\quad\quad \wedge c_i \prec c_j))$ $\quad$**then** add $prec(c_i, c_j)$
Uniqueness: the set of categories that cannot be repeated in a right-hand side	$\forall\ rhs_m \in RHS(XP)$ $\quad \forall\ (c_i, c_j) \in rhs_m$ $\quad\quad$**if** $c_i \neq c_j$ **then** add $uniq(c_i)$
Requirement: identification of two categories that co-occur systematically in all constructions of an XP	$\forall\ rhs_m \in RHS(XP)$ $\quad bool \leftarrow ((c_i \in rhs_m) \wedge (c_j \in rhs_m))$ $\quad$**if** $bool$ **then** add $req(c_i, c_j)$
Exclusion: when two categories never co-occur in the entire set of constructions, they are supposed to be mutually exclusive; this is a strong interpretation, which causes an overgeneration of such constraints, but there is no other way to identify this phenomenon automatically	$\forall\ rhs_m \in RHS(XP)$ $\quad bool \leftarrow \neg((c_i \in rhs_m) \wedge (c_j \in rhs_m))$ $\quad$**if** $bool$ **then** add $excl(c_i, c_j)$

Figure 5: Property extraction procedures

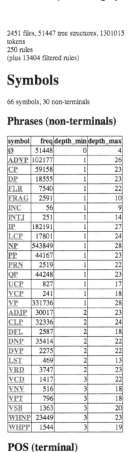

2451 files, 51447 tree structures, 1301015 tokens
250 rules
(plus 13404 filtered rules)

Symbols

66 symbols, 30 non-terminals

Phrases (non-terminals)

symbol	freq	depth_min	depth_max
Ø	51448	0	4
ADVP	102177	1	26
CP	59158	1	23
DP	18555	1	23
FLR	7540	1	22
FRAG	2591	1	10
INC	56	1	9
INTJ	251	1	14
IP	182191	1	27
LCP	17801	1	24
NP	543849	1	28
PP	44167	1	23
PRN	2519	1	22
QP	44248	1	23
UCP	827	1	17
VCP	241	1	18
VP	331736	1	28
ADJP	30017	2	23
CLP	32336	2	24
DFL	2587	2	18
DNP	35414	2	22
DVP	2275	2	22
LST	469	2	13
VRD	3747	2	23
VCD	1417	3	22
VNV	516	3	18
VPT	796	3	18
VSB	1363	3	20
WHNP	23449	3	23
WHPP	1544	3	19

POS (terminal)

symbol	freq	depth_min	depth_max
PU	176047	1	24

1 rules A 'alway succeeds' {B}' (DAG)

symbol	succeeds				
NP		nb_rules	occurrences	frequence	rules
	CP	1	14762	3.69%	6
	DP	1	11009	2.75%	9
	QP	1	11704	2.93%	8
	ADJP	1	10788	2.70%	10
	DNP	1	22966	5.75%	5

Obligation

This set of 5 symbols covers all rules and they are mutually exclusive

symbol	nb_rules	occurrences	frequence	rules
NR	1	48692	12.18%	1
NN	3	208565	52.19%	0 2 11
NT	1	12712	3.18%	7
PN	1	30572	7.65%	3
NP	6	99119	24.80%	4 5 6 8 9 10

Uniqueness

8 symbols that occurs only one time per rule

symbol	nb_rules	occurrences	frequence	rules
ADJP	1	10788	2.70%	10
NR	1	48692	12.18%	1
NT	1	12712	3.18%	7
DP	1	11009	2.75%	9
PN	1	30572	7.65%	3
QP	1	11704	2.93%	8
CP	1	14762	3.69%	6
DNP	1	22966	5.75%	5

Figure 6: Properties from the *Chinese Treebank*

with a link to a corresponding example in the treebank. Figure 6 illustrates some properties of a *NP* extracted from the *Chinese Treebank*.

In our interface, the left part of the window lists the set of categories of the grammar, together with frequency information. Non-terminals are hyperlinked to their corresponding syntactic description (corresponding PS-rules and properties). This information is displayed in the top right of the window. Each property (in this example *Obligation* and *Uniqueness*) comes with the set of rules starting from which it has been generated. Links to the different occurrences of the corresponding trees in the treebank are also listed. The lower right side of the window contains a graphical representation of the tree structure.

7   CONCLUSION

Describing linguistic phenomena by means of atomic, low-level, and independent properties makes possible the joining of formal and descriptive linguistics. We are now in position to propose a general account of language processing, capable of integrating the description of local phenomena into a global architecture and making it possible to benefit from the best of the descriptive and formal approaches.

Usage-based theories describe language starting from the data, identifying different linguistic phenomena and gathering them into a set of descriptions. In the same perspective, *Construction Grammars* represent phenomena in terms of constructions. We have proposed in this paper an extended version of *Property Grammars* (PG), that represents all syntactic information by means of properties that can interact. *PG* has the advantage of being very flexible: properties are local and independent of each other, able to represent any local relation between words or categories. This characteristic solves the issue raised by Pullum and Scholz (2001), showing the limits of a *holistic* approach in grammars, in which all statements are dependent on each other (for example, a phrase-structure rule is not considered in and of itself, but rather as a step in the derivation process corresponding to a piece of the final syntactic tree). In *PG* all information is described by means of properties; these can remain local or can interact with other properties.

PG thus offers a formal framework for representing *constructions*, which are considered as a set of interacting properties. It also constitutes a homogeneous approach integrating both views of syntactic description: a usage-based one, aimed at describing specific phenomena; and a formal one that proposes a general organization in terms of grammars. Moreover, a syntactic description given in terms of properties makes it possible to describe ill-formed inputs: a property graph is not necessarily connected, and can even contain violated properties.

As a perspective, on top of being an adequate framework for a precise description of unrestricted linguistic material, *Property Grammars* also offer a framework for an evaluation of the quality of syntactic information associated to an input, based on an analysis of the syntactic description (the quantity and the importance of satisfied properties, their coverage, etc.). This also paves the way towards a cognitive account of language processing, capable of evaluating the relative importance of local phenomena within a general description.

REFERENCES

Bas AARTS (2004), Modelling Linguistic Gradience, *Studies in Language*, 28(1):1–49.

Anne ABEILLÉ, Lionel CLÉMENT, and François TOUSSENEL (2003), Building a Treebank for French, in A. ABEILLÉ, editor, *Treebanks*, Kluwer, Dordrecht.

Rolf BACKOFEN, James ROGERS, and K. VIJAY-SHANKER (1995), A First-Order Axiomatization of the Theory of Finite Trees, *Journal of Logic, Language, and Information*, 4(1).

Philippe BLACHE (2000), Constraints, Linguistic Theories and Natural Language Processing, in D. CHRISTODOULAKIS, editor, *Natural Language Processing*, volume 1835 of *Lecture Notes in Artificial Intelligence (LNAI)*, Springer-Verlag.

Philippe BLACHE (2007), Model Theoretic Syntax is not Generative Enumerative Syntax with Constraints: at what Condition?, in *Proceedings of CSLP07*.

Philippe BLACHE (2011), Evaluating Language Complexity in Context: New Parameters for a Constraint-Based Model, in *CSLP-11, Workshop on Constraint Solving and Language Processing*.

Philippe BLACHE, Barbara HEMFORTH, and Stéphane RAUZY (2006), Acceptability Prediction by Means of Grammaticality Quantification, in *Proceedings of the 21st International Conference on Computational Linguistics and 44th Annual Meeting of the Association for Computational Linguistics*, pp. 57–64, Association for Computational Linguistics, Sydney, Australia, http://www.aclweb.org/anthology/P/P06/P06-1008.

Philippe BLACHE and Laurent PRÉVOT (2010), A Formal Scheme for Multimodal Grammars, in *Proceedings of COLING-2010*.

Philippe BLACHE and Jean-Philippe PROST (2005), Gradience, Constructions and Constraint Systems, in Henning CHRISTIANSEN, Peter Rossen SKADHAUGE, and Jorgen VILLADSEN, editors, *Constraint Solving and Language Processing - CSLP 2004*, volume 3438 of *Lecture Notes in Artificial Intelligence (LNAI)*, pp. 74–89, Springer, Roskilde, Denmark.

Philippe BLACHE and Jean-Philippe PROST (2014), Model-Theoretic Syntax: Property Grammar, Status and Directions, in P. BLACHE, H. CHRISTIANSEN, V. DAHL, D. DUCHIER, and J. VILLADSEN, editors, *Constraints and Language*, pp. 37–60, Cambridge Scholar Publishers.

Philippe BLACHE, S. RAUZY, and G. MONTCHEUIL (2016), MarsaGram: an Excursion in the Forests of Parsing Trees, in *Proceedings of LREC16*.

Patrick BLACKBURN and Wilfried MEYER-VIOL (1997), Modal Logic and Model-Theoretic Syntax, in M. DE RIJKE, editor, *Advances in Intensional Logic*, pp. 29–60, Kluwer.

Joan BRESNAN (1982), *The Mental Representation of Grammatical Relations*, MIT Press Series on Cognitive Theory and Mental Representation, MIT Press.

Joan BRESNAN (2007), Is Syntactic Knowledge Probabilistic? Experiments with the English Dative Alternation, in Sam FEATHERSTON and Wolfgang STERNEFELD, editors, *Roots: Linguistics in Search of Its Evidential Base*, pp. 75–96, Mouton de Gruyter.

Joan BYBEE (2010), *Language, Usage and Cognition*, Cambridge University Press.

Eugene CHARNIAK (1996), Tree-bank Grammars, in *Proceedings of the Thirteenth National Conference on Artificial Intelligence*, pp. 1031–1036.

Thomas CORNELL and James ROGERS (2000), Model Theoretic Syntax, in Cheng L. LAI-SHEN and R. SYBESMA, editors, *The Glot International State of the Article Book I*, Holland Academic Graphics.

Denys DUCHIER, Thi-Bich-Hanh DAO, Yannick PARMENTIER, and Willy LESAINT (2010), Property Grammar Parsing Seen as a Constraint Optimization Problem, in *Proceedings of Formal Grammar 2010*, pp. 82–96.

Gisbert FANSELOW, Caroline FÉRY, Ralph VOGEL, and Matthias SCHLESEWSKY, editors (2005), *Gradience in Grammar: Generative Perspectives*, Oxford University Press, Oxford.

Fernanda FERREIRA and Nikole D. PATSON (2007), The 'Good Enough' Approach to Language Comprehension, *Language and Linguistics Compass*, 1(1).

Charles J. FILLMORE (1988), The Mechanisms of "Construction Grammar", in *Proceedings of the Fourteenth Annual Meeting of the Berkeley Linguistics Society*, pp. 35–55.

Gerald GAZDAR, Ewan KLEIN, Geoffrey PULLUM, and Ivan SAG (1985), *Generalized Phrase Structure Grammars*, Blackwell.

Adele E GOLDBERG (2003), Constructions: a New Theoretical Approach to Language, *Trends in Cognitive Sciences*, 7(5):219–224.

Adele E GOLDBERG (2009), The Nature of Generalization in Language, *Cognitive Linguistics*, 20(1):1–35.

Ray JACKENDOFF (2007), A Parallel Architecture Perspective on Language Processing, *Brain Research*, 1146(2-22).

Aravind JOSHI, Leon LEVY, and M. TAKAHASHI (1975), Tree Adjunct Grammars, *Journal Computer Systems Science*, 10(1).

Paul KAY and Charles FILLMORE (1999), Grammatical Constructions and Linguistic Generalizations: the *What's X doing Y?* Construction, *Language*, 75(1):1–33.

Knud LAMBRECHT (1995), Compositional vs. Constructional Meaning: The Case of French "comme-N", in M. SIMONS and T. GALLOWAY, editors, *SALT V*.

Ronald LANGACKER (1987), *Foundations of Cognitive Grammar, vol. 1 : Theoretical Prerequisites*, Stanford University Press.

Mohamed MAAMOURI, Ann BIES, Hubert JIN, and Tim BUCKWALTER (2003), Arabic Treebank, Technical report, Distributed by the Linguistic Data Consortium. LDC Catalog No.: LDC2003T06.

Mitchell P. MARCUS, Beatrice SANTORINI, and Mary Ann MAREINKIEWICZ (1994), Building a Large Annotated Corpus of English: the Penn Treebank, *Computational Linguistics*, 19(2):313–330.

Joakim NIVRE, C. BOSCO, J. CHOI, M.-C. DE MARNEFFE, T. DOZAT, R. FARKAS, J. FOSTER, F. GINTER, Y. GOLDBERG, J. HAJIC, J. KANERVA, V. LAIPPALA, A. LENCI, T. LYNN, C. MANNING, R. MCDONALD, A. MISSILÄ, S. MONTEMAGNI, S. PETROV, S. PYYSALO, N. SILVEIRA, M. SIMI, A. SMITH, R. TSARFATY, V. VINCZE, and D. ZEMAN (2015), Universal Dependencies 1.0., Technical report, http://hdl.handle.net/11234/1-1464.

Carl POLLARD and Ivan SAG (1994), *Head-driven Phrase Structure Grammars*, Center for the Study of Language and Information Publication (CSLI), Chicago University Press.

Alan PRINCE and Paul SMOLENSKY (1993), *Optimality Theory: Constraint Interaction in Generative Grammars*, Technical Report RUCCS TR-2, Rutgers Optimality Archive 537.

Geoffrey PULLUM and Barbara SCHOLZ (2001), On the Distinction Between Model-Theoretic and Generative-Enumerative Syntactic Frameworks, in Philippe DE GROOTE, Glyn MORRILL, and Christian RÉTORÉ, editors, *Logical Aspects of Computational Linguistics: 4th International Conference*, number 2099 in Lecture Notes in Artificial Intelligence, pp. 17–43, Springer Verlag, Berlin.

Ivan SAG (2012), Sign-Based Construction Grammar: An Informal Synopsis, in H. BOAS and I. SAG, editors, *Sign-Based Construction Grammar*, pp. 69–200, CSLI.

Ivan SAG, Hans BOAS, and Paul KAY (2012), Introducing Sign-Based Construction Grammar, in H. BOAS and I. SAG, editors, *Sign-Based Construction Grammar*, pp. 1–30, CSLI.

Ivan SAG and T. WASOW (1999), *Syntactic Theory. A Formal Introduction*, CSLI.

Benjamin SWETS, Timothy DESMET, Charles CLIFTON, and Fernanda FERREIRA (2008), Underspecification of Syntactic Ambiguities: Evidence from Self-Paced Reading, *Memory and Cognition*, 36(1):201–216.

6

On regular languages over power sets

Tim Fernando
Trinity College Dublin, Ireland

Keywords: regular language, power set, MSO, institution

ABSTRACT

The power set of a finite set is used as the alphabet of a string interpreting a sentence of Monadic Second-Order Logic so that the string can be reduced (in straightforward ways) to the symbols occurring in the sentence. Simple extensions to regular expressions are described matching the succinctness of Monadic Second-Order Logic. A link to Goguen and Burstall's notion of an institution is forged, and applied to conceptions within natural language semantics of time based on change. Various reductions of strings are described, along which models can be miniaturized as strings.

1   INTRODUCTION

Working with more than one alphabet is established practice in finite-state language processing, attested by the popularity of auxiliary symbols (e.g., Kaplan and Kay 1994; Beesley and Karttunen 2003; Yli-Jyrä and Koskenniemi 2004; Hulden 2009). To avoid choosing an alphabet prematurely, implementations commonly treat the alphabet Σ as a dynamic entity that is left underspecified before the finite automaton is constructed in full.[1] Fixing Σ is not always necessary to determine the language denoted by an expression. This is the case with regular expressions; the expression $\emptyset$ denotes the empty set for any alphabet Σ, and the expression ab denotes the singleton set $\{ab\}$ for any alphabet $\Sigma \supseteq \{a, b\}$. Beyond regular expressions, however, there are expressions that denote different languages given different choices of

---

[1] I am indebted to an anonymous referee for raising this point.

the alphabet Σ. Consider ab's negation (or complement) $\overline{ab}$, which denotes a language

$$\Sigma^* - \{ab\} = \{s \in \Sigma^* \mid s \neq ab\}$$

that is regular iff Σ is a finite set. To delay fixing Σ to some finite set is to leave open just what the denotation $\Sigma^* - \{ab\}$ of $\overline{ab}$ is. Relative to an alphabet Σ, a symbol c, understood as a string of length one, belongs to that denotation if and only if $c \in \Sigma$. (Σ contains *any* symbol, including c, in the open alphabet system implemented in Beesley and Karttunen 2003.)

Apart from negations, there are many more extensions to regular expressions describing denotations that vary with the choice of alphabet. Consider the sentences of Monadic Second-Order Logic (MSO), which, under a model-theoretic interpretation against strings, capture the regular languages, by a fundamental theorem due independently to Büchi, Elgot and Trakhtenbrot (e.g., Theorem 3.2.11, page 145 in Grädel 2007; Theorem 7.21, page 124 in Libkin 2010). Leaving the precise details of MSO for Section 2 below, suffice it to say (for now) that occurrences of a string symbol a are encoded in a unary predicate symbol P_a for an MSO-sentence such as $\forall x P_a(x)$, saying a occurs at every string position (satisfied by the string aaa but not by the string ab unless $a = b$). We can check if a string over any finite alphabet Σ (hereafter, a Σ-string) satisfies an MSO-sentence φ, but the computation gets costlier as Σ is enlarged. Surely, however, only the symbols that appear in φ matter in satisfying φ or its negation? To investigate this question, let the *vocabulary of* φ be the set

$$voc(\varphi) := \{a \mid P_a \text{ occurs in } \varphi\}$$

of subscripts of unary predicate symbols appearing in φ. (For example, $\forall x P_a(x)$'s vocabulary $voc(\forall x P_a(x))$ is $\{a\}$.) Now the question is: can we not reduce satisfaction of φ by a Σ-string to satisfaction of φ by a $voc(\varphi)$-string? A simple form such a reduction might take is a function $f : \Sigma^* \to voc(\varphi)^*$ mapping a Σ-string s to a $voc(\varphi)$-string $f(s)$ that satisfies φ if and only if s does

$$s \models \varphi \iff f(s) \models \varphi. \tag{1}$$

Unfortunately, already for φ equal to $\forall x P_a(x)$ and Σ to $\{a, b\}$, it is clear no such function f can exist; the lefthand side of (1) fails for $s = ab$, whereas the righthand side cannot: $a^n \models \forall x P_a(x)$ for all integers $n \geq 0$. Evidently, $voc(\varphi)^*$ is too small to provide the variation necessary for the reduction (1). Enter $(2^{voc(\varphi)})^*$, where the power set 2^A of a set A is the set of all subsets of A. For any MSO-sentence φ and string $s = \alpha_1 \cdots \alpha_n$ of sets α_i, we intersect s componentwise with $voc(\varphi)$ for the $2^{voc(\varphi)}$-string

$$\rho_{voc(\varphi)}(\alpha_1 \cdots \alpha_n) := (\alpha_1 \cap voc(\varphi)) \cdots (\alpha_n \cap voc(\varphi)).$$

Then for any finite set Σ, we let MSO_Σ be the set of MSO-sentences with vocabulary contained in Σ

$$MSO_\Sigma := \{\varphi \mid \varphi \text{ is an MSO-sentence and } voc(\varphi) \subseteq \Sigma\}$$

and interpret sentences $\varphi \in MSO_\Sigma$ relative to 2^Σ-strings s using a binary relation $\models_\Sigma$ (defined in Section 2) such that

$$s \models_\Sigma \varphi \iff \rho_{voc(\varphi)}(s) \models_{voc(\varphi)} \varphi. \tag{2}$$

The subscripts Σ and $voc(\varphi)$ on $\models$ in the lefthand and righthand sides of (2) track the reduction effected by $\rho_{voc(\varphi)}$ but could otherwise be dropped, had we not already used $\models$ for the satisfaction relation mentioned in (1). Fixing φ's denotation relative to Σ as the set

$$\mathscr{L}_\Sigma(\varphi) = \{s \in (2^\Sigma)^* \mid s \models_\Sigma \varphi\}$$

of 2^Σ-strings that $\models_\Sigma$-satisfy φ, we may conclude from (2) that

(†)   whatever finite set Σ we use to fix the denotation of φ, it all comes down to $voc(\varphi)$.

Our argument for (†) via (2) rests on modifying MSO-satisfaction $\models$ as it is usually presented over Σ-strings (e.g., Libkin 2010) to one $\models_\Sigma$ over 2^Σ-strings. Without appealing to (†), which might be made precise some other way, we motivate the step from Σ to 2^Σ in our presentation of MSO-models in Section 2, showing, among other things, how that step clarifies what predication and quantification amount to on strings (essentially, preimages and images under $\rho_{voc(\varphi)}$).

Beyond MSO, the reduction (2) is an instance of a general condition built into an abstract model-theoretic approach to specification and programming based on *institutions* (Goguen and Burstall 1992). We adopt this perspective to generalize (2) in Section 3 from $\rho_{voc(\varphi)}$

to functions on strings of sets, manipulating not only the vocabulary but also the length of strings (yielding, at the limit, infinite strings). At the center of this perspective are declarative methods for specifying sets of strings over different alphabets. We focus on methods, including but not limited to MSO, where the alphabets are power sets 2^Σ of finite sets Σ.

A multiplicity of such alphabets is useful in the semantics of tense and aspect to measure time at different bounded granularities Σ, tracking finite sets of unary predicates named in Σ. Consider, for instance, Reichenbach's well-known account based on a reference time R, an event time E and a speech time S (Reichenbach 1947). We can picture various temporal relations between an event and a speech as strings of boxes that may or may not contain E or S. For example, the string $\boxed{E}\boxed{S}$ portrays S after E (much like a film or comic strip), which we can verbalize using the simple past or the present perfect, illustrated by (a) and (b) respectively (where the event with time E is Ed's exhalation).

(a)   Ed exhaled.
(b)   Ed has exhaled.

To represent the difference between (a) and (b), we bring the reference time R into the picture, expanding $\Sigma = \{E,S\}$ to $\Sigma = \{R,E,S\}$ with

(‡) $\boxed{R,E}\boxed{S}$ for the simple past (a), and
        $\boxed{E}\boxed{R,S}$ for the present perfect (b),

where a box is drawn instead of the usual curly braces $\{,\}$ for a set construed as a symbol in a string of sets. The difference brought out in (‡) carries significance for anaphora (e.g., Kamp and Reyle 1993, where R is split many ways) and event structure (including an event's consequent state, in Moens and Steedman 1988). Both strings in (‡) can be constructed from simpler strings representing a Reichenbachian analysis of

(i) tense as a relation between R and S, with $\Sigma = \{R,S\}$ and

   $\boxed{R}\boxed{S}$ for the past (a), and $\boxed{R,S}$ for the present (b)

and

(ii) aspect as a relation between R and E, with $\Sigma = \{R,E\}$ and

   $\boxed{R,E}$ for the simple (a), and $\boxed{E}\boxed{R}$ for the perfect (b).

Complicating the picture, there are finer analyses of E into aspectual classes going back to Aristotle, Ryle and Vendler (e.g., Dowty 1979) that call for an expansion of $\Sigma = \{R,E,S\}$ to refine the level of granularity (Fernando 2014). A wide ranging hypothesis that the semantics of tense and aspect is finite-state is defended in Fernando (2015), deploying regular languages over power sets, of the kind described below.

Applications to temporal semantics aside, the reader expecting a discussion of finite-state methods applied to phonology, morphology and/or syntax should be warned that such a discussion has been left for someone competent in such matters to take up elsewhere. The present paper claims neither to be the first nor the last word on regular languages over power sets. Its aim simply is to show how to get a handle on the dependence of certain declarative methods on the choice of a finite set Σ of symbols by stepping up to the power set 2^Σ of Σ and reducing a string through some function $\rho_{voc(\varphi)}$ or other. MSO provides an obvious point of departure (Section 2), leading to further declarative methods (Section 3).

2 MSO AND RELATED EXTENSIONS OF REGULAR EXPRESSIONS

It is convenient to fix an infinite set Z of symbols a that can appear in unary predicate symbols P_a, from which sentences of MSO are formed. An MSO-sentence φ can have within it only finitely many unary predicate symbols P_a, allowing us to break MSO up into fragments given by finite subsets Σ of Z (no single one of which encompasses all of MSO). In addition to the P_a's, we assume a binary relation symbol S (for successors), from which we can form, for example, the MSO-sentence

$$\forall x\big(P_a(x) \supset \exists y(S(x,y) \wedge P_b(y))\big)$$

saying that every a-occurrence is succeeded by a b-occurrence. Formal definitions are given in Subsection 2.1 of a satisfaction relation $\models_\Sigma$ between (finite) MSO_Σ-models and MSO_Σ-sentences, built from MSO_Σ-formulas with free variables analyzed by suitable expansions of Σ. These expansions are undone by functions ρ_Σ on strings that arguably provide the key to predication and quantification over strings. Indeed, the ρ_Σ's pave an easy route to the regularity of MSO, as we show in Subsection 2.2. The functions can be tweaked for useful extensions in Subsection 2.3 of regular expressions, and declarative methods in Section 3 that, like our presentation of MSO via $\models_\Sigma$, meet abstract requirements from Goguen and Burstall (1992).

In what follows, we write $Fin(A)$ for the set of finite subsets of a set A. Often but not always, A is Z.

2.1   *MSO-models, formulas and satisfaction*

We restrict our attention to finite models, defining for any integer $n \geq 0$, $[n]$ to be the set of integers from 1 to n,

$$[n] := \{1, 2, \ldots, n\}$$

and S_n to be the successor (next) relation from i to $i+1$ for $i \in [n-1]$

$$S_n := \{(1, 2), (2, 3), \ldots, (n-1, n)\}.$$

Given $\Sigma \in Fin(Z)$, let us agree that an MSO_Σ-*model* M is a tuple

$$\langle [n], S_n, \{\llbracket P_a \rrbracket\}_{a\in\Sigma}\rangle$$

for some integer $n \geq 0$,[2] such that for each $a \in \Sigma$, $\llbracket P_a \rrbracket$ is a subset of $[n]$ interpreting the unary relation symbol P_a. For $A \subseteq \Sigma$, the A-*reduct of* M is the MSO_A-model $\langle [n], S_n, \{\llbracket P_a \rrbracket\}_{a\in A}\rangle$, keeping only the interpretations $\llbracket P_a \rrbracket$ for $a \in A$.

There is a simple bijection *str* from MSO_Σ-models to 2^Σ-strings, picturing an MSO_Σ-model $M = \langle [n], S_n, \{\llbracket P_a \rrbracket\}_{a\in\Sigma}\rangle$ as the 2^Σ-string $str(M) = \alpha_1 \cdots \alpha_n$ with

$$\alpha_i := \{a \in \Sigma \mid i \in \llbracket P_a \rrbracket\} \qquad \text{(for } i \in [n]),$$

which inverts to

$$\llbracket P_a \rrbracket = \{i \in [n] \mid a \in \alpha_i\} \qquad \text{(for } a \in \Sigma).$$

For example, if $\Sigma = \{a, b\}$ and M is $\langle [4], S_4, \{\llbracket P_c \rrbracket\}_{c\in\Sigma}\rangle$ with $\llbracket P_a \rrbracket = \{1, 2\}$ and $\llbracket P_b \rrbracket = \{1, 3\}$, then

$$str(M) = \boxed{a, b} \boxed{a} \boxed{b} \boxed{}$$

(with α_i boxed, as noted in the introduction, to mark them out as string symbols). Strings of boxes with exactly one $a \in \Sigma$ embed Σ^* into $(2^\Sigma)^*$; let $\iota : \Sigma^* \to (2^\Sigma)^*$ map $a_1 \cdots a_n \in \Sigma^n$ to

$$\iota(a_1 \cdots a_n) := \boxed{a_1} \cdots \boxed{a_n}.$$

---

[2] We follow Libkin (2010) in allowing a model to have an empty domain/universe.

An advantage in working with $(2^\Sigma)^*$ rather than Σ^* is that we can intersect a 2^Σ-string $\alpha_1 \cdots \alpha_n$ componentwise with any subset A of Σ for the 2^A-string

$$\rho_A(\alpha_1 \cdots \alpha_n) := (\alpha_1 \cap A) \cdots (\alpha_n \cap A)$$

(generalizing $\rho_{voc(\varphi)}$ in the introduction). The A-reduct of the MSO_Σ-model given by the string $\alpha_1 \cdots \alpha_n$ is represented by $\rho_A(\alpha_1 \cdots \alpha_n)$; i.e., for any MSO_Σ-model M and MSO_A-model M',

$$\rho_A(str(M)) = str(M') \iff M' \text{ is the } A\text{-reduct of } M.$$

The difference between an MSO_Σ-model M and the string $str(M)$ is so slight that we can confuse M harmlessly with $str(M)$ and refer to a 2^Σ-string as an MSO_Σ-model.

To form MSO-formulas with free variables, let us fix an infinite set Var disjoint from Z, $Var \cap Z = \emptyset$, treating each $x \in Var$ as a first-order variable. Given finite subsets Σ of Z and V of Var, we define a $\text{MSO}_{\Sigma,V}$-*model* to be a $2^{\Sigma \cup V}$-string in which each $x \in V$ occurs exactly once, and collect these in the set $Mod_V(\Sigma)$

$$Mod_V(\Sigma) := \left\{ s \in (2^{\Sigma \cup V})^* \mid (\forall x \in V)\, \rho_{\{x\}}(s) \in \boxed{}^{*}\boxed{x}\boxed{}^{*} \right\}.$$

We define the set $MSO_{\Sigma,V}$ of MSO_Σ-formulas φ with free variables in V by induction, alongside sets $\mathscr{L}_{\Sigma,V}(\varphi)$ of strings in $Mod_V(\Sigma)$ that satisfy φ, determining a satisfaction relation

$$\models_{\Sigma,V} \subseteq Mod_V(\Sigma) \times MSO_{\Sigma,V}$$

between strings $s \in Mod_V(\Sigma)$ and formulas $\varphi \in MSO_{\Sigma,V}$ according to

$$s \models_{\Sigma,V} \varphi \iff s \in \mathscr{L}_{\Sigma,V}(\varphi).$$

The inductive definition consists of six clauses.

(a) If $\{x, y\} \subseteq V$, then $x = y$ and $S(x, y)$ are in $MSO_{\Sigma,V}$, with $x = y$ satisfied by strings in $Mod_V(\Sigma)$ where x and y occur in the same position

$$\mathscr{L}_{\Sigma,V}(x = y) := \left\{ s \in Mod_V(\Sigma) \mid \rho_{\{x,y\}}(s) \in \boxed{}^{*}\boxed{x, y}\boxed{}^{*} \right\}$$

and $S(x, y)$ satisfied by strings in $Mod_V(\Sigma)$ where x occurs immediately before y

$$\mathscr{L}_{\Sigma,V}(S(x, y)) := \left\{ s \in Mod_V(\Sigma) \mid \rho_{\{x,y\}}(s) \in \boxed{}^{*}\boxed{x}\boxed{y}\boxed{}^{*} \right\}.$$

(b) If $a \in \Sigma$ and $x \in V$, then $P_a(x)$ is in $MSO_{\Sigma,V}$ and is satisfied by strings in $Mod_V(\Sigma)$ where the occurrence of x coincides with one of a

$$\mathscr{L}_{\Sigma,V}(P_a(x))$$
$$:= \left\{ s \in Mod_V(\Sigma) \mid \rho_{\{a,x\}}(s) \in \left\{ \boxed{\;}, \boxed{a} \right\}^* \boxed{a,x} \left\{ \boxed{\;}, \boxed{a} \right\}^* \right\}.$$

(c) If $\varphi \in MSO_{\Sigma,V}$ then so is $\neg \varphi$ with $\neg \varphi$ satisfied by strings in $Mod_V(\Sigma)$ that do not satisfy φ

$$\mathscr{L}_{\Sigma,V}(\neg \varphi) := Mod_V(\Sigma) - \mathscr{L}_{\Sigma,V}(\varphi).$$

(d) If φ and ψ are in $MSO_{\Sigma,V}$ then so is $\varphi \wedge \psi$ with $\varphi \wedge \psi$ satisfied by strings in $Mod_V(\Sigma)$ that satisfy both φ and ψ

$$\mathscr{L}_{\Sigma,V}(\varphi \wedge \psi) := \mathscr{L}_{\Sigma,V}(\varphi) \cap \mathscr{L}_{\Sigma,V}(\psi).$$

For quantification, we must be careful that a variable can be reused, as in

$$P_b(x) \wedge \exists x P_a(x),$$

which is equivalent to $P_b(x) \wedge \exists y P_a(y)$ since $\exists x P_a(x)$ and $\exists y P_a(y)$ are.[3] To cater for reuse of $q \in Var \cup Z$, we define an equivalence relation $\sim_q$ between strings s and s' of sets that differ at most on q, putting

$$s' \sim_q s \iff \hat{\rho}_q(s') = \hat{\rho}_q(s),$$

where the function $\hat{\rho}_q$ removes q from a string $\alpha_1 \cdots \alpha_n$ of sets

$$\hat{\rho}_q(\alpha_1 \cdots \alpha_n) := (\alpha_1 - \{q\}) \cdots (\alpha_n - \{q\}).$$

We can now state the last two clauses of our inductive definition of $MSO_{\Sigma,V}$ and $\mathscr{L}_{\Sigma,V}(\varphi)$.

(e) If $\varphi \in MSO_{\Sigma,V \cup \{x\}}$ then $\exists x \varphi$ is in $MSO_{\Sigma,V}$ with $\exists x \varphi$ satisfied by strings in $Mod_V(\Sigma)$ that are $\sim_x$-equivalent to strings in $Mod_{V \cup \{x\}}(\Sigma)$ satisfying φ :

$$\mathscr{L}_{\Sigma,V}(\exists x \varphi) := \left\{ s \in Mod_V(\Sigma) \mid (\exists s' \in \mathscr{L}_{\Sigma,V \cup \{x\}}(\varphi)) \, s' \sim_x s \right\},$$

which simplifies in case x is not reused

$$\mathscr{L}_{\Sigma,V}(\exists x \varphi) = \left\{ \rho_{\Sigma \cup V}(s) \mid s \in \mathscr{L}_{\Sigma,V \cup \{x\}}(\varphi) \right\} \qquad \text{if } x \notin V.$$

---

[3] We can always avoid reuse in finite formulas, working with finitely many variables.

(f) If $\varphi \in MSO_{\Sigma \cup \{a\}, V}$ then $\exists P_a \varphi$ is in $MSO_{\Sigma, V}$ with $\exists P_a \varphi$ satisfied by strings in $Mod_V(\Sigma)$ that are $\sim_a$-equivalent to strings in $Mod_V(\Sigma \cup \{a\})$ satisfying φ :

$$\mathscr{L}_{\Sigma, V}(\exists P_a \varphi) := \{s \in Mod_V(\Sigma) \mid (\exists s' \in \mathscr{L}_{\Sigma \cup \{a\}, V}(\varphi)) \, s' \sim_a s\},$$

which simplifies in case P_a is not reused

$$\mathscr{L}_{\Sigma, V}(\exists P_a \varphi) = \{\rho_{\Sigma \cup V}(s) \mid s \in \mathscr{L}_{\Sigma \cup \{a\}, V}(\varphi)\} \qquad \text{if } a \notin \Sigma.$$

We adopt the usual abbreviations: $\varphi \vee \psi$ for $\neg(\neg \varphi \wedge \neg \psi)$, $\forall x \varphi$ for $\neg \exists x \neg \varphi$, etc. Also, we render second-order quantification $\exists P_a$ as $\exists X$, writing $\exists X \varphi$ for $\exists P_a \varphi_a^X$ where a does not occur in φ, and φ_a^X is φ with P_a replacing every occurrence of X. For example, we can express $x < y$ as $\exists X (X(y) \wedge \neg X(x) \wedge \text{closed}(X))$ where $\text{closed}(X)$ abbreviates $\forall x \forall y (X(x) \wedge S(x, y) \supset X(y))$, which we can picture as

$$\mathscr{L}_{\{a\}, \emptyset}(\text{closed}(P_a)) = \boxed{}^* \boxed{a}^*$$

for the picture

$$\mathscr{L}_{\emptyset, \{x, y\}}(\exists P_a(P_a(y) \wedge \neg P_a(x) \wedge \text{closed}(P_a)))$$
$$= \{\rho_{\{x, y\}}(s) \mid s \in \mathscr{L}_{\{a\}, \{x, y\}}(P_a(y) \wedge \neg P_a(x) \wedge \text{closed}(P_a))\}$$
$$= \{\rho_{\{x, y\}}(s) \mid s \in \boxed{}^* \boxed{x} \boxed{}^* \boxed{a} \boxed{a, y} \boxed{a}^*\}$$
$$= \boxed{}^* \boxed{x} \boxed{}^* \boxed{y} \boxed{}^*$$

of $x < y$.

Next comes the pay-off in interpreting MSO-sentences over not just Z-strings but strings of sets. An easy proof by induction on $\varphi \in MSO_{\Sigma, V}$ establishes

Proposition 1 *Let $\Sigma \in Fin(Z)$ and $V \in Fin(Var)$. Then for all sets $A \subseteq \Sigma$ and $U \subseteq V$,*

$$MSO_{A, U} \subseteq MSO_{\Sigma, V}$$

and for all $\varphi \in MSO_{A, U}$,

$$\mathscr{L}_{\Sigma, V}(\varphi) = \{s \in Mod_V(\Sigma) \mid \rho_{A \cup U}(s) \in \mathscr{L}_{A, U}(\varphi)\}.$$

To pick out $MSO_{\Sigma, V}$-formulas with *no* free variables, we let $V = \emptyset$ for the set

$$MSO_{\Sigma} = MSO_{\Sigma, \emptyset}$$

of MSO_Σ-sentences, and write $\models_\Sigma$ for $\models_{\Sigma,\emptyset}$, and $\mathscr{L}_\Sigma(\varphi)$ for $\mathscr{L}_{\Sigma,\emptyset}(\varphi)$ (where $\varphi \in MSO_\Sigma$). An immediate corollary to Proposition 1 is that for all $\varphi \in MSO_\Sigma$ and $s \in Mod_\emptyset(\Sigma) = (2^\Sigma)^*$,

$$s \models_\Sigma \varphi \iff \rho_{voc(\varphi)}(s) \models_{voc(\varphi)} \varphi \tag{2}$$

where $voc(\varphi)$ is the smallest subset A of Z such that $\varphi \in MSO_A$

$$voc(\varphi) = \bigcap \{A \in Fin(Z) \mid \varphi \in MSO_A\}$$

(sharpening the description of $voc(\varphi)$ in the introduction).

2.2   *Regularity*

For any finite sets A and B, the restriction

$$\rho_A^B := \rho_A \cap \left((2^B)^* \times (2^B)^*\right)$$

of ρ_A to $(2^B)^*$ is a regular relation – i.e. computed by a finite-state transducer (with one state, mapping $\alpha \subseteq B$ to $\alpha \cap A$). For the preimage (or inverse image) of a language L under a relation R, we borrow the notation

$$\langle R \rangle L := \left\{ s \mid (\exists s' \in L)\, sRs' \right\}$$

from dynamic logic, instead of $R^{-1}L$ which becomes awkward for long R's. We can then rephrase the definition of $Mod_V(\Sigma)$ as

$$Mod_V(\Sigma) = \bigcap_{x \in V} \left\langle \rho_{\{x\}}^{\Sigma \cup V} \right\rangle \boxed{}^* \boxed{x} \boxed{}^*. \tag{3}$$

Similarly we have

$$\mathscr{L}_{\Sigma,V}(S(x,y)) = Mod_V(\Sigma) \cap \left\langle \rho_{\{x,y\}}^{\Sigma \cup V} \right\rangle \boxed{}^* \boxed{x}\boxed{y}\boxed{}^* \quad \text{for } x,y \in V$$

and writing θ_A^B for the inverse of ρ_A^B,

$$\mathscr{L}_{\Sigma,V}(\exists x \varphi) = Mod_V(\Sigma) \cap \left\langle \rho_{\Sigma \cup V - \{x\}}^{\Sigma \cup V} \right\rangle \left\langle \theta_{\Sigma \cup V - \{x\}}^{\Sigma \cup V \cup \{x\}} \right\rangle \mathscr{L}_{\Sigma,V \cup \{x\}}(\varphi)$$

$$= Mod_V(\Sigma) \cap \left\langle \theta_{\Sigma \cup V}^{\Sigma \cup V \cup \{x\}} \right\rangle \mathscr{L}_{\Sigma,V \cup \{x\}}(\varphi) \qquad \text{for } x \notin V.$$

As regular languages are closed under intersection, complementation and preimages under regular relations (which are themselves closed under inverses), it follows that

Proposition 2 *For every $\Sigma \in Fin(Z)$, $V \in Fin(Var)$ and $\varphi \in MSO_{\Sigma,V}$, the set $\mathscr{L}_{\Sigma,V}(\varphi)$ of strings in $Mod_V(\Sigma)$ that satisfy φ is a regular language.*

The aforementioned Büchi–Elgot–Trakhtenbrot theorem (BET) side-steps free variables, making do with $MSO_\Sigma = MSO_{\Sigma,\emptyset}$ and a fragment $\models^\Sigma \subseteq \Sigma^* \times MSO_\Sigma$ of $\models_\Sigma \subseteq (2^\Sigma)^* \times MSO_\Sigma$ given by Σ-strings s and $\varphi \in MSO_\Sigma$ such that

$$s \models^\Sigma \varphi \iff \iota(s) \models_\Sigma \varphi$$

(recalling from Subsection 2.1 that $\iota(a_1 \cdots a_n) = \boxed{a_1} \cdots \boxed{a_n}$ for $a_1 \cdots a_n \in \Sigma^n$). A language $L \subseteq \Sigma^*$ is then characterized by BET as regular iff for some sentence $\varphi \in MSO_\Sigma$,

$$L = \left\{ s \in \Sigma^* \mid s \models^\Sigma \varphi \right\}.$$

There is a sense in which the difference between s and $\iota(s)$ is purely cosmetic; a simple one-state finite-state transducer computes ι. But the MSO_Σ-sentences valid in $\models^\Sigma$ need not be valid in $\models_\Sigma$; take the MSO_Σ-sentence

$$spec(\Sigma) := \forall x \bigvee_{a \in \Sigma} \left(P_a(x) \wedge \bigwedge_{a' \in \Sigma - \{a\}} \neg P_{a'}(x) \right)$$

specifying in every string position x, exactly one symbol a from Σ. BET effectively presupposes $spec(\Sigma)$ to extract from $\varphi \in MSO_\Sigma$ the regular language $\{s \in \Sigma^* \mid \iota(s) \models_\Sigma \varphi\}$ over Σ, rather than the full regular language $\mathscr{L}_\Sigma(\varphi)$ over 2^Σ from Proposition 2. To represent a regular language over 2^Σ, BET provides a sentence *not* in MSO_Σ but in MSO_{2^Σ}, which we can translate into MSO_Σ by replacing every subformula $P_\alpha(x)$ (for $\alpha \subseteq \Sigma$) with the conjunction

$$\bigwedge_{a \in \alpha} P_a(x) \wedge \bigwedge_{a' \in \Sigma - \alpha} \neg P_{a'}(x)$$

in $MSO_{\Sigma,\{x\}}$ interpretable by $\models_{\Sigma,V}$.[4] Insofar as computations are carried out on syntactic representations (e.g., MSO-formulas) rather than on semantic models (designed largely as theoretical aids to understanding), the explosion from Σ to 2^Σ is computationally worrying in the syntactic step from MSO_Σ to MSO_{2^Σ} rather than in the semantic enrichment of Σ^* to $(2^\Sigma)^*$.

---

[4] Conversely, we can translate MSO_Σ to MSO_{2^Σ} by replacing subformulas $P_a(x)$, for $a \in \Sigma$, with the disjunction $\bigvee\{P_\alpha(x) \mid \alpha \subseteq \Sigma \text{ and } a \in \alpha\}$ in $MSO_{2^\Sigma,\{x\}}$.

Underlying Proposition 2 is a recipe from $MSO_{\Sigma,V}$ to the regular expressions

$$\mathscr{L}_{\emptyset,\{x,y\}}(x=y) = \boxed{}^{*}\boxed{x,y}\boxed{}^{*}$$

$$\mathscr{L}_{\emptyset,\{x,y\}}(S(x,y)) = \boxed{}^{*}\boxed{x}\boxed{y}\boxed{}^{*}$$

$$\mathscr{L}_{\{a\},\{x\}}(P_a(x)) = \left\{\boxed{},\boxed{a}\right\}^{*}\boxed{a,x}\left\{\boxed{},\boxed{a}\right\}^{*}$$

closed under conjunction, complementation and preimages under ρ_A^B and θ_A^B. These extended regular expressions are as succinct as the formulas in $MSO_{\Sigma,V}$ they represent (up to a constant factor). That said, if we take the example of $spec(\Sigma)$, we can simplify the recipe for $\mathscr{L}_\Sigma(spec(\Sigma))$ considerably to the image of Σ^* under ι

$$\mathscr{L}_\Sigma(spec(\Sigma)) = \left\{\boxed{a} \mid a \in \Sigma\right\}^{*}$$

linear in the size of Σ (as opposed to $spec(\Sigma)$ with quadratically many occurrences of the variable x). The representability of regular languages by regular expressions in general (i.e., Kleene's theorem) raises the question: what useful finite-state tools does MSO add to the usual regular operations? Apart from intersection and complementation (the usual extensions to regular expressions), one tool that MSO_Σ introduces is the idea of a string as a model, the proper formulation of which blows Σ up to its power set 2^Σ (to represent all finite MSO_Σ-models, whether or not they satisfy $spec(\Sigma)$). Exploiting that blow up, we can define regular relations such as ρ_A^B under which preimages of regular languages are also regular. We modify the relations ρ_A^B in the next subsection, Subsection 2.3, examining the MSO representation of accepting runs of a finite automaton, which is demonstrably more succinct than any available with regular expressions.

2.3 *Some parts and sorts*

Using sets as symbols provides a ready approach to meronymy (i.e., parts); we drop the subscript A on ρ_A for the non-deterministic relation $\unrhd$ of componentwise inclusion between strings of the same length

$$\alpha_1 \cdots \alpha_n \unrhd \beta_1 \cdots \beta_m \iff n=m \text{ and } \alpha_i \supseteq \beta_i \text{ for } i \in [n]$$

called *subsumption* in Fernando (2004). For example, $s \unrhd \rho_A(s)$ for all strings s of sets. A part of reduced length can be obtained by truncating a string s from the front for a suffix s'

$$s \text{ suffix } s' \iff (\exists s'') \, s = s''s'$$

or from the back for a prefix s'

$$s \text{ prefix } s' \iff (\exists s'') \, s = s's''.$$

We can then compose the relations $\trianglerighteq$, *suffix* and *prefix* for a notion $\sqsupseteq$ of *containment*

$$s \sqsupseteq s' \iff (\exists s_1, s_2) \, s \trianglerighteq s_1 \text{ and } s_1 \text{ suffix } s_2 \text{ and } s_2 \text{ prefix } s'$$
$$\iff (\exists u, v) \, s \trianglerighteq us'v$$

between strings of possibly different lengths. For every atomic $MSO_{\Sigma,V}$-formula φ, the satisfaction set $\mathscr{L}_{\Sigma,V}(\varphi)$ consists of the strings in $Mod_V(\Sigma)$ with characteristic $\sqsupseteq$-parts, given as follows.

Proposition 3 *For all disjoint finite sets Σ and V,*

$$\mathscr{L}_{\Sigma,V}(x = y) = Mod_V(\Sigma) \cap \langle \sqsupseteq \rangle \boxed{x, y} \qquad \text{for } x, y \in V$$

$$\mathscr{L}_{\Sigma,V}(S(x, y)) = Mod_V(\Sigma) \cap \langle \sqsupseteq \rangle \boxed{x}\boxed{y} \qquad \text{for } x, y \in V$$

$$\mathscr{L}_{\Sigma,V}(P_a(x)) = Mod_V(\Sigma) \cap \langle \sqsupseteq \rangle \boxed{a, x} \qquad \text{for } a \in \Sigma, \quad x \in V.$$

Under Proposition 3, each set $\mathscr{L}_{\Sigma,V}(\varphi)$ is the intersection of $Mod_V(\Sigma)$ with a language $\langle \sqsupseteq \rangle s_\varphi$, where s_φ is a string of length ≤ 2 that pictures φ. The obvious picture of $x < y$ is the set $\boxed{x}\boxed{}^*\boxed{y}$ of arbitrarily long strings

$$\mathscr{L}_{\Sigma,V}(x < y) = Mod_V(\Sigma) \cap \langle \sqsupseteq \rangle \boxed{x}\boxed{}^*\boxed{y} \qquad \text{for } x, y \in V$$

which is nonetheless easier to visualize (if not read) than the $MSO_{\emptyset,\{x,y\}}$-formula

$$\exists X \, (X(y) \wedge \neg X(x) \wedge (\forall u, v)(X(u) \wedge S(u, v) \supset X(v)))$$

expressing $x < y$. To compress the language $\boxed{x}\boxed{}^*\boxed{y}$ to the string $\boxed{x}\boxed{y}$, we can replace containment $\sqsupseteq$ by *weak containment*

$$\succeq := \{(\alpha_1 \cdots \alpha_n, x_1 \cdots x_n) \mid x_i = \epsilon \text{ or } x_i \subseteq \alpha_i \text{ for } i \in [n]\}$$

with deletions (x_i equal to the empty string ϵ) allowed anywhere, not just in the front or back of $\alpha_1 \cdots \alpha_n$ or inside any box α_i. (For example, $\boxed{x,a}\,\boxed{}^n\boxed{y} \succeq \boxed{x}\,\boxed{y}$ for all integers $n \geq 0$.) Proposition 3 holds with $\sqsupseteq$ and $S(x, y)$ replaced by $\succeq$ and $x < y$ respectively

$$\mathscr{L}_{\Sigma,V}(x = y) = Mod_V(\Sigma) \cap \langle \succeq \rangle \boxed{x, y} \qquad \text{for } x, y \in V$$

$$\mathscr{L}_{\Sigma,V}(x < y) = Mod_V(\Sigma) \cap \langle \succeq \rangle \boxed{x}\,\boxed{y} \qquad \text{for } x, y \in V$$

$$\mathscr{L}_{\Sigma,V}(P_a(x)) = Mod_V(\Sigma) \cap \langle \succeq \rangle \boxed{a, x} \qquad \text{for } a \in \Sigma,\ x \in V.$$

Whether the part relation R is $\sqsupseteq$ or $\succeq$,[5] what matters for the regularity of $\mathscr{L}_{\Sigma,V}(\varphi)$ is that the restriction of R to $(2^{\Sigma \cup V})^*$

$$R \cap ((2^{\Sigma \cup V})^* \times (2^{\Sigma \cup V})^*)$$

is computable by a finite-state transducer (for all finite sets Σ and V). Within $Mod_V(\Sigma)$ are part relations $\rho_{\{x\}}$ (for $x \in V$) revealed by the equation

$$Mod_V(\Sigma) = \bigcap_{x \in V} \left\langle \rho_{\{x\}}^{\Sigma \cup V} \right\rangle \boxed{}^* \boxed{x} \boxed{}^*. \tag{3}$$

Moving from MSO to finite automata, let us rewrite pairs Σ, V as pairs A, Q of disjoint finite sets A and Q, and define an (A, Q)-*automaton* to be a triple $\mathscr{A} = (\to_{\mathscr{A}}, F_{\mathscr{A}}, q_{\mathscr{A}})$ consisting of

(i) a set $\to_{\mathscr{A}}$ of triples in $Q \times A \times Q$ specifying $\mathscr{A}$-transitions (where we write $q \xrightarrow{a}_{\mathscr{A}} q'$ instead of $(q, a, q') \in \to_{\mathscr{A}}$)

(ii) a set $F_{\mathscr{A}} \subseteq Q$ of $\mathscr{A}$-final states, and

(iii) an $\mathscr{A}$-initial state $q_{\mathscr{A}} \in Q$.

Given an (A, Q)-automaton $\mathscr{A}$, an $\mathscr{A}$-*accepting run* is a string

$$\boxed{a_1, q_1}\,\boxed{a_2, q_2} \cdots \boxed{a_n, q_n} \in (2^{A \cup Q})^*$$

such that $q_{\mathscr{A}} \xrightarrow{a_1}_{\mathscr{A}} q_1$ and $q_n \in F_{\mathscr{A}}$ and

$$q_{i-1} \xrightarrow{a_i}_{\mathscr{A}} q_i \quad \text{for } 1 < i \leq n$$

---

[5] For the present purposes, we can take a *part relation* to be any fragment R of $\succeq$ (i.e., whenever sRs', $s \succeq s'$). Thus, ρ_A, *suffix*, *prefix*, $\sqsupseteq$ and $\succeq$ are all part relations.

(where for $n = 0$, the empty string ϵ is an $\mathscr{A}$-accepting run iff $q_{\mathscr{A}} \in F_{\mathscr{A}}$). Let $AccRuns(\mathscr{A})$ be the set of $\mathscr{A}$-accepting runs. Clearly, for all $s \in A^*$,

$$\mathscr{A} \text{ accepts } s \iff (\exists s' \in AccRuns(\mathscr{A}))\, \iota(s) = \rho_A(s')$$

(recalling $\iota(a_1 \cdots a_n) = \boxed{a_1} \cdots \boxed{a_n}$). That is, $\mathscr{A}$ accepts the language

$$\mathscr{L}(\mathscr{A}) \;=\; \langle \iota_A \rangle \langle \theta_A^{A \cup Q} \rangle\, AccRuns(\mathscr{A})$$

(recalling θ_A^B is the inverse of ρ_A^B). As for the set $AccRuns(\mathscr{A})$ of $\mathscr{A}$-accepting runs, we start by collecting strings of pairs from A and Q in

$$Pairs(A, Q) \;:=\; \bigcup_{n \geq 0} \left\{ \boxed{a_1, q_1} \cdots \boxed{a_n, q_n} \;\middle|\; a_1 \cdots a_n \in A^n \text{ and } q_1 \cdots q_n \in Q^n \right\}.$$

We refine $Pairs(A, Q)$ to $AccRuns(\mathscr{A})$, taking into account

(i) the set $Init[\mathscr{A}]$ of strings that start with a pair a, q such that $q_{\mathscr{A}} \overset{a}{\rightsquigarrow}_{\mathscr{A}} q$

$$Init[\mathscr{A}] \;:=\; \langle prefix \rangle \left\{ \boxed{a, q} \;\middle|\; q_{\mathscr{A}} \overset{a}{\rightsquigarrow}_{\mathscr{A}} q \right\}$$

(ii) the set $Final[\mathscr{A}]$ of strings ending with an $\mathscr{A}$-final state

$$Final[\mathscr{A}] \;:=\; \langle \trianglerighteq \rangle\, \langle suffix \rangle \left\{ \boxed{q} \;\middle|\; q \in F_{\mathscr{A}} \right\}$$

and

(iii) the set $Bad[\mathscr{A}]$ of strings containing $\boxed{q \mid a, q'}$ for triples (q, a, q') outside the set $\rightsquigarrow_{\mathscr{A}}$ of $\mathscr{A}$-transitions

$$Bad[\mathscr{A}] \;:=\; \langle \trianglerighteq \rangle\, \langle suffix \rangle\, \langle prefix \rangle \left\{ \boxed{q \mid a, q'} \;\middle|\; (q, a, q') \in Q \times A \times Q \right.$$
$$\left. \text{and not } q \overset{a}{\rightsquigarrow}_{\mathscr{A}} q' \right\}.$$

Note that $\langle R \rangle \langle R' \rangle L = \langle R; R' \rangle L$ for all relations R and R' and sets L, where $R; R'$ is the *relational composition of R and R'*

$$R; R' \;:=\; \left\{ (s, s') \;\middle|\; (\exists s'')\, sRs'' \text{ and } s''R's' \right\}$$

(and containment $\sqsupseteq$ is the relational composition of $\trianglerighteq$, *suffix* and *prefix*).

Proposition 4 *For all disjoint finite sets A and Q, and all (A,Q)-automata $\mathscr{A}$, the set AccRuns($\mathscr{A}$) of $\mathscr{A}$-accepting runs consists of all strings in Pairs(A,Q) that belong to Init$[\mathscr{A}]$ and Final$[\mathscr{A}]$ but not to Bad$[\mathscr{A}]$*

$$AccRuns(\mathscr{A}) \;=\; Pairs(A,Q) \cap Init[\mathscr{A}] \cap Final[\mathscr{A}] - Bad[\mathscr{A}].$$

Note that the language $Pairs(A,Q)$ can be formed by defining for any finite sets C and D, the set

$$Spec_D(C) \;:=\; \mathscr{L}_{C\cup D}(spec(C)) \;=\; \langle \rho_C^{C\cup D}\rangle \left\{ \boxed{c} \mid c \in C \right\}^*$$

of $2^{C\cup D}$-strings with exactly one element of C in each box, making

$$Pairs(A,Q) \;=\; Spec_Q(A) \cap Spec_A(Q).$$

The language $\left\{ \boxed{c} \mid c \in C \right\}$ of ρ_C-parts of strings in $Spec_D(C)$ includes strings of any finite length, whereas all strings $\boxed{a,q}$, $\boxed{q}$ and $\boxed{q\,|\,a,q'}$ pictured in $Init_{\mathscr{A}}$, $Final_{\mathscr{A}}$ and $Bad_{\mathscr{A}}$ have length ≤ 2. This is one sense in which the constraint $Pairs(A,Q)$ is global (wide), while $Init[\mathscr{A}] \cap Final[\mathscr{A}] - Bad[\mathscr{A}]$ is local (narrow). A second sense is that $Pairs(A,Q)$ captures accepting runs of all (A,Q)-automata, just as $Mod_V(\Sigma)$ in Proposition 3 captures all $MSO_{\Sigma,V}$-models. That is, $Pairs(A,Q)$ and $Mod_V(\Sigma)$ are general, sortal constraints that provide a context (or background) for more specific constraints to differentiate strings of the same sort; this differentiation is effected in Propositions 4 and 3 by attributes or parts that pick out substrings of length bounded by 2. Table 1 outlines the situation.

Table 1:

	sortal (taxonomic)	differential (meronymic)
Proposition 3	$Mod_V(\Sigma)$	$\langle \sqsupseteq \rangle s_\varphi$
Proposition 4	$Pairs(A,Q)$	$Init[\mathscr{A}] \cap Final[\mathscr{A}] - Bad[\mathscr{A}]$
	general	specific (to φ, $\mathscr{A}$)
length of part	unbounded (ρ_A)	bounded (≤ 2)

A further difference between the second and third columns of Table 1 is that whereas the sortal constraints $Mod_V(\Sigma)$ and $Pairs(A,Q)$ employ deterministic part relations ρ_A, the differential constraints $\langle \sqsupseteq \rangle s_\varphi$ and $Init[\mathscr{A}] \cap Final[\mathscr{A}] - Bad[\mathscr{A}]$ employ non-deterministic relations $\sqsupseteq$, *prefix* and the relational composition $\trianglerighteq$; *suffix*. Although it is clear from Subsection 2.1 that the work done by $\sqsupseteq$, *prefix* and $\unrhd$; *suffix* can be done by ρ_A, non-determinism nevertheless arises when introducing existential quantification through the inverse θ_A^B of ρ_A^B (used for the step from $\mathscr{A}$-accepting runs to the language $\mathscr{L}(\mathscr{A})$ accepted by $\mathscr{A}$). But while $\sqsupseteq$, *prefix* and $\unrhd$; *suffix* search inside a string, θ_A^B searches outside. The search by θ_A^B is bounded only because the set B (that serves as its superscript) is finite (with elements of B not in A amounting to auxiliary symbols).

Non-determinism aside, the relations $\sqsupseteq$, *prefix* and $\unrhd$; *suffix* differ from ρ_A and its inverse in relating strings of different lengths. Indeed, Table 1 arose above from the observation that parts with length ≤ 2 suffice for the constraints in the third column. That said, in the next section, we compress strings deterministically without setting any predetermined bounds (such as 2) on the resulting length, for sorts and parts alike.

3   COMPRESSION AND INSTITUTIONS

Having established through Proposition 1 the reduction

$$ s \models_\Sigma \varphi \iff \rho_{voc(\varphi)}(s) \models_{voc(\varphi)} \varphi \tag{2} $$

(for all $\varphi \in MSO_\Sigma$ and $s \in (2^\Sigma)^*$), we proceeded to part relations other than ρ_A in Table 1. The present section calls attention to string functions that can (unlike ρ_A) shorten a string, pointing the equivalence (2) and Table 1 in the direction of institutions (Goguen and Burstall 1992). As the length n of a string determines the domain $[n] = \{1, \ldots, n\}$ of the model encoded by the string, compression alters ontology over and above A-reducts produced by ρ_A.

3.1   *From compression to inverse limits*

We can strip off empty boxes at the front and back of a string s by defining

$$ unpad(s) \;:=\; \begin{cases} unpad(s') & \text{if } s = \boxempty s' \text{ or else } s = s'\boxempty \\ s & \text{otherwise} \end{cases} $$

so that $unpad(s)$ neither begins nor ends with $\boxempty$, making

$$ \boxempty^* \boxed{x} \boxempty^* \;=\; \langle unpad \rangle \boxed{x}. $$

Using *unpad*-preimages, we can eliminate Kleene stars from the right side of

$$Mod_V(\Sigma) = \bigcap_{x \in V} \left\langle \rho_{\{x\}}^{\Sigma \cup V} \right\rangle \boxed{}^* \boxed{x}^* \tag{3}$$

and from the extended regular expressions from Proposition 3 for the sets $\mathscr{L}_{\Sigma,V}(\varphi)$ of strings satisfying formulas $\varphi \in MSO_{\Sigma,V}$. Regular expressions with complementation instead of Kleene star are known in the literature as *star-free regular expressions*, denoting, by a theorem of McNaughton and Papert, the first-order definable sets (Theorem 7.26, page 127, Libkin 2010). We can formulate a notion of Σ-*extended star-free expressions* matching the regular expressions over 2^Σ, but while it is easy enough to introduce the constructs $\langle \sqsupseteq \rangle$ and $\langle unpad \rangle$, we need subsets and supersets of Σ to relativize complementation and define the constructs $\left\langle \rho_A^B \right\rangle$ and $\left\langle \theta_A^B \right\rangle$, where θ_A^B is the inverse of ρ_A^B. On the positive side, this complication is potentially interesting as it suggests a hierarchy between the star-free regular languages and regular languages over 2^Σ. Be that as it may, our present concerns lie elsewhere.

Rather than separating the set *Var* of first-order variables from the set Z of subscripts a on unary predicates P_a, we can formulate the requirement on a symbol a that it occur exactly once in $MSO_{\{a\}}$

$$nom(a) := \exists x \forall y (P_a(y) \equiv x = y)$$

characteristic of *nominals* in the sense of Hybrid Logic (e.g., Braüner 2014, or "world variables" in Prior 1967, pages 187–197), with

$$\mathscr{L}_{\{a\}}(nom(a)) = \langle unpad \rangle \boxed{a}.$$

From $nom(a)$, it is a small step to the condition *interval*(a) that a occur in a string without gaps, which we can express in $MSO_{\{a\}}$ as

$$interval(a) := \exists x \, P_a(x) \land \neg \exists y \, gap_a(y)$$

where $gap_a(y)$ says a does not occur at position y even though it occurs before and after y

$$gap_a(y) := \neg P_a(y) \land \exists u \exists v \, (u < y \land y < v \land P_a(u) \land P_a(v))$$

so that

$$\mathscr{L}_{\{a\}}(interval(a)) = \langle unpad \rangle \boxed{a}^+. \tag{4}$$

We can eliminate $\cdot^{+}$ from the right of (4) by defining a function bc that given a string s, compresses blocks α^{n} of $n > 1$ consecutive occurrences in s of the same symbol α to a single α, leaving s otherwise unchanged

$$bc(s) \; := \; \begin{cases} bc(\alpha s') & \text{if } s = \alpha\alpha s' \\ \alpha \, bc(\beta s') & \text{if } s = \alpha\beta s' \text{ with } \alpha \neq \beta \\ s & \text{otherwise} \end{cases}$$

so that $\boxed{a}^{+}$ is $\langle bc \rangle \boxed{a}$. In general, bc outputs only stutter-free strings, where a string $\alpha_1\alpha_2\cdots\alpha_n$ is *stutter-free* if $\alpha_i \neq \alpha_{i+1}$ for i from 1 to $n-1$. Construing boxes in a string as moments of time, we can view bc as implementing "McTaggart's dictum that 'there could be no time if nothing changed'" (Prior 1967, page 85). The restriction of bc to any finite alphabet is computable by a finite-state transducer, as are, for all $\Sigma \in Fin(Z)$ and $A \subseteq \Sigma$, the composition $\rho_A^{\Sigma}; bc$ for bc_A^{Σ}

$$bc_A^{\Sigma}(s) \; := \; bc\big(\rho_A^{\Sigma}(s)\big) \qquad \text{for } s \in (2^{\Sigma})^{*}$$

and the composition $bc_A^{\Sigma}; unpad$ for π_A^{Σ}

$$\pi_A^{\Sigma}(s) \; := \; unpad\big(bc_A^{\Sigma}(s)\big) \; = \; bc\big(unpad(\rho_A^{\Sigma}(s))\big) \qquad \text{for } s \in (2^{\Sigma})^{*}.$$

For $a \in \Sigma$, the (2^{Σ})-strings in which a is an interval are those that $\pi_{\{a\}}^{\Sigma}$ maps to $\boxed{a}$

$$\mathscr{L}_{\Sigma}(interval(a)) \; = \; \big\langle \pi_{\{a\}}^{\Sigma} \big\rangle \boxed{a}.$$

The functions π_A^{Σ} compose nicely

$$\text{whenever } A \subseteq B \subseteq \Sigma, \quad \pi_A^{\Sigma} \; = \; \pi_B^{\Sigma}; \pi_A^{B} \tag{5}$$

from which it follows that

$$\mathscr{L}_{\Sigma}\Big(\bigwedge_{a \in A} interval(a)\Big) = \bigcap_{a \in A} \mathscr{L}_{\Sigma}(interval(a))$$

$$= \bigcap_{a \in A} \big\langle \pi_{\{a\}}^{\Sigma} \big\rangle \boxed{a}$$

$$= \big\langle \pi_A^{\Sigma} \big\rangle \, Interval(A)$$

where $Interval(A)$ is the π_A^{A}-image of $\bigcap_{a \in A} \big\langle \pi_{\{a\}}^{A} \big\rangle \boxed{a}$

$$Interval(A) \; := \; \Big\{ \pi_A^{A}(s) \mid s \in \bigcap_{a \in A} \big\langle \pi_{\{a\}}^{A} \big\rangle \boxed{a} \Big\}.$$

Conflating a string s with the language $\{s\}$, observe that $Interval(\{a\}) = \boxed{a}$. For $a \neq a'$, the set $Interval(\{a, a'\})$ consists of thirteen strings, one per interval relation in Allen (1983), which can be partitioned

$$Interval(\{a, a'\}) = \mathscr{L}\left(a \bigcirc a'\right) \cup \mathscr{L}(a \prec a') \cup \mathscr{L}(a' \prec a)$$

between the nine-element set

$$\mathscr{L}\left(a \bigcirc a'\right) := \left\{\boxed{a}, \boxed{a'}, \epsilon\right\}\boxed{a,a'}\left\{\boxed{a}, \boxed{a'}, \epsilon\right\}$$

describing overlap $\bigcirc$ between a and a' insofar as for all $s \in Interval(\Sigma)$ with $a, a' \in \Sigma$,

$$s \models_\Sigma \exists x \, (P_a(x) \wedge P_{a'}(x)) \iff \pi^\Sigma_{\{a,a'\}}(s) \in \mathscr{L}\left(a \bigcirc a'\right)$$

and the two-element sets

$$\mathscr{L}(a \prec a') := \left\{\boxed{a\,|\,a'}, \boxed{a\,|\,|\,a'}\right\}$$

$$\mathscr{L}(a' \prec a) := \left\{\boxed{a'\,|\,a}, \boxed{a'\,|\,|\,a}\right\}$$

describing complete precedence $\prec$ insofar as for all $s \in Interval(\Sigma)$ with $a, a' \in \Sigma$,

$$s \models_\Sigma \forall x \forall y \big((P_a(x) \wedge P_{a'}(y)) \supset x < y\big) \iff \pi^\Sigma_{\{a,a'\}}(s) \in \mathscr{L}(a \prec a')$$

and similarly for $a' \prec a$. Event structures are built around the relations $\bigcirc$ and $\prec$ in Kamp and Reyle (1993) (pages 667–674) to express the Russell-Wiener event-based conception of time, a particular elaboration of McTaggart's dictum mentioned above. The sets $Interval(A)$ above provide representations of finite event structures (Fernando 2011).

Requiring that event structures be finite flies against the popularity of, for instance, the real line $\mathbb{R}$ in temporal semantics (e.g., Kamp and Reyle 1993, page 670). But we can approximate any infinite set Z by its set $Fin(Z)$ of finite subsets, using the inverse system $(Interval(A))_{A \in Fin(Z)}$,

$$\pi_{A,B} : Interval(B) \to Interval(A), \quad s \mapsto \pi^B_A(s) \qquad \text{for } A \subseteq B \in Fin(Z)$$

for the *inverse limit*

$$\{\mathbf{a} : Fin(Z) \to Fin(Z)^* \mid \mathbf{a}(A) = \pi_{A,B}(\mathbf{a}(B)) \text{ whenever } A \subseteq B \in Fin(Z)\}$$

consisting of maps $\mathbf{a} : Fin(Z) \to Fin(Z)^*$ that respect the projections $\pi_{A,B}$. An element of that inverse limit, in case $\mathbb{R} \subseteq Z$, is the map $\mathbf{a}_{\mathbb{R}}$ such that for all $r_1 \cdots r_n \in \mathbb{R}^*$,

$$\mathbf{a}_{\mathbb{R}}(\{r_1, r_2, \ldots, r_n\}) = \boxed{r_1}\boxed{r_2}\cdots\boxed{r_n} \qquad \text{for } r_1 < r_2 < \cdots < r_n$$

copying $\mathbb{R}$. Notice that compressing strings via $\pi_{A,B}$ allows us to lengthen the strings in the inverse limit. If we remove the compression bc in $\pi_{A,B}$, we are left with the map ρ_A that leaves the ontology intact (insofar as the domain of an MSO-model is given by the string length), whilst restricting the vocabulary (for A-reducts).

3.2   *From inverse systems to institutions*

We have left out from the language $Interval(\{a\}) = \boxed{a}$ the string $\boxed{ \, }\boxed{a}$ (among many others) that satisfies $interval(a)$, having built *unpad* into π_A^A. Notice that a is bounded to the left in $\boxed{\,}\boxed{a}$

$$\boxed{\,}\boxed{a} \models_{\{a\}} \exists x \exists y (S(x,y) \wedge P_a(y) \wedge \neg P_a(x))$$

but not in $\boxed{a}$. The functions π_A^B underlying $Interval(A)$ abstract away information about boundedness, which is fine if we assume intervals are bounded (as in Allen 1983). But what if we wish to study intervals that may or may not be left-bounded? Or, for that matter, strings where a may or may not be an interval? The line we pursue in this subsection harks back to Table 1 at the end of Section 2, encoding presuppositions in the second column (e.g., $Mod_V(\Sigma)$), and assertions in the third column (e.g., $\langle \sqsupseteq \rangle s_\varphi$). For instance, we presuppose a string s is stutter-free (i.e., $s = bc(s)$) and assert that a is an interval in s, to replace $Interval(A)$ by the intersection

$$\underbrace{\{bc(s) \mid s \in (2^A)^*\}}_{\text{presupposition}} \cap \underbrace{\bigcap\{\langle \pi_{\{a\}}^A \rangle \boxed{a} \mid a \in A\}}_{\text{assertion}}$$

of which $\boxed{\,}\boxed{a}$ and $\boxed{a}$ are members, for $a \in A$. More generally, the idea is to refine the inverse system from the previous subsection to certain concrete instances of institutions (in the sense of Goguen and Burstall 1992) given by suitable functions on strings.

More precisely, let Z be a large set of symbols, and f be a function on $Fin(Z)$-strings (e.g., bc). For any finite subset A of Z, let $P_f(A)$ be the image of $(2^A)^*$ under f

$$P_f(A) := \{f(s) \mid s \in (2^A)^*\}$$

and let f_A be the composition $f_A = \rho_A; f$

$$f_A(s) := f(\rho_A(s)) \qquad \text{for } s \in Fin(Z)^*.$$

Thus, $P_f(A)$ is the image of $Fin(Z)^*$ under f_A. More importantly, for every pair (B,A) of finite subsets of Z such that $A \subseteq B$, we define the function $P_f(B,A) : P_f(B) \to P_f(A)$ sending $s \in P_f(B)$ to $f_A(s) \in P_f(A)$

$$P_f(B,A)(s) := f_A(s) \qquad \text{for } s \in P_f(B).$$

Now, to say P_f is an inverse system over $Fin(Z)$ is to require that for all $A \in Fin(Z)$,

(c1) $P_f(A,A)$ is the identity function on $P_f(A)$; i.e.,

$$f_A(f(s)) = f(s) \qquad \text{for all } s \in (2^A)^*$$

and whenever $A \subseteq B \subseteq C \in Fin(Z)$,

(c2) $P_f(C,A)$ is the composition $P_f(C,B); P_f(B,A)$; i.e.,

$$f_A(f(s)) = f_A(f_B(f(s))) \qquad \text{for all } s \in (2^C)^*.$$

Functions f validating conditions (c1) and (c2) include the identity function on $Fin(Z)^*$ (in which case f_A is ρ_A), $unpad$ and bc (see Fernando 2014, where inverse systems P_f are referred to as presheaves). The condition (c2) reduces to the condition

$$\text{whenever } A \subseteq B \subseteq \Sigma, \quad \pi_A^\Sigma = \pi_B^\Sigma; \pi_A^B \tag{5}$$

from the previous subsection, for f equal to the composition $bc; unpad$ (meeting also the requirement (c1)). To capture the entry $Mod_V(\Sigma)$ in the second column and row of Table 1 in terms of P_f, we must treat a first-order variable in V as a symbol $a \in Z$ (as in the previous subsection), and build into f both the uniqueness and existence conditions that $nom(a)$ expresses, for $a \in V$. To ensure that no $a \in V$ occur more than once in a string s, we delete occurrences in s of a after its first, setting for all $\alpha_1 \cdots \alpha_n \in Fin(Z)^*$,

$$u_V(\alpha_1 \cdots \alpha_n) := \beta_1 \cdots \beta_n \qquad \text{where } \beta_i := \alpha_i - \left(V \cap \bigcup_{j=1}^{i-1} \alpha_j\right) \text{ for } i \in [n].$$

To ensure each $a \in V$ occurs at least once in the string, we put V at the very end

$$e_V(s\alpha) := s(\alpha \cup V)$$

with $e_V(\epsilon) := V$ for the empty string ϵ. Now, if f is the composition $e^V; u^V$ then

$$Mod_V(\Sigma) = \mathsf{P}_f(\Sigma \cup V)$$

and (c1) and (c2) hold.

The third column of Table 1 calls for further ingredients. Let us define a Z-*form* to be a function *sen* with domain $Fin(Z)$ mapping $A \in Fin(Z)$ to a set $sen(A)$ such that for all $B \in Fin(Z)$,

$$sen(A) \cap sen(B) \subseteq sen(A \cap B)$$

and

$$sen(A) \subseteq sen(B) \text{ whenever } A \subseteq B.$$

Given a Z-form *sen*, we can associate every $\varphi \in \bigcup\{sen(A) \mid A \in Fin(Z)\}$ with the finite subset

$$voc(\varphi) = \bigcap\{A \in Fin(Z) \mid \varphi \in sen(A)\}$$

of Z such that

$$\varphi \in sen(A) \iff voc(\varphi) \subseteq A$$

for all $A \in Fin(Z)$. Next, given a function f on $Fin(Z)^*$ and a Z-form *sen*, let us agree that a (f, sen)-*specification* $\mathscr{L}$ is a function with domain $Fin(Z)$ mapping $A \in Fin(Z)$ to a function $\mathscr{L}_A$ with domain $sen(A)$ mapping $\varphi \in sen(A)$ to a set $\mathscr{L}_A(\varphi)$ of strings in $\mathsf{P}_f(A)$. The intuition is that $\mathscr{L}_A(\varphi)$ consists of the strings in $\mathsf{P}_f(A)$ that A-satisfy φ

$$s \in \mathscr{L}_A(\varphi) \iff s \text{ } A\text{-satisfies } \varphi \qquad (\text{for all } s \in \mathsf{P}_f(A)).$$

Putting the ingredients together, let us define a (Z, f)-*quadriplex* to be a 4-tuple $(Fin(Z), \mathsf{P}_f, sen, \mathscr{L})$ such that

(i) P_f is an inverse system over $Fin(Z)$

(ii) *sen* is a Z-form, and

(iii) $\mathscr{L}$ is a (f, sen)-specification.

Note that once Z and f are fixed, only the third and fourth components *sen* and $\mathscr{L}$ of a (Z, f)-quadriplex $(Fin(Z), \mathsf{P}_f, sen, \mathscr{L})$ may vary. To link up with institutions, as defined in Goguen and Burstall (1992), we view

  (i) *Fin(Z)* as a category with morphisms given by $\subseteq$

 (ii) P_f as a contravariant functor from *Fin(Z)* to the category **Set** of sets and functions, and

(iii) *sen* as a (covariant) functor from $Fin(\Phi)$ to **Set** such that whenever $A \subseteq B \in Fin(Z)$, $sen(A, B)$ is the inclusion $sen(A) \hookrightarrow sen(B)$.

The one remaining condition a (Z, f)-quadriplex must meet to be an institution is that for all $A \subseteq B \in Fin(Z)$ and $\varphi \in sen(A)$,

$$s \in \mathscr{L}_B(\varphi) \iff f_A(s) \in \mathscr{L}_A(\varphi) \qquad (\text{for all } s \in \mathsf{P}_f(B))$$

which we can put as the equation

$$\mathscr{L}_B(\varphi) = \mathsf{P}_f(B) \cap \langle f_A \rangle \, \mathscr{L}_A(\varphi).$$

In fact, the special case $A = voc(\varphi)$ suffices.

Proposition 5 *Given a set Z and function f on $Fin(Z)^*$, a (Z, f)-quadriplex $(Fin(Z), \mathsf{P}_f, sen, \mathscr{L})$ is an institution iff for all $\Sigma \in Fin(Z)$ and $\varphi \in sen(\Sigma)$,*

$$\mathscr{L}_\Sigma(\varphi) = \mathsf{P}_f(\Sigma) \cap \langle f_{voc(\varphi)} \rangle \, \mathscr{L}_{voc(\varphi)}(\varphi) . \tag{6}$$

If f is the identity on $Fin(Z)^*$, and $sen(\Sigma)$ is MSO_Σ, then (6) becomes the equivalence

$$s \models_\Sigma \varphi \iff \rho_{voc(\varphi)}(s) \models_{voc(\varphi)} \varphi \tag{2}$$

for all $\varphi \in MSO_\Sigma$ and $s \in (2^\Sigma)^*$. (6) also represents the division in Table 1 between column 2 ($\mathsf{P}_f(\Sigma)$) and column 3 ($\langle f_{voc(\varphi)} \rangle \, \mathscr{L}_{voc(\varphi)}(\varphi)$), whilst leaving open the possibility that f is not the identity function on $Fin(Z)^*$ nor is φ an MSO-formula.

    Under (6), we may assume without loss of generality that *sen* and $\mathscr{L}$ have the following form. For every $\Sigma \in Fin(Z)$, there is a set $\mathrm{Expr}(\Sigma)$ of expressions e with denotations $[\![e]\!] \subseteq (2^\Sigma)^*$ such that $sen(\Sigma) = 2^\Sigma \times \mathrm{Expr}(\Sigma)$ consists of pairs (A, e) of subsets $A \subseteq \Sigma$ and $e \in \mathrm{Expr}(\Sigma)$ with $voc(A, e) = A$ and

$$\mathscr{L}_\Sigma(A, e) = \mathsf{P}_f(\Sigma) \cap \langle f_A \rangle [\![e]\!]. \tag{7}$$

An instructive example is provided by A equal to $\{a\}$, and e equal to the extended regular expression $\langle\sqsupseteq\rangle\,\boxed{a\,|\,a}$ or equivalently, the $\mathrm{MSO}_{\{a\}}$-sentence

$$\exists x\exists y\ (S(x,y)\wedge P_a(x)\wedge P_a(y)).$$

The righthand side of (7) can never hold with $f=bc$; there is *no* $s\in(2^\Sigma)^+$ such that $bc_{\{a\}}(s)\sqsupseteq\boxed{a\,|\,a}$. A slight revision, however, makes the right hand side bc-satisfiable; introduce a symbol $b\neq a$ for A equal to $\{a,b\}$ and e equal to $\langle\sqsupseteq\rangle\,\boxed{a,b\,|\,a}$ or the $\mathrm{MSO}_{\{a,b\}}$-sentence

$$\exists x\exists y\ (S(x,y)\wedge P_a(x)\wedge P_a(y)\wedge P_b(x)).$$

In general, we can neutralize block compression bc on a string s by adding a fresh symbol to alternating boxes in s, which bc then leaves unchanged, since

$$bc(s)=s\iff s\text{ is stutter-free}$$

(recalling that $\alpha_1\cdots\alpha_n$ is *stutter-free* if $\alpha_i\neq\alpha_{i+1}$ for $1\le i<n$). Similarly, we can add negations $\overline{a}$ of symbols a in A through a function cl_A

$$cl_A(\alpha_1\cdots\alpha_n):=\beta_1\cdots\beta_n\ \text{ where }\beta_i:=\alpha_i\cup\{\overline{a}\mid a\in A-\alpha_i\}\ \text{ for }i\in[n]$$

to express bc_A^Σ in terms of π_B^Σ

$$bc_A^\Sigma\ =\ cl_A;\pi_{c(A)}^\Sigma;\rho_A\ \text{ where }\ c(A):=A\cup\{\overline{a}\mid a\in A\}$$

treating $\overline{a}\in c(A)-A$ as an auxiliary symbol, and

$$bc_A^\Sigma;cl_A\ =\ cl_A;\pi_{c(A)}^\Sigma.$$

Returning to (7) with $f=bc$, we can say a is bounded to the left

$$\mathscr{L}_\Sigma(\{a\},\exists x(\neg P_a(x)\wedge\forall y(P_a(y)\supset x<y)))\ =\ \left\langle bc_{\{a\}}^\Sigma\right\rangle\langle\mathit{prefix}\rangle\,\boxed{\ }$$

applying *prefix* after bc, and say a overlaps a'

$$\mathscr{L}_\Sigma(\{a,a'\},\exists x(P_a(x)\wedge P_{a'}(x)))\ =\ \left\langle bc_{\{a,a'\}}^\Sigma\right\rangle\langle\sqsupseteq\rangle\,\boxed{a,a'}$$

applying containment $\sqsupseteq$ after bc. It is clear that *unpad* is just one of many relations that can come after bc_A^Σ (leading, in this case, to $\pi_A^\Sigma=bc_A^\Sigma;\mathit{unpad}$). The projection ρ_A^Σ in $bc_A^\Sigma=\rho_A^\Sigma;bc$ changes the granularity from Σ to A before bc reduces the ontology to suit A, and part relations (such as *prefix*, containment $\sqsupseteq$ or *unpad*) pick out a temporal span to frame a string (such as ⬚ or ⎡a, a'⎤) picturing an assertion (e.g., left-boundedness, overlap). We are dividing here the choice of an expression e_φ denoting the language $\mathscr{L}_{voc(\varphi)}(\varphi)$ in Proposition 5 between a relation R and a string s for $e_\varphi = \langle R \rangle\, s$. Such a choice presupposes the finite approximability of the model of interest via the inverse limit of P_f (the discreteness of strings mirroring the bounded granularity of natural language statements, rife with talk of "the next moment"). Finite approximability is not only plausible but arguably implicit in accounts such as Reichenbach (1947) of tense and aspect.

4   CONCLUSION

There is no question that as declarative devices specifying sets of strings accepted by finite automata, regular expressions are more popular than MSO. What MSO offers, however, is a model-theoretic perspective on strings with computable notions of entailment (inclusions between regular languages being decidable), in addition to Boolean connectives that expose deficiencies in succinctness of regular expressions (e.g., Gelade and Neven 2012). Mapping a finite automaton $\mathscr{A}$ to a regular expression denoting the language $\mathscr{L}(\mathscr{A})$ accepted by $\mathscr{A}$ can have exponential cost (Ehrenfeucht and Zeiger 1976; Holzer and Kutrib 2010). A more concise representation of $\mathscr{L}(\mathscr{A})$ existentially quantifies away the internal states from the accepting runs of $\mathscr{A}$ (analyzed in Proposition 4 above). Not only can this be carried out in MSO (proving one half of the Büchi–Elgot–Trakhtenbrot theorem), but it is well-known that MSO-sentences can be far more succinct than finite automata (e.g., Libkin 2010, pages 124–125, and 135–136). To match the succinctness of MSO, regular expressions over alphabets 2^Σ (for finite sets Σ) are extended with preimages and images under homomorphisms ρ_A that output A-reducts, for $A \subseteq \Sigma$.

    The step from Σ up to 2^Σ is justified by the various notions of part between strings of sets, given by ρ_A, subsumption $\trianglerighteq$, *prefix*, *suffix*, block compression *bc* and *unpad*, all computable (over 2^Σ) by finite-state transducers. Reducts between vocabularies are composed with compression within a fixed vocabulary to fit ontology against the vocabulary. An inverse limit construction (turning compression around to extension) takes us beyond the finite models of MSO to infinite timelines, approximated at granularity Σ by strings over the alphabet 2^{Σ}. Different finite sets Σ induce different notions $\models_{\Sigma}$ of satisfaction that form institutions, under certain minimal smoothness conditions (used to establish the Büchi–Elgot–Trakhtenbrot theorem in Section 2).

ACKNOWLEDGEMENTS

My thanks to Mark-Jan Nederhof for his editorship and four anonymous journal referees for their comments and help.

REFERENCES

James F. ALLEN (1983), Maintaining knowledge about temporal intervals, *Communications of the ACM*, 26(11):832–843.

Kenneth R. BEESLEY and Lauri KARTTUNEN (2003), *Finite State Morphology*, CSLI Publications, Stanford.

Torben BRAÜNER (2014), Hybrid Logic, The Stanford Encyclopedia of Philosophy, http://plato.stanford.edu/archives/spr2014/entries/logic-hybrid/.

David R. DOWTY (1979), *Word Meaning and Montague Grammar*, Reidel, Dordrecht.

Andrzej EHRENFEUCHT and Paul ZEIGER (1976), Complexity measures for regular expressions, *J. Comput. Syst. Sci.*, 12(2):134–146.

Tim FERNANDO (2004), A finite-state approach to events in natural language semantics, *Journal of Logic and Computation*, 14(1):79–92.

Tim FERNANDO (2011), Finite-state representations embodying temporal relations, in *Proceedings 9th International Workshop on Finite State Methods and Natural Language Processing*, pp. 12–20.

Tim FERNANDO (2014), Incremental semantic scales by strings, in *Proceedings EACL 2014 Workshop on Type Theory and Natural Language Semantics (TTNLS)*, pp. 63–71.

Tim FERNANDO (2015), The semantics of tense and aspect: A finite-state perspective, in S. LAPPIN and C. FOX, editors, *Handbook of Contemporary Semantic Theory*, pp. 203–236, Wiley-Blackwell, second edition.

Wouter GELADE and Frank NEVEN (2012), Succinctness of the complement and negation of regular expressions, *ACM Trans. Comput. Log.*, 13(1):4.1–4.19.

Joseph GOGUEN and Rod BURSTALL (1992), Institutions: Abstract model theory for specification and programming, *J. ACM*, 39(1):95–146.

Erich GRÄDEL (2007), Finite model theory and descriptive complexity, in *Finite Model Theory and Its Applications*, pp. 125–230, Springer.

Markus HOLZER and Martin KUTRIB (2010), The complexity of regular(-like) expressions, in *Developments in Language Theory*, pp. 16–30, Springer.

Mans HULDEN (2009), Regular expressions and predicate logic in finite-state language processing, in *Finite-State Methods and Natural Language Processing*, pp. 82–97, IOS Press.

Hans KAMP and Uwe REYLE (1993), *From Discourse to Logic*, Kluwer Academic Publishers, Dordrecht.

Ronald M. KAPLAN and Martin KAY (1994), Regular models of phonological rule systems, *Computational Linguistics*, 20(3):331–378.

Leonid LIBKIN (2010), *Elements of Finite Model Theory*, Springer.

Marc MOENS and Mark STEEDMAN (1988), Temporal ontology and temporal reference, *Computational Linguistics*, 14(2):15–28.

Arthur N. PRIOR (1967), *Past, Present and Future*, Clarendon Press, Oxford.

Hans REICHENBACH (1947), *Elements of Symbolic Logic*, London, Macmillan.

Anssi YLI-JYRÄ and Kimmo KOSKENNIEMI (2004), Compiling contextual restrictions on strings into finite-state automata, in *Proceedings of the Eindhoven FASTAR Days*.

Permissions

All chapters in this book were first published in JLM, by Institute of Computer Science of the Polish Academy of Sciences; hereby published with permission under the Creative Commons Attribution License or equivalent. Every chapter published in this book has been scrutinized by our experts. Their significance has been extensively debated. The topics covered herein carry significant findings which will fuel the growth of the discipline. They may even be implemented as practical applications or may be referred to as a beginning point for another development.

The contributors of this book come from diverse backgrounds, making this book a truly international effort. This book will bring forth new frontiers with its revolutionizing research information and detailed analysis of the nascent developments around the world.

We would like to thank all the contributing authors for lending their expertise to make the book truly unique. They have played a crucial role in the development of this book. Without their invaluable contributions this book wouldn't have been possible. They have made vital efforts to compile up to date information on the varied aspects of this subject to make this book a valuable addition to the collection of many professionals and students.

This book was conceptualized with the vision of imparting up-to-date information and advanced data in this field. To ensure the same, a matchless editorial board was set up. Every individual on the board went through rigorous rounds of assessment to prove their worth. After which they invested a large part of their time researching and compiling the most relevant data for our readers.

The editorial board has been involved in producing this book since its inception. They have spent rigorous hours researching and exploring the diverse topics which have resulted in the successful publishing of this book. They have passed on their knowledge of decades through this book. To expedite this challenging task, the publisher supported the team at every step. A small team of assistant editors was also appointed to further simplify the editing procedure and attain best results for the readers.

Apart from the editorial board, the designing team has also invested a significant amount of their time in understanding the subject and creating the most relevant covers. They scrutinized every image to scout for the most suitable representation of the subject and create an appropriate cover for the book.

The publishing team has been an ardent support to the editorial, designing and production team. Their endless efforts to recruit the best for this project, has resulted in the accomplishment of this book. They are a veteran in the field of academics and their pool of knowledge is as vast as their experience in printing. Their expertise and guidance has proved useful at every step. Their uncompromising quality standards have made this book an exceptional effort. Their encouragement from time to time has been an inspiration for everyone.

The publisher and the editorial board hope that this book will prove to be a valuable piece of knowledge for researchers, students, practitioners and scholars across the globe.

List of Contributors

Stuart M. Shieber
School of Engineering and Applied Sciences
Harvard University, Cambridge MA, USA

Gijs Jasper Wijnholds
School of Electronic Engineering and Computer Science, Queen Mary University of London

Thomas Graf, James Monette and Chong Zhang
Department of Linguistics, Stony Brook University, USA

Ribeka Tanaka
Ochanomizu University

Koji Mineshima and Daisuke Bekki
Ochanomizu University
CREST, Japan Science and Technology Agency

Philippe Blache
CNRS & Aix-Marseille Université Laboratoire Parole et Langage

Tim Fernando
Trinity College Dublin, Ireland

Index

Printed in the USA
CPSIA information can be obtained
at www.ICGtesting.com
JSHW051408221024
72173JS00006B/1319